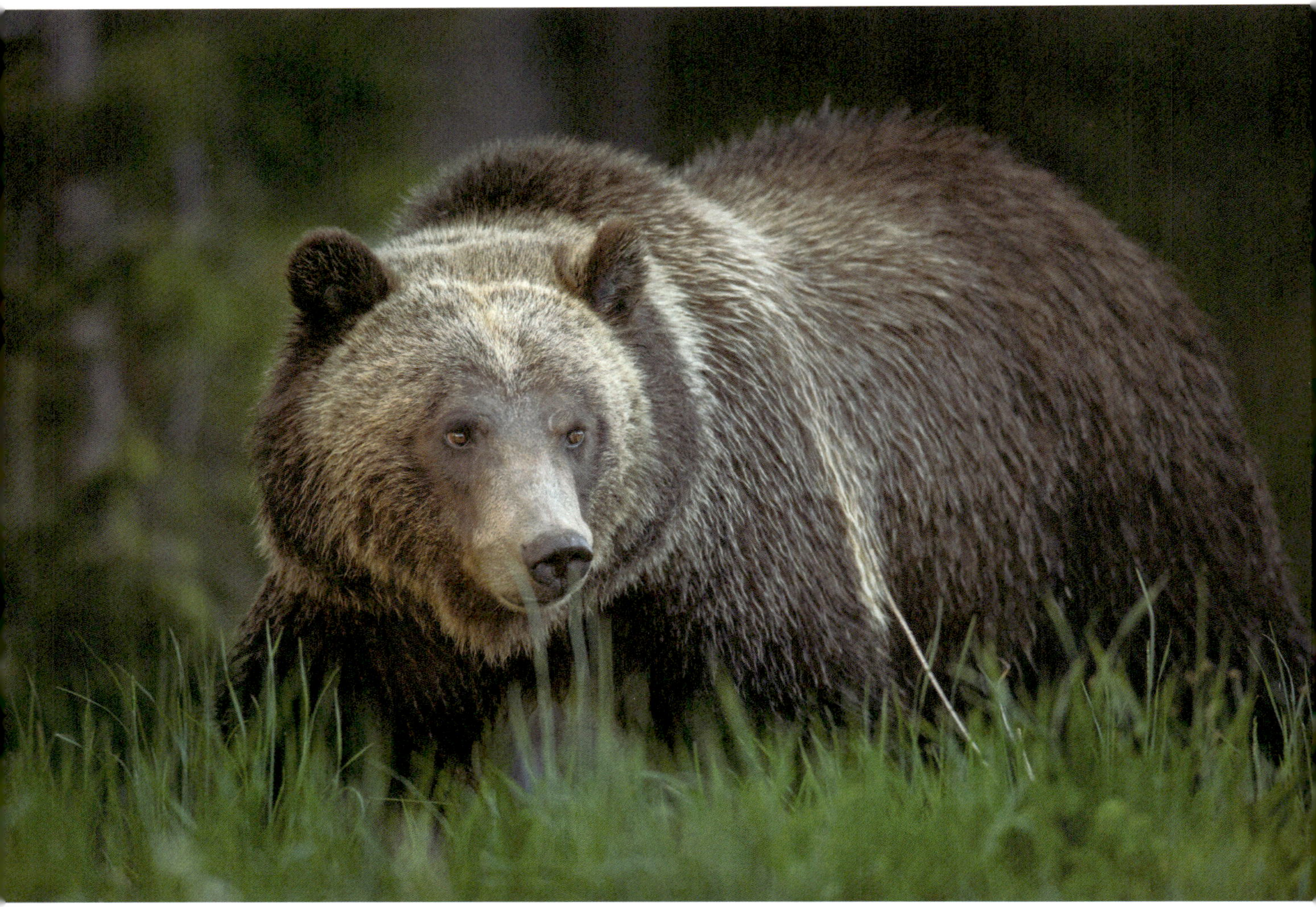

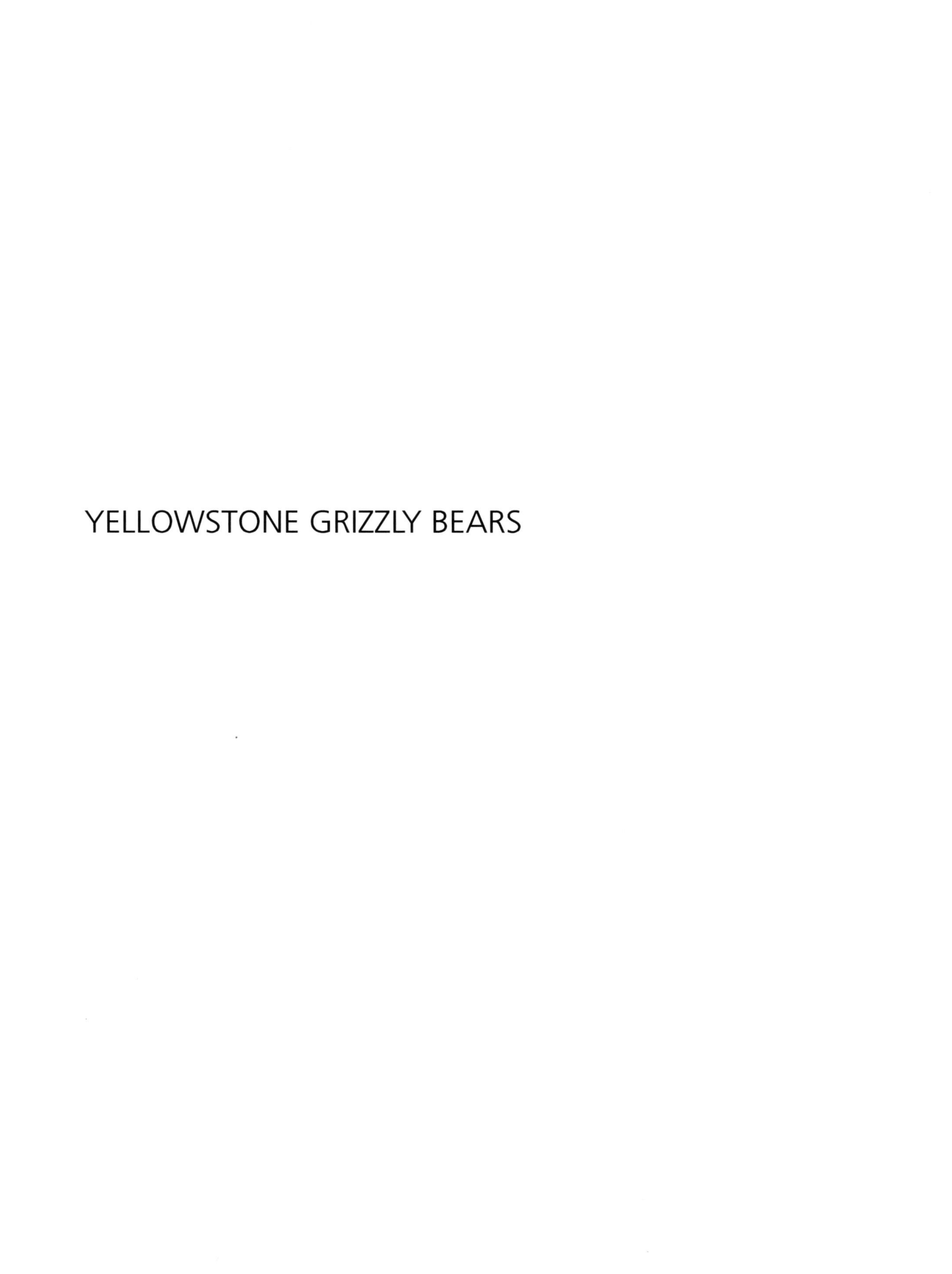

YELLOWSTONE GRIZZLY BEARS

# Yellowstone Grizzly Bears: Ecology and Conservation of an Icon of Wildness

*Editors*
P. J. White, Kerry A. Gunther, and Frank T. van Manen

Contributing Authors
Daniel D. Bjornlie, Amanda M. Bramblett, Steven L. Cain, Tyler H. Coleman, Jennifer K. Fortin-Noreus, Kevin L. Frey, Mark A. Haroldson, Pauline L. Kamath, Eric G. Reinertson, Charles T. Robbins, Daniel J. Thompson, Daniel B. Tyers, Katharine R. Wilmot, and Travis C. Wyman

Managing Editor
Jennifer A. Jerrett

YELLOWSTONE FOREVER, YELLOWSTONE NATIONAL PARK
AND
U.S. GEOLOGICAL SURVEY, NORTHERN ROCKY MOUNTAIN SCIENCE CENTER

Yellowstone Forever, Yellowstone National Park 82190
Published 2017
Printed in the United States of America

All chapters are prepared solely by officers or employees of the United States government as part of their official duties and are not subject to copyright protection in the United States. Foreign copyrights may apply. National Park Service (NPS) photographs are not subject to copyright protection in the United States. Foreign copyrights may apply. However, because this work may contain other copyrighted images or other incorporated material, permission from the copyright holder may be necessary. Cover and half title images: www.revealedinnature.com by Jake Davis.

Library of Congress Cataloging-in-Publication Data

Names: White, P. J. (Patrick James), editor. | Gunther, Kerry A., editor. | van Manen, Frank T., editor. | Bjornlie, Daniel D.
Title: Yellowstone grizzly bears : ecology and conservation of an icon of wildness / editors, P.J. White, Kerry A. Gunther, and Frank T. van Manen ; contributing authors, Daniel D. Bjornlie [and thirteen others] ; managing editor, Jennifer A. Jerrett.
Description: Yellowstone National Park, [Wyoming] : National Park Service, Yellowstone National Park ; [Bozeman, Montana] : U.S. Geological Survey, Northern Rocky Mountain Science Center, 2017. | Includes bibliographical references and index.
Identifiers: LCCN 2016058699 | ISBN 9780934948463 (pbk. : alk. paper)
Subjects: LCSH: Grizzly bear--Yellowstone National Park. | Grizzly bear--Habitat--Yellowstone National Park Region. | Grizzly bear--Conservation--Yellowstone National Park Region. | Bear populations--Yellowstone National Park. | Yellowstone National Park.
Classification: LCC QL737.C27 Y45 2017 | DDC 599.784--dc23
LC record available at https://lccn.loc.gov/2016058699

The authors gratefully acknowledge the generous contribution of Yellowstone Forever, whose publication grant enabled the production of this book.

# Contents

Preface ix
*Daniel N. Wenk*

Introduction xv
*P. J. White, Kerry A. Gunther, and Frank T. van Manen*

Chapter 1: The Population 1
*P. J. White, Kerry A. Gunther, and Travis C. Wyman*

Chapter 2: Historical Perspective 13
*P. J. White and Kerry A. Gunther*

Chapter 3: Reproduction, Survival, and Population Growth 29
*Frank T. van Manen and Mark A. Haroldson*

Chapter 4: Nutritional Ecology 47
*Charles T. Robbins and Jennifer K. Fortin-Noreus*

Chapter 5: Movements and Occupied Range 63
*Daniel D. Bjornlie and Mark A. Haroldson*

Chapter 6: Ecological Niche 75
*Frank T. van Manen, Mark A. Haroldson, and Kerry A. Gunther*

Chapter 7: Genetics and Adaptive Capabilities 91
*Mark A. Haroldson, Pauline L. Kamath, and Frank T. van Manen*

Chapter 8: Human-Bear Interactions                               103
 *Kerry A. Gunther, Katherine R. Wilmot, Travis C. Wyman, and Eric G. Reinertson*

Chapter 9: Bear Viewing in Yellowstone and
Grand Teton National Parks                                      117
 *Kerry A. Gunther, Katharine R. Wilmot, Steven L. Cain, Travis C. Wyman,*
 *Eric G. Reinertson, and Amanda M. Bramblett*

Chapter 10: Current Management Strategy                         131
 *Kerry A. Gunther, Daniel B. Tyers, Tyler H. Coleman, Katharine R. Wilmot,*
 *and P. J. White*

Chapter 11: The Future                                          153
 *P. J. White, Kerry A. Gunther, Frank T. van Manen, Mark A. Haroldson,*
 *and Daniel J. Thompson*

Yellowstone Grizzly Bear Facts                                  169
 *Kerry A. Gunther, Mark A. Haroldson, and Frank T. van Manen*

History of Yellowstone Grizzly Bear
Conservation and Management                                     177
 *Daniel B. Tyers, Kevin L. Frey, and Kerry A. Gunther*

Acknowledgments                                                 195

Glossary of Terms                                               197

Scientific Names                                                211

References                                                      215

Index                                                           255

Author Affiliations                                             274

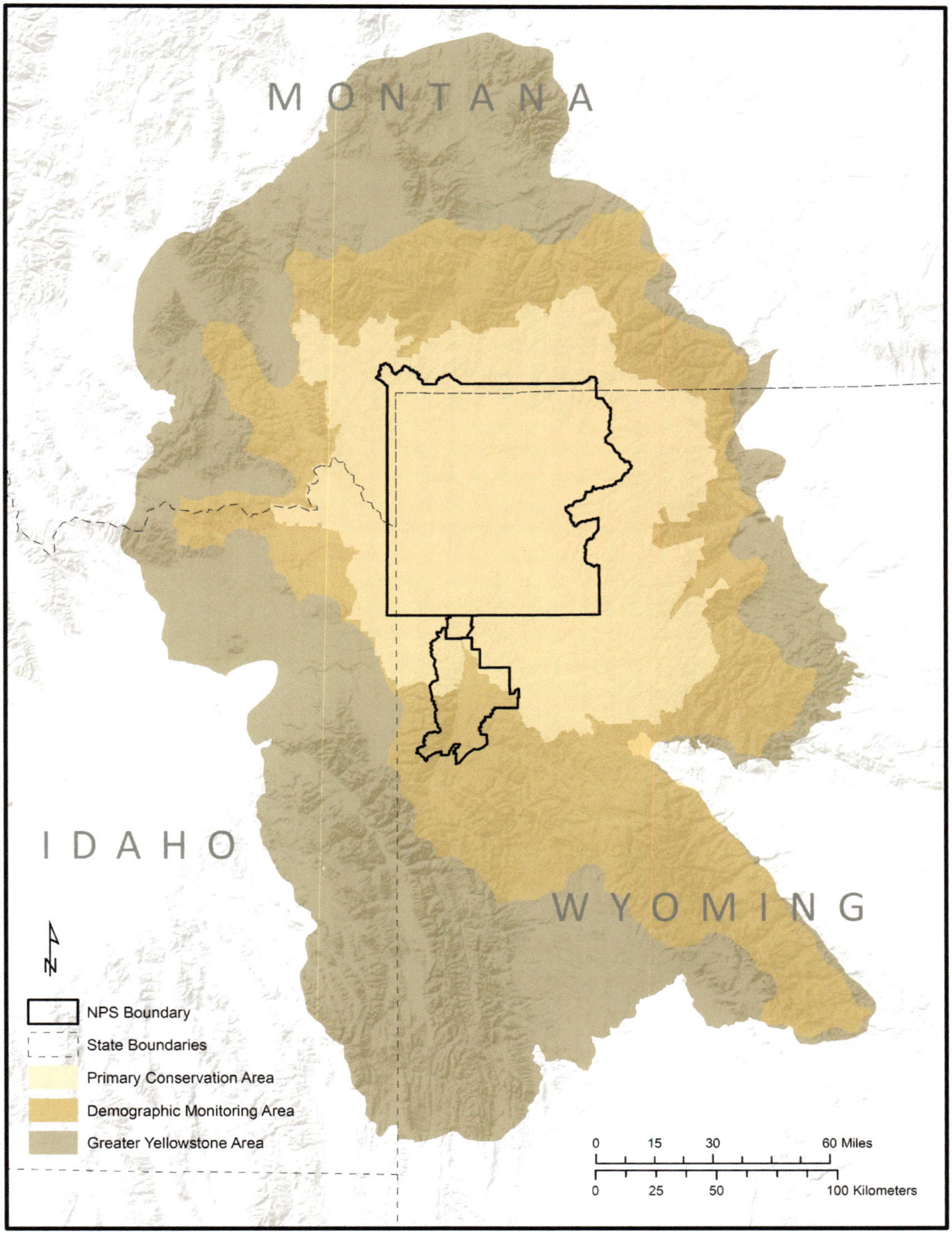
MONTANA
IDAHO
WYOMING
NPS Boundary
State Boundaries
Primary Conservation Area
Demographic Monitoring Area
Greater Yellowstone Area
N
0 15 30 60 Miles
0 25 50 100 Kilometers

Photograph by Jake Davis

*Grizzly bear in autumn. Grizzly bears go through a period of copious food consumption prior to entering their winter dens. Referred to as autumn hyperphagia, this stage allows bears to build up sufficient fat reserves before hibernation.*

# Preface

*Daniel N. Wenk, Superintendent, Yellowstone National Park*

GRIZZLY BEARS ARE one of the most iconic wildlife species in Yellowstone National Park. They are the species that evokes the greatest emotions in visitors from great elation at seeing bears along roadsides to the awe of a surprise encounter in the backcountry. Grizzly bears are the species that, for many people around the world, best represents the wild natural history of the west.

My knowledge of grizzly bears and their management in Yellowstone National Park goes back almost 40 years. There were perhaps fewer than 250 grizzly bears in the Yellowstone area during 1975, when they were protected as a threatened species under the Endangered Species Act. I worked in Yellowstone for Superintendents John Townsley and Bob Barbee from the fall of 1979 until the fall of 1984, and over that 5-year span I traveled the roads throughout the park on a near-daily basis. I observed only 5 grizzly bears in the wild during that entire 5-year period.

In the early 1980s, the grizzly bear population was still declining following the high human-caused mortality associated with the closing of garbage dumps, both inside and outside of Yellowstone National Park, where bears had fed for decades. The decisions by the National Park Service to take these actions were the subject of much discussion and heated debate among both advocates and critics of those decisions. It was rare for visitors to the area to see grizzly bears, so it was difficult to understand why any bears—even problem bears—would be removed. At that time, the population seemed utterly at risk.

Much has changed since then. I believe Yellowstone is ecologically healthier today than it was in the early 1980s. Many reasons have contributed to this, including the reintroduction of wolves, management of fire on the landscape, and native fish restoration, but equally or more significant is the recovery of grizzly bears in this ecosystem. Thanks to the interdisciplinary efforts to restore a population of grizzly bears to this landscape, grizzly bears had increased significantly in numbers and range by the time I returned as Superintendent in 2011. What's more, they had become a significant draw for tourism.

I personally saw grizzly bears along the roadside on many occasions during that first spring back in Yellowstone. Over the Memorial Day weekend, I toured the park with my family and we saw 10 grizzly bears just on one day. It was abundantly clear that this was a different park than the one I left more than 25 years earlier. Grizzly bears had become abundant enough that they were regularly observed foraging for natural foods in roadside meadows. Wildlife viewing, and in particular viewing of grizzly bears, had become as important to visitor experience as the thermal features or the incredible geology of the park. Yellowstone had become the premiere wildlife and grizzly bear viewing opportunity in the contiguous 48 states and grizzly bear recovery contributed significantly to the visitor appreciation and understanding of natural processes and healthy ecosystems.

This is something I had never imagined back in the early 1980s, but there was a tricky side to the recovery. An unintended consequence of this recovery was the development of large traffic jams, called "bear jams," created by visitors that just wanted the chance to view, photograph, or simply enjoy bears that could be seen easily in roadside meadows. This new development had become both a bear management and people management challenge for the park, requiring hundreds of staff hours to manage traffic, people, and bears.

Grizzly bear management had been so successful over the previous three decades that the Yellowstone population had been removed from threatened species status in the spring of 2007 and continued to expand in both numbers and range. However, in the fall of 2009, they were returned to threatened species status by court order due to uncertainty regarding the future of whitebark pine, a high-quality food source for grizzly bears. In 2013, the Interagency Grizzly Bear Study Team completed an analysis of the whitebark pine issues and concluded that changes in food resources had not had a profound negative effect on grizzly bears at the population or the individual level. The population, now numbering possibly as many as 1,000 bears, had continued to increase during a period of marked whitebark pine mortality. Later that fall, the Yellowstone Ecosystem Grizzly Bear Subcommittee voted to recommend that the U.S. Fish and Wildlife Service once again consider removing grizzly bears from threatened species status.

The science, well-articulated by the authors in this book, suggests grizzly bears have recovered biologically. However, they will likely always need careful management, warranting a conservative approach strongly rooted in science-based decision-making. The challenge for future management will be to maintain a viable population of grizzly bears within the Yellowstone ecosystem, including their ecological function on the landscape. Equally important will be managing the grizzly bear population to protect the values of people, a great many of whom treasure the opportunity to experience bears in their natural environment. This is going to be delicate work, but we must find a way to preserve the bears' role in ecosystem processes, while at the same time protecting multiple uses of these landscapes. Engendering public support across a spectrum of values will be critical for the continued survival of grizzly bears.

Grizzly bears are the icon of wildness in Yellowstone National Park. The American people's willingness to recover a species with such an intimidating reputation is a remarkable conservation achievement. This book outlines the fascinating history of the conservation of grizzly bears, from the early 1870s to the management challenges of today's human-dominated landscape. The authors reveal the latest findings about the role grizzly bears play in Yellowstone National Park and the Greater Yellowstone Ecosystem, and contemplate the diverse stakeholder interests and issues in grizzly bear management. Most importantly, this book illustrates our collective commitment to sustain a viable population of wild grizzly bears on the landscape.

*Grizzly bear walking toward a remote camera along Pelican Creek, Yellowstone National Park.*

Photograph by Ronan Donovan

Photograph by Drew Rush

*This grizzly bear inspects a camera trap left at the site of a red squirrel midden in the mountains of Wyoming.*

# Introduction

*P. J. White, Kerry A. Gunther, and Frank T. van Manen*

TO MANY PEOPLE, grizzly bears symbolize wildness because they dominate the landscape. Their intelligence, size, speed, strength, and resourcefulness evoke awe and wonder while, in certain situations, their explosive aggression in defense of food or young can create terror. As a result, grizzly bears remind us of an ancestral world filled with natural dangers and difficulties rarely experienced by most people today.

Perhaps a few hundred grizzly bears survived Euro-American colonization and predator eradication efforts in the Yellowstone area during the mid-1800s to the mid-1900s, with the national park providing refuge to many of these bears after 1872. Early in the park's history, black bears and grizzly bears were viewed as cute, though troublesome, garbage raiders whose begging along roadways, congregations at garbage dumps, and plundering through campgrounds and residential areas attracted people from around the world. Initially, managers tolerated and even facilitated these sideshows due to their popularity with visitors. Over time, however, increasing injuries to people and property damage from bears accustomed to obtaining human foods led to changes in management to eliminate this dependence and restore bears as wildlife.

This transition took many decades and was not without conflict, but eventually reestablished grizzly bears as awe-inspiring symbols of power and wildness, rather than conjuring images of Yogi Bear attempting to steal picnic baskets from campers in Jellystone Park. Today, grizzly bear attacks on people (1 per year) and incidents of property damage (5 per year) in Yellowstone National Park are quite low, despite more than 4 million visits to the park annually. There are about 150 to 200 grizzly bears that primarily live in the park and at least another 500 to 600 in surrounding portions of the Greater Yellowstone Ecosystem, which encompasses portions of Idaho, Montana, and Wyoming. These grizzly bears now occupy more than 22,000 square miles (58,000 square kilometers), including many areas from which they were absent for numerous decades. The high visibility of bears foraging for foods in roadside meadows has made Yellowstone National Park and other portions of the ecosystem some of the most popular bear viewing destinations in the world.

Despite this success, there are lingering issues about how to conserve and manage grizzly bears into the future, including their appropriate abundance and distribution, reducing human-induced mortalities, access to (and protection of) available habitat, connectivity and immigration of bears (gene flow) from other populations, and protecting people and property. Also, there are new biological, political, and social concerns about grizzly bear recovery, including climate warming and its possible effects on key food resources, habitat encroachment and increasing human-bear conflicts, and the possible initiation and effects of sport harvests.

In this book, we provide updated information on grizzly bears in the Greater Yellowstone Ecosystem. This information was compiled from numerous published and unpublished sources and organized into a concise, readable format. The original sources of information are cited at the end of each paragraph. People can refer to these references to review details regarding data collection methods and statistical analyses. Similar wording was often maintained from these source documents to preserve original intent and avoid misrepresentation. Also, a glossary of terms and a history of grizzly bear management are included for reference.

Chapters 1 and 2 provide background information on Yellowstone grizzly bears and the history of their management. Chapters 3 through 5 discuss their demographics (reproduction, survival), nutrition, movements, and occupied range. Chapters 6 and 7 explore the ecological niche and genetic integrity of these bears, while Chapters 8 and 9 discuss human-bear interactions and bear viewing. Chapters 10 and 11 address current strategies for reducing conflicts and provide management considerations for the continued conservation of grizzly bears in the ecosystem. We describe factors affecting grizzly bears and opportunities for natural resource managers, wildlife ecologists, and others to enhance the conservation of grizzly bears. This information should benefit professionals and students of wildlife conservation, as well as the millions of people that visit the Yellowstone area each year to observe bears or monitor their conservation and management via the Internet or other outreach avenues.

Some information included in this book was originally presented in a 2015 issue of *Yellowstone Science*. Also, much of the information in Chapter 1 has been included in the Yellowstone Resources and Issues Handbook, collaboratively written and edited by personnel from the Yellowstone Center for Resources and the Division of Resource Education and Youth Programs. In addition, portions of the glossary of terms were adopted from previously published articles and texts. References for definitions in the glossary are provided in the text. (Morrison and Hall 2002, Hopkins et al. 2010, Gunther et al. 2015c, White et al. 2015, National Park Service 2016b)

NPS Photo/Jim Peaco

*Grizzly bear in the sagebrush, Yellowstone National Park. Grizzly bears move widely across the landscape, using a variety of habitats.*

# Chapter 1

## THE POPULATION—ATTRIBUTES, BEHAVIOR, GENETICS, NUTRITION, AND STATUS

*P. J. White, Kerry A. Gunther, and Travis C. Wyman*

### Attributes

THE SPECIES *Ursus arctos* is widely distributed across Asia and Europe, where it is called the brown bear. It is also found in portions of western North America, where it is called the grizzly bear (although coastal bears in Alaska and Canada are also called brown bears). Grizzly bears have a concave facial profile, long and slightly curving fore-claws (3 inches; 8 centimeters), and a prominent shoulder hump extending about 3 feet (1 meter) above-ground. They use their large shoulder muscles and long claws for digging foods such as bulbs, corms, roots, tubers, and rodents from the ground. Fur color can be brown, black, or blonde; often with white-colored tips that contribute to a silver or grayish sheen. Their dentition is characterized by large canines and other teeth with cusps in the front of the mouth for cutting and tearing, coupled with flatter molar surfaces for chewing and grinding in the rear. (Herrero 1978, Schwartz et al. 2003b)

Grizzly bears are quadrupedal and walk with a lumbering gait on the soles of all 4 feet. They have tremendous strength, can swim many miles, and can run 35 miles (45 kilometers) per hour. They have sensitive hearing, vision similar to humans, and an incredible sense of smell due to millions of nerves in their large snout. They also have a remarkable spatial memory, likely tied to smell, that enables them to remember for decades the locations of key foods and other resources essential for survival. (Schwartz et al. 2003b, Peterson 2005)

Yellowstone grizzly bears are large animals, with adult males generally weighing more than females of similar age (males: 265 to 720 pounds [120 to 325 kilograms]; females: 200 to 440 pounds [90 to 200 kilograms]). Males and females are nearly full-grown by 5 years of age, but continue to grow at a slower rate thereafter. Males reach their maximum size later in life than females. Cubs-of-the-year (hereafter cubs) weigh about 0.9 to 1.4 pounds (0.4 to 0.7 kilograms) at birth and 10 to 20 pounds (4.5 to 9.0 kilograms) by 10 weeks of age. Yearlings weigh about 128 to 139 pounds (58 to 63 kilograms) in spring and 2-year-olds weigh about 187 to 217 pounds (84 to 98 kilograms). (Blanchard 1987, Schwartz et al. 2003b)

## Behavior and Occupied Range

Yellowstone grizzly bears live in the Greater Yellowstone Ecosystem, which encompasses about 19 million acres (7.7 million hectares) of relatively undeveloped lands, including Grand Teton and Yellowstone national parks, portions of 5 national forests, 3 national wildlife refuges, Bureau of Land Management and Bureau of Reclamation lands, and private and state lands in Idaho, Montana, and Wyoming. Currently, grizzly bears occupy about two-thirds of this area, with 150 to 200 of these bears having all or a significant portion of their home range inside Yellowstone National Park. Grizzly bears move widely across the landscape, using forests, geothermal areas, meadows, river corridors, subalpine areas, talus slopes, and valleys. Their movements are influenced by factors such as age and sex, breeding, changes in food availability and quality, disturbance by humans, denning, and the avoidance of larger, more dangerous bears. More information on the movements and occupied range of Yellowstone grizzly bears is provided in Chapter 5. (Blanchard and Knight 1991, Keiter and Boyce 1991, Schwartz et al. 2003b, Coleman et al. 2013b, Bjornlie et al. 2014a, Haroldson et al. 2015b)

Yellowstone grizzly bears are primarily active from dusk to dawn, though they can be active at any time. When active, bears spend most of their time feeding. Other activities include breeding, raising young, resting, and interacting with other animals. Mating occurs during May through July, with males competing for females through displays and occasional fights. Dominant males attempt to isolate females, but females often mate with multiple males and vice versa. As a result, cubs in a single litter may be sired by 1 or more males. (Schleyer 1983, Harting 1985, Craighead et al. 1995, Schwartz et al. 2003b, Coleman et al. 2013b)

Yellowstone grizzly bears enter dens from late October to December as snow accumulates across the landscape, food becomes limited, and temperatures become frigid. Pregnant females usually den earliest, followed by females with cubs, subadults, and adult males. Dens generally consist of an entrance, a short tunnel, and a chamber with some type of bedding material such as grass. Bears emerge from hibernation in these dens after 4 to 6 months when temperatures and food availability increase. Males emerge during early March, followed by females without newborn cubs during late March to mid-April, and females with newborn cubs during mid-April to early May. (Craighead and Craighead 1972, Lindzey and Meslow 1976, Jonkel 1980, Judd et al. 1986, Linnell et al. 2000, Haroldson et al. 2002, Schwartz et al. 2003b)

The strongest relationship in grizzly bear society is between a mother and her cubs, which depend on her for food and protection. Cubs are born in the den during winter and spend up to 4 years

*Today, there are at least 690 grizzly bears inhabiting more than 14.3 million acres (5.8 million hectares) of the Greater Yellowstone Ecosystem.*

with their mother before weaning and separation. Most offspring are weaned as 2-year-olds, though separation occasionally occurs as yearlings or 3-year-olds. Female grizzly bears aggressively protect their cubs from predators or other threats, including humans and adult male grizzly bears. Males do not help raise cubs and, in fact, sometimes kill younger bears, which is referred to as infanticide. Most other grizzly bears are solitary, though aggregations of up to 2 dozen bears may occur near quality food sites such as carcasses of hoofed animals (called ungulates). Large males dominate interactions with other bears, sometimes driving them from quality habitats and food sources. As a result, subadult bears and females with young cubs may avoid areas frequented by larger males. (Mattson et al. 1987, Schwartz et al. 2003b, Gunther and Wyman 2008, Gunther 2016)

## Nutritional Ecology

Yellowstone grizzly bears have a generalist diet, which means they can eat a wide variety of foods. They have been documented eating 175 different plants, 37 invertebrates, 34 mammals, 7 birds, and 4 species of fish. Bears have a single stomach and a relatively short intestinal tract to extract nutrients from this assortment of foods. They do not have a cecum or rumen and, as a result, cannot digest plant fiber efficiently. To compensate, bears typically eat succulent plants low in fiber and high in digestibility and nutrients. However, they cannot increase fat reserves solely by eating plants and, for this reason, army cutworm moths, cutthroat trout, meat from ungulates, and whitebark pine nuts (seeds) are seasonally eaten due to their high nutritional value. Grizzly bears in the Greater Yellowstone Ecosystem eat more meat than bears in most other populations, with a diet that consists of about 40% meat and 60% plants. (Mealey 1975, Herrero 1978, Mattson et al. 1991a, Craighead et al. 1995, Mattson 1997a, Mattson 1997b, Jacoby et al. 1999, Herrero 2002, Schwartz et al. 2003b, Mowat and Heard 2006, Fortin et al. 2013, Schwartz et al. 2013, Gunther et al. 2014)

The generalist diet of Yellowstone grizzly bears enables them to feed across diverse habitats and adjust to variations in forage availability within and among seasons and years. Bears feed opportunistically on bison and elk carcasses left from accidents, injuries, starvation (winter-kill), and wolf predation. In spring, many bears hunt newborn elk calves, while some feed on spawning cutthroat trout in the tributaries of Yellowstone Lake. Other food items eaten through summer and autumn include ants, army cutworm moths, forbs, grasses and grass-like plants, and whitebark pine nuts from red squirrel caches. More information on the diet, nutritional ecology, and energetics of grizzly bears is provided in Chapter 4. (Mealey 1980, Gunther and Renkin 1990, Reinhart 1990, Mattson et al. 1991a, Green et al. 1997, Mattson 1997a, Jacoby et al. 1999, Koel et al. 2005, Barber-Meyer et al. 2008, Fortin et al. 2013, Middleton et al. 2013, Schwartz et al. 2013, Gunther et al. 2014)

**Population Dynamics**

Perhaps fewer than 250 grizzly bears remained in the Greater Yellowstone Ecosystem during the mid-1970s (Figure 1.1). Bear numbers were decreasing as many adult females were killed due to conflicts with humans and, in turn, the recruitment of young bears into the population decreased. Grizzly bears have a low reproductive rate compared to other mammals and, as a result, higher survival was needed to increase numbers. In 1975, Yellowstone grizzly bears were protected as threatened pursuant to the federal Endangered Species Act and managers began implementing measures to decrease human-caused bear mortality, protect habitat on public lands, and reduce conflicts between bears and people. These measures included preventing bears from getting human foods, reducing management removals of bears, protecting undeveloped habitat, and educating and managing people to ensure their safety. (Cowan et al. 1974, Craighead et al. 1974, U.S. Fish and Wildlife Service 1975, Knight and

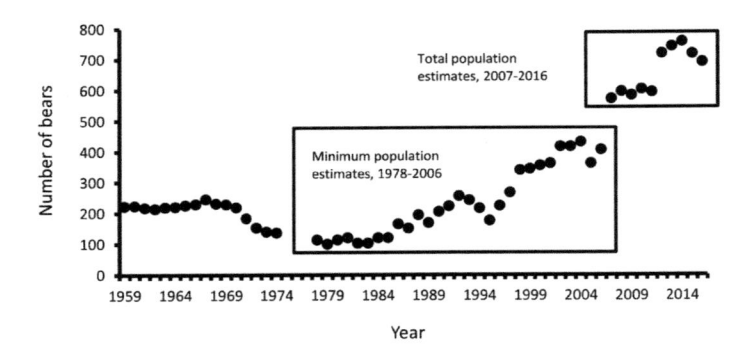

*Figure 1.1. Counts or estimates of the number of grizzly bears in the Greater Yellowstone Ecosystem, 1959-2016. Numbers were estimated from counts of bears at open-pit garbage dumps during 1959 to 1974, extrapolated from the number of females with cubs observed in the ecosystem during 1978 to 2006, and estimated using the Chao2 model during 2007 to 2016. (Craighead et al. 1974, Schwartz et al. 2008, Haroldson et al. 2015b)*

Eberhardt 1985, Craighead et al. 1988, Craighead et al. 1995, Gunther 2008, Servheen and Shoemaker 2008)

There were signs of recovery starting in the late 1980s, with higher adult female survival, population growth between 4% and 7% each year, and the recolonization of habitats outside Yellowstone National Park. This recovery continued as managers focused on increasing bear survival and recruitment by minimizing conflicts with humans. By 2002, there were about 560 grizzly bears living across more than 8.1 million acres (3.3 million hectares) of the Greater Yellowstone Ecosystem. Also, the number of females producing cubs increased and then stabilized in the early 2000s, suggesting bear numbers in the core of the ecosystem were near the capacity of the environment to support them. (Schwartz et al. 2002, Haroldson and Frey 2005, Schwartz et al. 2006a, Schwartz et al. 2006b, Schwartz et al. 2006d, Harris et al. 2007, Haroldson and Frey 2008, Haroldson et al. 2008b, Servheen and Shoemaker 2008, Servheen and Cross 2010, Schwartz et al. 2013, van Manen et al. 2016a)

Today, there are at least 690 grizzly bears within the area monitored by the Interagency Grizzly Bear Study Team (called the Demographic Monitoring Area) inhabiting more than 14.3 million acres (5.8 million hectares) of the Greater Yellowstone Ecosystem. In reality, this estimate is probably much lower than the actual number of bears because it was derived from counts of unique females with cubs that may underestimate true bear numbers by 40% to 50% at the current population size. Bears continue to disperse into new areas, and abundance, reproduction, and survival are high enough that grizzly bears should continue to be well-distributed throughout the ecosystem for the foreseeable future. However, conditions in the ecosystem continue to change with increasing visitation and residential development, as well as recent decreases in some food resources that could increase human-bear interactions and complicate bear conservation. Also, humans continue to be the primary source of mortality for grizzly bears, causing 87% of 61 deaths during 2015, primarily due to management removals for livestock depredation or other conflicts and defensive shootings by ungulate hunters. Therefore, public attitudes and their influence on future decisions will have a tremendous impact on the further recovery of the Yellowstone grizzly bear population. More information on the historical management and population trends of Yellowstone grizzly bears is provided in Chapter 2. (Cherry et al. 2007, Gunther 2008, Schwartz et al. 2008, Servheen and Shoemaker 2008, Bjornlie et al. 2014a, van Manen et al. 2014, Haroldson et al. 2015b, Haroldson and Frey 2016, van Manen et al. 2016a)

## Ecological Niche

Grizzly bears influence the function and structure of the Greater Yellowstone Ecosystem by limiting elk numbers in certain areas through predation on newborn calves, influencing the distribution of predators and scavengers through competition, and redistributing energy and nutrients across the landscape. Historically, as many as 60 grizzly bears transferred energy and nutrients from aquatic to terrestrial systems during spring foraging on spawning cutthroat trout in tributaries of Yellowstone Lake, though this food source has decreased substantially in recent decades. (Reinhart and Mattson 1990, Schwartz et al. 2003b, Barber-Meyer et al. 2008, Fortin et al. 2013, Middleton et al. 2013, Schwartz et al. 2013, Center for Biological Diversity 2014)

Ungulate carcasses from predation or starvation are an important food source for grizzly bears, particularly before and after hibernation, as well as during years when other important food sources such as whitebark pine nuts are sparse. Bears use their heightened sense of smell to locate carcasses and then compete with other predators and scavengers for them. Adult grizzly bears are usually victorious in usurping ungulate carcasses from mountain lions and wolves due to their aggressiveness and larger size. However, female grizzly bears with cubs are less effective at stealing carcasses from wolves because wolves may attempt to kill the cubs, sometimes successfully. (Green et al. 1997, Ballard et al. 2003, Felicetti et al. 2003, Gunther and Smith 2004, Hebblewhite and Smith 2010, Garrott et al. 2013, Schwartz et al. 2013)

Black bears are numerous throughout much of the Greater Yellowstone Ecosystem and may compete with grizzly bears for food during certain times of year, especially in spring when both species are attracted to succulent new plant growth and ungulate carcasses. Their diets are different during summer and autumn when black bears eat more berries and grizzly bears eat more meat and roots. Black bears are more adept at acquiring smaller, scattered foods such as berries, whereas grizzly bears can defend concentrated food sources such as clover patches and ungulate carcasses. Grizzly bears occasionally prey on black bears, and large males of both species sometimes kill smaller bears. More information on the relationships between grizzly bears and other animals, and the effects of grizzly bears on ecosystem processes, is provided in Chapter 6. (Herrero

1978, Gunther et al. 2002, Schwartz et al. 2003b, Mattson et al. 2005, Belant et al. 2006, Schwartz et al. 2013, Costello et al. 2016a)

## Adaptive Capabilities and Genetics

Yellowstone grizzly bears live in a challenging environment where they compete for food, mates, and other resources. Consequently, they retain behaviors, capabilities, and traits that embody wildness. However, the population has been geographically isolated from other populations for about 100 years and may have experienced a bottleneck when numbers were reduced to less than 250 bears during the mid-1970s. A population reduced to a small number of animals contains less genetic variation than the original larger population, which can result in further losses of genetic diversity due to chance and inbreeding if there is no immigration of breeding bears (gene flow) from other populations. These circumstances eventually reduce the abilities of animals to adapt to new environmental challenges. (Darwin 1859, Craighead et al. 1995, Mattson 1997a, Miller and Waits 2003, Allendorf and Luikart 2007, U.S. Fish and Wildlife Service 2007a, Kamath et al. 2015, van Manen et al. 2015)

The isolation of Yellowstone grizzly bears contributed to a slight decrease in genetic diversity during the 1900s. As a result, there were concerns about the long-term persistence, or viability, of the population. However, recent genetic analyses indicate a low rate of inbreeding (0.2%) and stable genetic diversity since 1985. Also, the 3- to 4-fold increase in population size since the 1980s should slow the future loss of genetic diversity, while periodic immigration or relocation of bears from other populations should forestall losses in the long term. More information on the genetics and adaptive capabilities of Yellowstone grizzly bears is provided in Chapter 7. (Miller and Waits 2003, Kamath et al. 2015)

## Human-Bear Interactions

Historically, human foods left unattended in campgrounds or developed areas, as well as refuse disposed in open-pit garbage dumps, were a significant portion of the diets of many grizzly bears in and near Yellowstone National Park. Bears readily visible along roadsides and within developed areas were quite popular with visitors, but eventually led to concerns because black bears and grizzly bears caused about 50 human injuries and 140 damages of property each year. As a result, the dumps were closed in the late 1960s and 1970s, and regulations prohibiting the feeding of bears and requiring proper food storage were strictly enforced. Many food-conditioned bears, which associated people with food and were dependent on human food sources, were removed from the population. Remaining bears subsisted on natural foods and, over time, bear numbers increased and surpassed abundance and distribution goals considered necessary for recovery and the persistence of a viable population. (Meagher and Phillips 1983, Schullery 1992, Gunther 1994, Craighead et al. 1995, Gunther and Hoekstra 1998, U.S. Fish and Wildlife Service 2007a, Haroldson et al. 2008b, Meagher 2008, Gunther 2015a)

Visitation to Yellowstone National Park consistently increased following World War II, with grizzly bears being a premier attraction. Visitors reported more than 41,000 bear sightings during 1980 through 2012. Today, there are more than 4 million visits to the park annually and, not surprisingly, some grizzly bears feeding in viewable areas such as roadside meadows attract a lot of attention from visitors. Because bears rarely experience injuries or pain during these frequent encounters, they often stop running away or visibly responding to people or traffic. In fact, these habituated bears, which include some females with cubs, often tolerate people at distances of less than 30 yards (27 meters), where they are capable of unexpectedly and quickly inflicting serious injury or death to visitors. Fortunately, most grizzly bears remain in backcountry areas where they are generally more wary of humans. However, managing ever larger numbers of visitors to prevent feeding, injuries, property damage, or unwanted encounters with bears at campsites, along trails, or along roadways has become a major concern and a complicated management issue for park staff. More information on bear viewing and interactions between grizzly bears and people is provided in Chapters 2, 8, and 9. (Schullery 1992, Gunther and Wyman 2008, Coleman et al. 2013a, Coleman et al. 2013b, Haroldson and Gunther 2013, Gunther et al. 2015c)

## Conclusions

Current conditions within the Greater Yellowstone Ecosystem present an opportunity for the continued recovery of grizzly bears in suitable habitats. Tourism has a large and increasing influence on the economy, and more and more residents see the environment and wildlife as valuable resources for recreation and viewing rather than extraction or harvesting. Regardless, humans will continue to be the overriding factor influencing the conservation of grizzly bears in the Greater Yellowstone Ecosystem and elsewhere in western North America. As a result, managers will continue efforts to minimize bear conflicts with people, while resolving human causes to decrease bear mortality and further degradation of habitat. The current management of Yellowstone grizzly bears and considerations for the future are discussed in Chapters 10 and 11. (Morris and McBeth 2003, Gunther 2008, Haroldson et al. 2008b, Servheen and Shoemaker 2008, Schwartz et al. 2013, Gunther et al. 2015c)

Bear feeding stations, like this one near Old Faithful (ca. 1920s), were popular attractions before they were closed in the early 1940s.

# Chapter 2

## HISTORICAL PERSPECTIVE—FROM PROTECTION TO FOOD DEPENDENCY TO RECOVERY AS WILDLIFE

*P. J. White and Kerry A. Gunther*

### Population Decrease and Protection

PERHAPS AS MANY as 100,000 grizzly bears lived in western North America from Alaska to northern Mexico before colonization and settlement by Euro-Americans in the 1800s. However, bear numbers were decimated across the Great Plains and Rocky Mountains in the contiguous United States by the late 1800s due to pervasive predator control by colonists. Thereafter, much habitat in this region was degraded or usurped by agriculture, dam building, livestock grazing, resource extraction, and residential development. Grizzly bears outside protected areas continued to be killed through the mid-1900s, with their geographic range in the western contiguous United States reduced by about 98% and most populations in this region eradicated by the 1970s. (Servheen 1990, Schullery 1992, U.S. Fish and Wildlife Service 1993, Mattson et al. 1995, Schwartz et al. 2003b, Haroldson et al. 2008b)

There are not sufficient historical accounts to accurately or precisely estimate the abundance of grizzly bears in the Greater Yellowstone Ecosystem prior to the designation of Yellowstone National Park in 1872. Written accounts compiled by park historians suggest bears were widespread in suitable habitats, including the area eventually encompassed by the park. Apparently, however, there was a massive slaughter of wildlife in the Yellowstone area during the 1870s and, as a result, the grizzly bear population was likely small and isolated by the mid-1880s. This remnant population was probably the largest south of the Northern Continental Divide Ecosystem in northern Montana and Canada. (Cowan et al. 1974, U.S. Fish and Wildlife Service 1993, Whittlesey et al. 2015)

Yellowstone National Park was established, in part, to prevent the further decimation of fish and wildlife populations in the area. Hunting in the park was prohibited in 1883 and a company of Army cavalry was sent to protect the park in 1886. However, poachers continued to kill wildlife therein until Congress passed the Lacey Act in 1894. Thereafter, the Army and subsequently the National Park Service had the authority to arrest and prosecute individuals for killing or transporting wildlife. As a result, poaching was curtailed and wildlife species were protected within the park. (Haines 1977)

## Food-conditioning and Feeding Sideshows

Soon after Yellowstone National Park was established, many black bears and grizzly bears were attracted to human foods left unattended in campgrounds and developments, discarded in open-pit dumps, or offered by visitors along roadways. These bears became a famous tourist attraction and enticed more and more visitors to the Yellowstone area. The tame, begging behavior of many black bears resulted in all bears being viewed as entertaining, gentle, and subservient, rather than fearless and formidable monarchs of the wilderness. Though the hand feeding of bears was prohibited in 1902, this regulation was not obeyed or enforced. Instead, the vaudevillian perception of bears was enhanced by visitors watching congregations of grizzly bears in dumps, which park staff facilitated by creating a show-like atmosphere with seating and commentary. By the 1960s, 40 different grizzly bears were attracted to both the Rabbit Creek and West Yellowstone dumps during summer, while more than 100 bears fed at the Trout Creek dump. (Hornocker 1962, Cole 1971a, Cole 1971b, Schullery 1992, Craighead et al. 1995, Haroldson et al. 2008b, Meagher 2008)

Food-conditioned bears were extremely popular with visitors, but conflicts arose as visitation increased. At the time, there were no bear-resistant garbage cans, dumpsters, incinerators, or pre-prepared foods. As a result, foods left unattended in campgrounds or deposited in garbage dumps contributed to more food-conditioned bears. As these bears attempted to obtain human foods, they caused 64 injuries to people and 128 damages of property for every 1 million visits to the park during 1931 to 1959. In turn, park rangers spent more time responding to problems and trapping bears for relocation or removal. However, most tourism through the 1960s was concentrated during mid-June to mid-August, and there was relatively little hiking in backcountry areas of the park. Thus, there were few interactions between people and bears emerging from (March-May) or preparing for (October-November) denning and hibernation. These are critical periods for bears focused on acquiring food resources to replenish their fat and protein reserves. (Schullery 1992, Schwartz et al. 2003b, Haroldson et al. 2008b, Meagher 2008, Gunther et al. 2015c)

## Restoration as Wildlife

The modern-day environmental movement, which began in the 1930s and 1940s with the teachings of Aldo Leopold, bloomed during the late 1950s and 1960s with changing attitudes and beliefs about the appropriate management of wildlife in national parks and wilderness areas. By that time, the relatively undeveloped Greater Yellowstone Ecosystem was one of the last areas inhabited by grizzly bears in the continental United States. Perhaps 220 to 360 bears occupied 5 million acres (2 million hectares) in and near Yellowstone National Park during 1959 to 1967. People killed about 15 grizzly bears each year, but abundance was relatively stable. Most of the grizzly bears killed by people during this period were dependent on human foods and garbage in developments and campgrounds. (Craighead and Craighead 1967, Cowan et al. 1974, Craighead et al. 1974, Cole 1976, Craighead et al. 1988, Schullery 1992, Meagher 2008, Servheen and Shoemaker 2008)

In 1959, Frank and John Craighead began the first scientific study of grizzly bears in the Yellowstone ecosystem, pioneering advancements in radio telemetry to learn about bear movements, reproduction, and survival, and using innovative population dynamics modeling to estimate and predict trends. Popular magazine articles and movies about their studies were very influential at stimulating public awareness and generating support for the conservation of grizzly bears. When the Craigheads began their studies, many (if not most) grizzly bears were feeding at garbage dumps in and near Yellowstone National Park. Their research indicated these concentrations of food were extremely important to the behavior, reproduction, and survival of grizzly bears. As a result, they cautioned that closing the dumps would lead to the deaths of many bears deprived of these food sources. (Craighead 1982, Craighead et al. 1995)

However, in 1969 a report by the Natural Sciences Advisory Committee of the National Park Service suggested a new approach for bear management in Yellowstone National Park that would prevent bears from obtaining human foods and return them to a wild existence. Park managers adopted this approach and implemented actions and regulations to keep bears from acquiring human foods and refuse. Four garbage dumps in Yellowstone National Park and 3 in nearby areas of Montana were closed during 1968 to 1979. These abrupt closures were controversial and unpopular, with the Craigheads fervently arguing against them. In fact, the debate became so acrimonious that

*John (left) and Frank Craighead fit a grizzly bear with an early radio collar, August 1966. The Craigheads were pioneers of grizzly bear research in the Yellowstone ecosystem.*

the National Park Service did not renew the Craigheads' research permit in 1971. Regulations forbidding the feeding of bears were enforced and bear-resistant garbage cans and dumpsters were placed throughout the park to prevent more bears from learning to subsist on human foods and transferring this behavior to their young. In addition, park interpreters began instructing visitors about proper food storage and disposal, and rangers began issuing citations for violations. (National Park Service 1960, Leopold et al. 1963, Craighead and Craighead 1967, Leopold et al. 1969, Cole 1976, Craighead 1982, Meagher and Phillips 1983, Schullery 1992, Craighead et al. 1995, Haroldson et al. 2008b, Meagher 2008)

Moreover, managers implemented measures to prevent bears from getting human foods in backcountry areas. In 1972, Yellowstone National Park converted from non-designated, dispersed camping in backcountry areas to a system with specific campsites in select areas along trails and lakeshores. Campers at each site were provided with food-hanging poles or bear-resistant food storage containers. These combined efforts in frontcountry and backcountry areas were successful at preventing bears from obtaining human foods and garbage. (Cole 1976, Meagher and Phillips 1983, Gunther 1994, National Park Service 1995)

Over time, changes in human behavior and removals of food-conditioned bears led to fewer injuries to people and less property damage as remaining bears subsisted on natural foods. In the short term, however, dump closures resulted in many food-conditioned bears searching for human foods in campgrounds and developments and eventually being captured and killed or sent to zoos. More than 229 grizzly bears were killed during 1967 to 1972 due to managers removing food-conditioned bears, landowners shooting bears to defend life or property, and hunters harvesting bears outside the park. Also, the removal of garbage as a steady, dependable food source contributed to smaller litter sizes and lower survival of cubs and adult females. (Meagher and Phillips 1983, Knight and Eberhardt

1985, Craighead et al. 1988, Gunther 1994, Craighead et al. 1995, Gunther and Hoekstra 1998, Haroldson et al. 2008b, Meagher 2008)

The high human-caused mortality resulted in grizzly bear numbers in the Greater Yellowstone Ecosystem decreasing to perhaps fewer than 250 bears by the mid-1970s. This decrease led to an evaluation of the population dynamics of Yellowstone grizzly bears by the National Academy of Sciences. One of the recommendations from this Committee on the Yellowstone Grizzlies was to limit removals of bears until more reliable information on bear reproduction, survival, and population trends was obtained. Thus, the Interagency Grizzly Bear Study Team was formed in 1973 to conduct monitoring and research on food resources, habitats, human-bear conflicts, and population dynamics. The Study Team originally consisted of biologists and researchers from the National Park Service, U.S. Fish and Wildlife Service, U.S. Forest Service, and the states of Idaho, Montana, and Wyoming. The U.S. Geological Survey became the coordinating agency in 1997 and the Eastern Shoshone and Northern Arapaho tribes from the Wind River Reservation joined in 2009. (Cowan et al. 1974, Craighead et al. 1974, Craighead et al. 1988, Craighead et al. 1995, Haroldson et al. 2008b)

In addition, grizzly bears in the Greater Yellowstone Ecosystem were protected in 1975 as threatened pursuant to the federal Endangered Species Act due to high mortality from people, low recruitment, and loss of habitat. Bear management necessarily transitioned to the prevention of mortality and protection of habitat rather than removing conflict bears and, before long, grizzly bears became a national symbol of the modern conservation and wilderness movements that proliferated in the 1960s and 1970s. In response, many people in areas where agriculture, mining, and timber harvest were traditional occupations became frustrated because they felt the legal protection for grizzly bears was used to thwart development and extraction activities. (U.S. Fish and Wildlife Service 1975, Schullery 1992, Simberloff 1999, Meagher 2008, Servheen and Shoemaker 2008)

*The modern-day environmental movement, which began in the 1930s and 1940s with the teachings of Aldo Leopold, bloomed during the late 1950s and 1960s with changing attitudes and beliefs about the appropriate management of wildlife in national parks and wilderness areas.*

## Recovery and Range Expansion

It took many years to wean bears from human foods, and the rapid dump closures and subsequent killing of many food-conditioned bears generated intense debate among managers, scientists, and the public. The 1970s and 1980s were a period of intense learning and adaptation to these changed circumstances by bears, managers, and visitors. In 1983, the Interagency Grizzly Bear Committee with a Yellowstone Ecosystem Subcommittee, comprised of high-level managers of federal and state agencies, was created to coordinate management, monitoring, and research efforts across jurisdictions. The Subcommittee has members from national forests, state wildlife agencies, Native American tribes, national parks, Bureau of Land Management, and county governments in the Greater Yellowstone Ecosystem. Several regional measures were implemented by the Subcommittee to reduce grizzly bear mortality, including the establishment of secure habitat through management of motorized access, better garbage management and food storage requirements, reduced sheep grazing on public lands, and rewards for identifying poachers. This coordinated, interagency implementation of conservation measures was effective. Eventually, the Yellowstone grizzly bear population began to recover, with about 276 grizzly bears in 1990 and 512 in 2000. Also, conflicts between bears and people inside Yellowstone National Park began to decrease, with less than 1 bear attack and 5 property damages for every 1 million visits during 1983 through 2012. (Craighead et al. 1995, Haroldson 1999, Haroldson et al. 2008b, Meagher 2008, Servheen and Shoemaker 2008, Gunther 2015b)

As bear numbers increased during the 1980s and 1990s, some black bears and grizzly bears began to occupy meadows adjacent to developed areas and roads in Yellowstone National Park. Grizzly bears using these areas included about 39% solitary adults, 34% subadults, and 27% females with cubs. Also, tourism to Yellowstone National Park increased to almost 3 million visits per summer by the mid-2000s. These changes led to more visitors stopping their cars along roadways to view and photograph bears. There were more than 4,000 bear jams from March through October during 1990 to 2004, with numbers increasing substantially after 2000. Bears stopped running away as they learned visitors would not harm them, which inevitably led to more frequent, larger, and longer bear jams along roadways. Initially, park rangers captured and relocated these habituated bears. They also implemented temporary closures and hazed bears away from roadside meadows using cracker shells, rubber bullets, and other methods. These efforts were rarely successful, however, possibly because access to high-quality natural foods without the risk of injury from more dominant bears outweighed the distraction or pain caused by these human deterrents. (Gunther and Wyman 2008, Haroldson and Gunther 2013)

Park managers realized they needed a different and more integrated management approach for dealing with roadside bears habituated to people, but not dependent on human foods. Visitors quickly became used to viewing and photographing these non-aggressive bears, which eventually led to people approaching bears too closely and sometimes trying to feed them. As a result, the park adopted a new strategy in 1990 that focused interpreters, rangers, and resource specialists on educating and managing people to ensure their safety, rather than trying to discourage bears from using roadside meadows. Initially, only black bears were tolerated near roadways but, over time, grizzly bears were tolerated as well. Also, beginning in 2001, seasonal rangers were hired to oversee visitors at bear jams and keep traffic moving along roadways. This management approach proved extremely successful, with no people being injured by bears during thousands of roadway traffic jams in subsequent decades. (Gunther and Wyman 2008, Haroldson and Gunther 2013)

Though roadside bears were a premier attraction for visitors, most grizzly bears remained in wilderness areas where they avoided encounters with people. However, hiking and camping in backcountry areas increased steadily after the 1960s, which raised concerns about disturbances by unsuspecting people resulting in aggressive responses from these wary bears. Therefore, managers initiated a Bear

Management Area program in 1982 to reduce conflicts by closing some areas, backcountry campsites, and trails to people during certain times of year. The program was designed to maintain undisturbed foraging opportunities for grizzly bears in key areas, while increasing the safety of backcountry visitors. (National Park Service 1982, Coleman et al. 2013a, Coleman et al. 2013b)

Monitoring by the Interagency Grizzly Bear Study Team indicated bear numbers increased 4 to 7% per year during 1983 to 2001, primarily due to higher adult female survival. In turn, grizzly bears began recolonizing habitats outside Yellowstone National Park, expanding their range by almost 50% from the 1980s to the 1990s. By 2005, there were about 630 grizzly bears living across more than 8.5 million acres (3.5 million hectares) of the Greater Yellowstone Ecosystem. Survival of adult females remained high in national parks and surrounding wilderness areas, but was lower in areas with higher densities of roads and developed sites. Conversely, cub survival and reproduction decreased somewhat in national parks and surrounding wilderness areas where grizzly bear densities were high. Collectively, these factors contributed to a slowing of population growth after 2001. (Schwartz et al. 2002, Haroldson and Frey 2005, Haroldson et al. 2006, Schwartz et al. 2006b, Harris et al. 2007, Haroldson et al. 2008b, Schwartz et al. 2010b, Bjornlie et al. 2014b, van Manen et al. 2016a)

In 2007, the U.S. Fish and Wildlife Service concluded the Yellowstone grizzly bear population was recovered and removed it from protection under the Endangered Species Act. However, this action was overturned in 2009 by the District Court of Montana, with the 9th U.S. Circuit Court of Appeals upholding this decision in 2011. These courts questioned the resiliency of grizzly bears to recent and predicted future decreases in food resources such as whitebark pine nuts. Regardless, the grizzly bear population continued to expand in numbers and range during 2007 to 2015. After the Interagency Grizzly Bear Study Team analyzed possible impacts from a substantial mortality of whitebark pine trees, the U.S. Fish and Wildlife Service again proposed to remove Yellowstone grizzly bears from the federal

*A grizzly bear foraging for whitebark pine nuts, Bridger-Teton National Forest. Whitebark pine trees have experienced substantial mortality throughout the Greater Yellowstone Ecosystem since the early 2000s, but continue to be an important fall food source during years of seed abundance.*

Photograph by Jake Davis

list of endangered and threatened wildlife in 2016. (Mattson 1997a, Paetkau et al. 1998, Jacoby et al. 1999, Miller and Waits 2003, U.S. Fish and Wildlife Service 2007a, U.S. Fish and Wildlife Service 2016)

## Cultural Importance

The Yellowstone area is home to various native peoples, including the Blackfeet, Crow, Eastern Shoshone, Gros Ventre and Assiniboine, Nez Perce, Salish and Kootenai, Shoshone-Bannock, and other tribal nations. Grizzly bears have a sacred place in their culture, being historically used for food, clothing, and jewelry, and having a prominent role in many ceremonies, competitions, legends, and paintings. Also, grizzly bears are revered as a spiritual source of guidance, medicine, power, regeneration, and renewal. In addition, grizzly bears symbolize many qualities such as bravery, courage, curiosity, protection, and strength. (Shepard and Sanders 1985, Rockwell 1991, Kellert et al. 1996, Nabokov and Loendorf 2004, GOAL 2014, Montana & Wyoming Tribal Leaders Council 2014, Native American Encyclopedia 2014, Old Coyote 2014)

Some tribal elders believe the exploitation and persecution of grizzly bears by colonizing Euro-Americans reflected sentiments towards native peoples. Also, the possibility of hunting grizzly bears in portions of the Greater Yellowstone Ecosystem after their removal from protection under the Endangered Species Act has evoked protests and opposition by several tribes. Many tribal leaders see the possible future hunting of grizzly bears as an infringement of their spiritual and religious rights guaranteed by the American Indian Religious Freedom Act. (Archambault 2014, Fisher 2014, GOAL 2014, Montana & Wyoming Tribal Leaders Council 2014, Old Coyote 2014, Pearson 2014, Small 2014, St. Clair 2014)

Grizzly bears were also an important part of the Euro-American experience. Accounts of interactions with grizzly bears by early colonists span a range of perceptions from awe to fear to respect that still persist in contemporary society, even though most Americans are far more removed from nature. Today, there is worldwide support for the conservation of grizzly bears in the Yellowstone area because they are viewed as threatened and Yellowstone National Park is considered their home by many people due to past visitation experiences, television shows such as Yogi Bear, and magazine articles. However, perceptions in the Greater Yellowstone Ecosystem are more variable and depend on a person's background, experiences, knowledge, occupation, and values regarding predators and wilderness. (Jobes 1991, Kellert et al. 1996, Whittlesey et al. 2015)

The Greater Yellowstone Ecosystem has become more demographically and economically diverse since the 1970s, with amenity living, recreation, and tourism confronting traditional agricultural, extraction (logging, mining), and ranching lifestyles. Many residents consider living near wilderness with grizzly bears an amenity and a valuable economic attraction for recreation and tourism. Thus, they generally support grizzly bear conservation as long as their livelihoods, property, and safety are protected. However, some residents with more utilitarian backgrounds view increases in the abundance and distribution of predators such as grizzly bears as a detriment to the economy and a threat to their way of life. As a result, regulations protecting predators such as bears, as well as resentment against perceived interference by outsiders, sometimes lead to illegal shootings. (Kellert et al. 1996, Hansen et al. 2002, Morris and McBeth 2003, Johnson and Stewart 2005, Bienen and Tabor 2006, Haggerty and Travis 2006, Hansen 2009, Bergstrom and Harrington 2013)

## Conclusions

The recovery of grizzly bears in the Greater Yellowstone Ecosystem was successful because a diverse group of agencies, organizations, and people, who often disagreed about specific management approaches, worked together toward a mutual goal to sustain grizzly bears and wildness in suitable areas. Coordinated efforts across various jurisdictions were necessary to remove human food attractants, reduce bear mortalities, and protect secure habitats. During these efforts, collectively managing the behavior of residents and visitors to prevent the food-conditioning of bears was as important as managing the bears themselves. In combination, these collaborative actions enabled grizzly bears to expand their distribution and numbers which, in turn, contributed to the viability of this wild population. (Gunther and Wyman 2008, Meagher 2008, Servheen and Shoemaker 2008)

However, there are several lingering and forthcoming threats to this conservation success story. Tourism to Yellowstone National Park and surrounding areas now exceeds 4 million visits per year and extends from March through November, thereby increasing the chance for people to disturb grizzly bears focused on obtaining foods to replenish their body condition before or after denning and hibernation. This intense and prolonged visitation has challenged the ability of staff to adequately manage traffic jams associated with roadside bears and increased concerns about visitor and bear safety. The habituation of some bears frequenting roadside meadows was likely an inevitable outcome in an intensely visited area like Yellowstone but, today, most bears remain in the backcountry where they generally avoid people. However, managing ever larger numbers of visitors to prevent feeding, injuries, property damage, or unwanted encounters with bears at campsites and along trails in the backcountry has become much more difficult as funding and staffing diminish in comparison. If visitation continues to increase, it is doubtful the success of the current management approach at preventing food-conditioning and aggressive encounters between grizzly bears and people will remain unchanged. Rather, resource protection personnel will likely need to try new methods to manage increasing numbers of visitors wanting to view and photograph bears or try to reverse and subsequently prevent the habituation of bears. (Gunther and Wyman 2008, Meagher 2008, Coleman et al. 2013a, Coleman et al. 2013b, Haroldson and Gunther 2013)

In addition, there are developing issues such as habitat encroachment with an increasing human populace and the development of unprotected portions of the ecosystem; climate warming and its possible future effects on food resources such as whitebark pine nuts, cutthroat trout, and native vegetation; and the possible removal of grizzly bears from protection under the Endangered Species Act, which would be followed by state management and, possibly, sport hunting and a reduction in bear numbers in some areas outside preserves. There is significant uncertainty regarding the extent of these changes, the magnitude of their effects on grizzly bears, and the resilience of bears to adapt to the changes. As a result, the Interagency Grizzly Bear Study Team is conducting monitoring and research, and federal, state, and tribal agencies are implementing additional management actions (see Chapters 10 and 11) to reduce these uncertainties. What is clear, however, is the continued recovery of the Yellowstone grizzly bear population will be overwhelmingly influenced by human behavior, values, and decisions. (Gunther 2008, Haroldson et al. 2008b, Servheen and Shoemaker 2008, Schwartz et al. 2013, van Manen et al. 2016a)

Photograph by Jake Davis

*A grizzly bear cub-of-the-year. Cubs are born in the den during winter and typically spend 2.5 years with their mother before weaning and separation.*

# Chapter 3

## REPRODUCTION, SURVIVAL, AND POPULATION GROWTH

*Frank T. van Manen and Mark A. Haroldson*

### Introduction

THE TRAJECTORY OF any wildlife population, or increase or decrease in size over time, is the result of births and deaths, as well as immigration and emigration. Evidence suggests the grizzly bear population in the Greater Yellowstone Ecosystem remains isolated, although there is a small chance that some emigration or immigration has gone undetected. Regardless, the trajectory of this population is based almost entirely on reproduction and survival, which are broadly governed by the life history characteristics of a species and influenced by many ecological processes. In this chapter, we examine patterns of reproduction and survival of grizzly bears in the ecosystem, how various ecological factors influence those patterns, and how these factors contributed to changes in the population trajectory. (Cole 1954, Caughley 1977, Haroldson et al. 2010)

## Reproductive Cycle

Reproductively active female grizzly bears that are not accompanied by cubs-of-the-year (cubs) or yearlings (between 1 and 2 years of age) have a single breeding season per year. Females are receptive to copulation for between 17 and 45 days. Copulations have been observed as early as May 18 and as late as July 11, with the mating season lasting approximately 63 days. Most successful copulations last less than 25 minutes, but some last as long as 60 minutes. Both male and female grizzly bears are promiscuous and litters may include siblings sired by different fathers. Males maximize breeding opportunities by following a female while she is receptive, with pair bonds sometimes lasting several days or weeks. This strategy is most successful among dominant males, and dominance generally correlates with body mass (weight). Male home ranges are large and overlap multiple female ranges, enhancing mating opportunities. (Dittrich and Kronberger 1963, Schleyer 1983, Hamer and Herrero 1990, Blanchard and Knight 1991, Craighead et al. 1995, Craighead et al. 1998, Schwartz et al. 2003b)

Like other species in the bear family, *Ursidae*, female grizzly bears experience seasonal delayed implantation in which eggs fertilized in spring remain in a stage of early development (blastocyst). Implantation into the uterine wall occurs in late November or early December. Normal fetal growth (gestation) then occurs for about 60 days, culminating in birth (parturition) in late January or early February. The combined period of delayed implantation and gestation is about 235 days. Newborn grizzly bear cubs are about 8 inches (20 centimeters) in length and weigh about 1.1 pounds (0.5 kilograms). Members of the *Ursidae* family have some of the smallest ratios of offspring to adult body mass among placental mammals. Given a typical litter size of 2 cubs and a female body mass of 250 pounds (113 kilograms), the body mass ratio of offspring to mother is less than 1%. For comparison, this ratio is typically around 5% for humans. (Renfree and Calaby 1981, Tsubota et al. 1987, Oftedal and Gittleman 1989, Pasitschniak-Arts 1993, Sibly and Brown 2009)

The period of maternal care and the timing of weaning vary among brown bear populations. In the Greater Yellowstone Ecosystem, offspring are typically weaned as 2-year-olds, at age 2.5. However, in Scandinavian brown bears almost equal numbers of litters are weaned as yearlings as 2-year-olds. Conversely, the average weaning age is 4.5 years on the North Slope of Alaska, where habitat productivity is low. Females typically breed again during the spring of the year offspring are weaned, but delays of one to several years may occur. For female grizzly bears in the Greater Yellowstone Ecosystem, a successful reproductive cycle is typically 3 years (Figure 3.1). However, several factors can disrupt this sequence, including the loss of a litter, the timing of separation between mother and offspring, and a delay in subsequent reproduction. Female grizzly bears show some flexibility in this reproductive sequence, as indicated by rare observations of mixed-age litters composed of cubs and yearlings. This phenomenon may occur when a female is temporarily separated from her cubs, mates while still maintaining lactation, and produces another litter in the subsequent year. (Reynolds 1976, Dahle and Swenson 2003a, Schwartz et al. 2003b, Swenson and Haroldson 2008)

The reproductive longevity of female brown bears is relatively high, but even a female surviving into her early 20s may only produce 4 to 5 litters of offspring in her lifetime. Consequently, the average time it takes a female grizzly bear in the Greater Yellowstone Ecosystem to replace herself in the population, or generation time, is relatively long; approximately 14 years in the most recent decade. (Schwartz et al. 2003a, Kamath et al. 2015)

## Reproductive Rates

Reproductive rates for grizzly bears, or fecundity, are commonly expressed as the number of female cubs produced per reproductive-age female per year. Much of what we know about reproductive parameters for grizzly bears in the Greater Yellowstone Ecosystem is based on long-term capture efforts and telemetry monitoring. Reproductive rates are

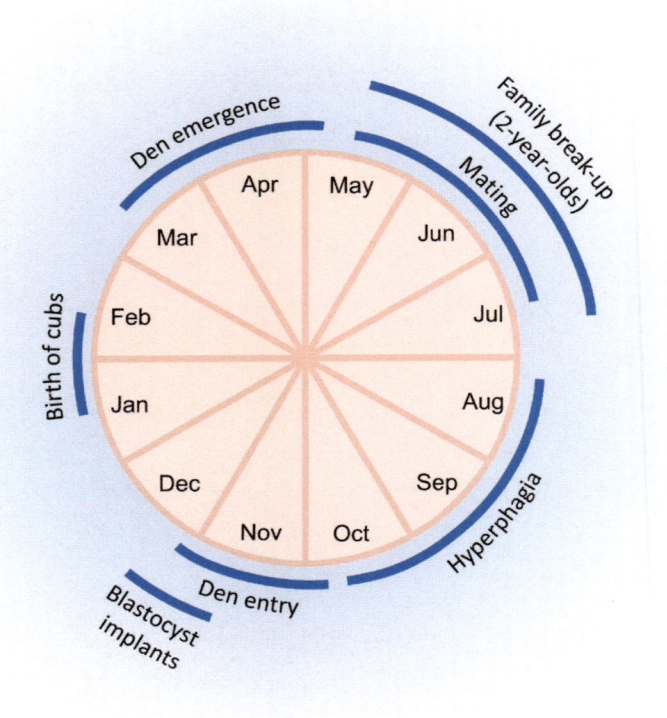

*Figure 3.1. Diagram of the typical reproductive cycle of grizzly bears in the Greater Yellowstone Ecosystem.*

a direct result of factors such as age of first reproduction, litter size, cub survival, inter-birth interval, and the age of reproductive senescence, after which reproduction wanes. In turn, these factors are influenced by habitat productivity, or food supply, as well as population density. Fecundity in this ecosystem is relatively high compared with 20 populations of brown bears studied worldwide. Yellowstone grizzly bears have access to abundant ungulate resources, so the quantity and quality of food supply may be a contributing factor. (Schwartz et al. 2003a)

In North America, the age of first reproduction varies geographically and among individuals, ranging from 4 years to as high as 10 years. This variation is primarily a function of habitat quality, but may also be influenced by population density and whether females disperse.

Researchers in Scandinavia have reported some of the lowest ages of first reproduction, ranging from a mean of 4.5 years in central Sweden to a mean of 5.4 years in northern Sweden, but with occasional observations of 3 years. In the Greater Yellowstone Ecosystem, the average age of first reproduction is 5.8 years, with 10% of females producing their first litter of cubs at age 4, 30% at age 5, and 56% at age 6. All Yellowstone females produce their first litter by age 7. (Nagy and Haroldson 1990, McLellan 1994, Swenson et al. 2001, Zedrosser et al. 2004, Kovach et al. 2006, Schwartz et al. 2006a, Støen et al. 2006b)

Brown bears typically have litters of 1 to 3 cubs, with occasional litters of 4. Average litter size is similar among populations, varying between 1.7 and 2.5 cubs for 17 study sites in North America. Litter size is associated with the age of the female producing the litter, as well as food production. In the Greater Yellowstone Ecosystem, average litter size has remained remarkably constant for several decades at 2.0 during 1983 to 2001 and 2.1 during 2002 to 2011. These estimates are based on initial sightings of radio-marked females with cubs during telemetry flights, which results in conservative estimates because cub mortality may have occurred prior to the first observation of a female with cubs. When adjusted for this possibility, average litter size was estimated at 2.5 cubs. In any given year, 2-cub litters are most common, followed by approximately equal proportions of litters with 1 and 3 cubs (Figure 3.2). Eight litters of quadruplets have been observed since 1983, with 6 of those litters occurring since 2009. Litter size increases with age of the mother and capture records indicate the average age of female bears has increased over the past 3 decades, which may be a factor contributing to more 4-cub litters. Also, we have documented at least one 4-cub litter that was the result of an adoption event. (Onoyama and Haga 1982, McLellan 1994, Schwartz et al. 2006a, Haroldson et al. 2008a, Interagency Grizzly Bear Study Team 2012, Haroldson et al. 2015a)

The inter-birth interval also influences reproductive rates. This interval is the period between subsequent litters produced by a female. For brown bear populations in North America, this interval is approximately 3 years or more, because the typical age of weaning is around 2.5 years.

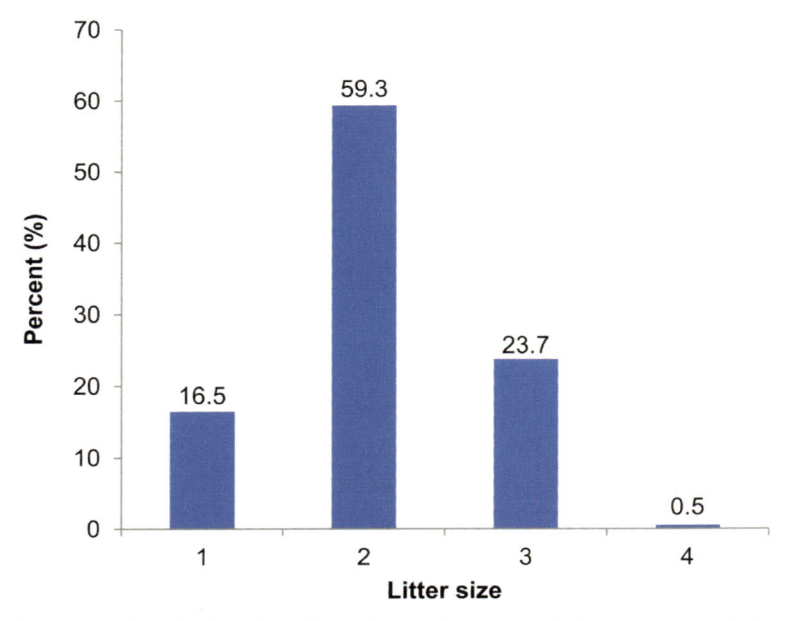

*Figure 3.2. Distribution of 194 litter sizes of female grizzly bears monitored via radio telemetry in the Greater Yellowstone Ecosystem, 1973-2011.*

A delay in subsequent reproduction is not uncommon and lengthens the interval. It is shorter on rare occasions when females lose their entire litter prior to weaning, or when they wean offspring as 1.5-year-olds and enter into estrus and breed again the same year. Therefore, interpretation of changes in the inter-birth interval should be made carefully. The average inter-birth interval in the Greater Yellowstone Ecosystem is 2.8 years. Given that this period is less than 3 years, and there is little evidence of offspring being weaned at 1.5 years, litter loss must play a role. (McLellan 1994, Schwartz et al. 2003b, Schwartz et al. 2006a)

Reproductive maturation and a reduction of reproduction with age (reproductive senescence) can play an important role in the life history of bears. Reproduction in female brown bears follows a classic mammalian productivity curve, with a rapid increase in productivity starting during sexual maturation at ages 4 to 5, followed by highest productivity during the ages of 9 to 20 years, and a rapid decrease in reproduction after age 25. In the Greater Yellowstone Ecosystem, however, the oldest documented female with cubs was 25 years. Among males, reproductive senescence may not be so much a function of physiological factors, but more due to a diminishing ability to physically compete for mates. Currently, reproductive senescence has little effect on population growth, but this may change in the future as the population ages further, particularly in Yellowstone National Park where the survival of adult bears has been high since the closure of open-pit garbage dumps more than 4 decades ago. (Schwartz et al. 2003a, van Manen et al. 2014)

Habitat and food productivity are other factors that can affect reproductive rates. For example, the seeds of whitebark pine trees are a variable, but calorie-rich, food resource for bears. In years following poor production of whitebark pine seeds the previous autumn, 1-cub litters were more likely than 3-cub litters compared to years with good seed crops the previous fall. However, recent research showed no relationship between the ability of females to produce cubs and the decline of healthy whitebark pine stands in their home ranges, which suggests reproduction by grizzly bears is resilient to major changes in this food resource. Thus far, studies of this relationship in the Greater Yellowstone Ecosystem have focused on whitebark pine because annual variation in cone production can be reliably measured; however, such relationships may also exist for other food resources or habitat productivity in general, which merits further investigation. (Schwartz et al. 2006a, van Manen et al. 2016a)

Finally, the population density of grizzly bears may affect reproductive parameters. In the Greater Yellowstone Ecosystem, smaller litter sizes were more likely as population size increased. Similarly, the probability of lone females producing cubs started decreasing during the mid-1990s and was associated with increasing grizzly bear density. This contributed to a moderate decrease in fecundity from 0.36 during 1983 to 2001 to 0.34 during 2002 to 2012. (Miller et al. 2003, Schwartz et al. 2006a, Interagency Grizzly Bear Study Team 2012, van Manen et al. 2016a)

*Survival rates are a major factor influencing the population dynamics of large mammals, including grizzly bears. Adult female survival is of particular interest because it typically has the greatest effect on population growth.*

## Maternal Care and Cub Growth

Grizzly bear cubs are born during the prolonged, winter denning period when the mother is hibernating. Newborn cubs are blind, have little fur, and are relatively helpless, requiring extensive maternal care in a secure environment. Hibernation is an effective adaptation to prolonged periods of food scarcity, but requires considerable energy storage to survive the 4 to 6 months of winter. Therefore, a period of copious food consumption prior to entering their dens, also referred to as autumn hyperphagia, is important for bears to build up sufficient energy reserves, especially fat. The ability to build fat reserves is particularly important for pregnant females. In studies at the Washington State University Bear Research Center, captive female brown bears with less than 20% body fat did not produce cubs. Additionally, for females giving birth to cubs in the den, energetic demands are greater than other bears because of lactation. Consequently, the loss of body mass during the hibernation period tends to be greatest for females that emerge from their dens with cubs. In captivity, females with more fat reserves gave birth earlier and their cubs grew faster and attained greater body mass at den emergence compared with those nursing from leaner mothers. These patterns are likely similar for female grizzly bears in the wild. (Robbins et al. 2012)

The growth of grizzly bear cubs is rapid. For wild grizzly bears, data on early cub growth are almost completely lacking, but studies on captive grizzly bears provide useful insights. While the mother is still hibernating, average milk intake among cubs is about 12.5 ounces (353 grams) per day and body mass gain is about 3.5 ounces (98 grams) per day. For twin litters, cub body mass increases to approximately 4.4 pounds (2 kilograms) after 30 days, 8.8 pounds (4 kilograms) after 60 days, and 22 pounds (10 kilograms) after 90 days. For triplet litters, growth was slower and body mass was only about 11 pounds (5 kilograms) at 90 days. Also, total litter mass at 90 days was 83% compared with twin litters. These data suggest a trade-off between litter size and body growth, which may be a function of sibling competition. By mid-summer (July-August), cubs typically have a body mass of 44 to

55 pounds (20 to 25 kilograms). By the time they enter dens with the mothers in late fall, they may reach as much as 115 pounds (52 kilograms). Yearling body mass is typically around 110 to 137 pounds (50 to 62 kilograms) by summer, whereas summer body mass of 2- and 3-year-olds may be 194 to 220 pounds (88 to 100 kilograms). Such impressive gains are likely promoted by the long period of time that offspring stay with the mother, another indicator of maternal investment. Most offspring are weaned after approximately 2.5 years, but we have observed mothers with their 3.5-year-old offspring. Such observations may reflect occasional reunions or an extended period of care. (Farley and Robbins 1995, Gonzalez et al. 2012, Robbins et al. 2012)

## Survival

Survival rates are a major factor influencing the population dynamics of large mammals, including grizzly bears. Adult female survival is of particular interest because it typically has the greatest effect on population growth. Low adult female survival was the critical factor causing a decrease in grizzly bear numbers in the Greater Yellowstone Ecosystem prior to the mid-1980s. Managers realized adult female survival was insufficient for population recovery and they needed to find effective ways to reduce mortality of adult females. This was one of the factors that led to the establishment of the Interagency Grizzly Bear Committee in 1983 to develop and implement effective conservation strategies. Such strategies included implementing food storage orders and reducing development, motorized access, and livestock grazing on public lands within the Grizzly Bear Recovery Zone. This zone was established by the U.S. Fish and Wildlife Service in 1982 and encompassed Yellowstone National Park and adjacent national forest areas. There was an increase in the survival of independent bears 2 years or older during 1983 to 2001, likely in response to these interagency management efforts which, in turn, contributed to an increasing population. Survival remains strongly influenced by human-related factors such as developed sites, roads, livestock grazing, and food attractants, and there is a distinct relationship with the amount of undeveloped, protected habitat where bears can avoid conflicts with humans. Survival is highest within Yellowstone National Park and surrounding wilderness areas, with females frequently living into their late 20s and males into their mid-20s, and generally decreases towards the periphery of the ecosystem. (Eberhardt 1977, Knight and Eberhardt 1985, Interagency Grizzly Bear Committee 1986, Eberhardt et al. 1994, Haroldson et al. 2006, Harris et al. 2006, Schwartz et al. 2006d, U.S. Fish and Wildlife Service 2007a, Schwartz et al. 2010b, Interagency Grizzly Bear Study Team 2012)

The survival of independent-age grizzly bears in the Greater Yellowstone Ecosystem is estimated from telemetry monitoring of a sample of bears in the population, also referred to as known-fate monitoring. The goal for the Interagency Grizzly Bear Study Team is to maintain at least 25 radio-collared females and a representative sample of males, all of which are located approximately twice per month. Each radio collar is equipped with a motion sensor that switches the pulse rate of the transmitted telemetry signal when the collar has been stationary for at least 4 hours. Biologists investigate the location of each stationary collar within 2 weeks to determine if the bear is alive or dead; though sometimes no radio collar or carcass is located and, as a result, the bear's fate is recorded as unknown. With a consistent sample of radio-collared bears over time, reliable estimates of survival are obtained. Survival of independent-age females has not changed for more than 3 decades, with annual survival estimated at 95% since 1983. A review of 41 studies on long-lived vertebrates suggested an annual survival rate of 95% is typical when populations experience relatively little impact from human activities. For independent-age males, annual survival was 87% from 1983 through 2001, but increased to 95% during 2002 to 2011. This trend was unexpected because males generally are more vulnerable to mortality than females. The increase in male survival may indicate conservation strategies initiated during the 1980s helped reduce mortality among males as well as females.

(Eberhardt 2002, Haroldson et al. 2006, Interagency Grizzly Bear Study Team 2012)

The survival of dependent young (cubs and yearlings) in the Greater Yellowstone Ecosystem is estimated differently than the survival of independent bears, though telemetry monitoring is still used. During ground monitoring or aerial telemetry flights of radio-collared females, visual observations of family groups are used to document the presence or loss of dependent young. Actual mortality events are rarely observed and, as a result, in most instances mortality is assumed when cubs or yearlings are no longer observed with their mother or after the mother dies. Cub survival is estimated for the period from den emergence in spring to the last cub observation prior to den entry (211 days), whereas yearling survival spans the dates of first and last observations of a litter of yearlings (199 days). Notable changes have occurred in these survival rates. Cub survival was 64% during 1983 to 2001, but decreased to 55% during 2002 to 2011. Yearling survival for these same time periods decreased from 82% to 54%. (Schwartz et al 2006b, Schwartz et al. 2006c, Interagency Grizzly Bear Study Team 2012, van Manen et al. 2016a)

## Causes of Mortality

The Interagency Grizzly Bear Study Team documents grizzly bear deaths due to natural causes, poaching, misidentification or self-defense shootings by black bear and ungulate hunters, accidents such as vehicle strikes, undetermined causes, and management removals following livestock depredation or conflicts with people in developed areas. Natural and undetermined causes represented 8% and 7%, respectively, of total reported mortality during 2006 to 2015. Natural causes included avalanches, injuries, killing by other bears or other wildlife species (bison, wolves), old age, and starvation. For several decades, about 85% of grizzly bear deaths have been due to human actions, though the relative contributions of various causes have changed over time. For example, poaching was the most common source of mortality during

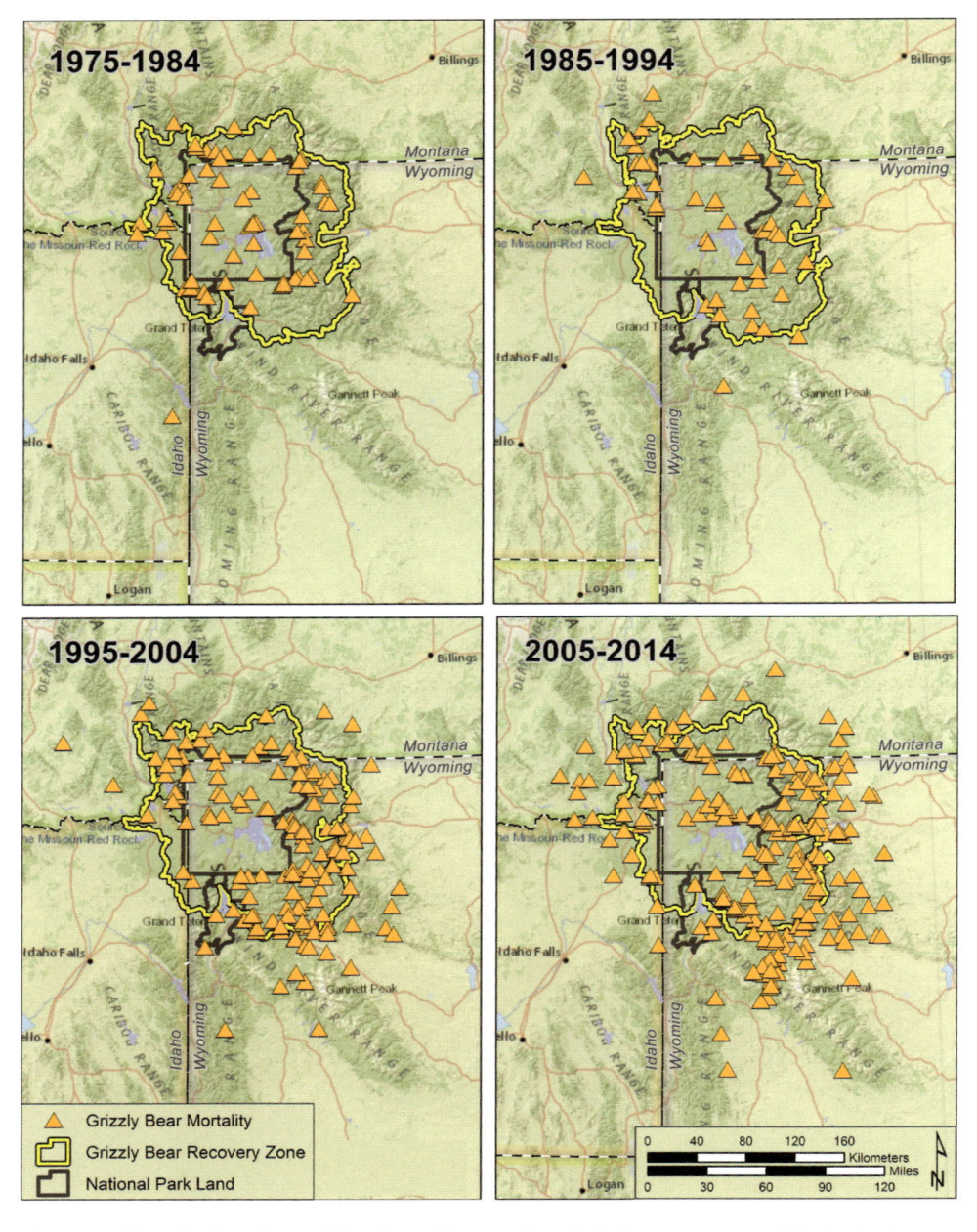

*Figure 3.3. Distribution of mortalities from all causes for grizzly bears 2 years or older in the Greater Yellowstone Ecosystem by decade, 1975-2014. Base map source: National Geographic World Map, ESRI, Redlands, California.*

the late 1970s and early 1980s, reaching over 20%, but decreased to 5% during 2006 to 2015. Bears removed due to conflicts with people in developed areas represented the largest proportion of mortalities during the late 1980s and early 1990s, but the proportion of hunting-related mortality was larger during the late 1990s and 2000s. Currently, the highest proportion (30%) of all reported grizzly bear mortalities is associated with shootings by ungulate hunters (mostly self-defense kills), followed by conflicts with humans in developed areas (25%) and livestock depredations (19%). Most deaths in the latter categories reflect management removals. (Haroldson et al. 2006, Haroldson and Frey 2016)

The trends in mortality were associated with an increasing distribution, or range expansion, of grizzly bears in the Greater Yellowstone Ecosystem. Mortalities mostly occurred within the Grizzly Bear Recovery Zone until the mid-1990s, but increased in the eastern and southeastern portions of the ecosystem as the distribution of grizzly bears expanded (Figure 3.3). The area encompassing reported mortalities increased by 85% between 1975-1984 and 2005-2014, or approximately 3,580 square miles (9,275 square kilometers) during every decade. Range expansion probably also contributed to the shift in proportional causes of mortality mentioned previously. For example, grizzly bear mortalities related to livestock depredations were almost eliminated within the Grizzly Bear Recovery Zone as livestock allotments were closed or retired during the 1980s. This was an effort supported by organizations such as the National Wildlife Federation, who compensated ranchers for voluntarily ending their leases on U.S. Forest Service grazing allotments in known conflict areas. However, with the grizzly bear population expanding well beyond the boundaries of the Recovery Zone, where livestock grazing is common, these types of mortalities again increased. The increase in hunter-related incidents may similarly be associated with range expansion. Human access in core areas of the ecosystem dominated by national parks and wilderness areas is generally lower compared with peripheral areas.

Consequently, the probability of hunters encountering grizzly bears during fall ungulate hunts has increased. (Bjornlie et al. 2014a)

Specific causes of mortality are often difficult to determine for cub and yearling grizzly bears because there is seldom direct evidence and many unresolved cases may reflect natural mortality due to starvation or predation. Human causes are easily documented and accounted for about one-third of all cub and yearling mortalities in the Greater Yellowstone Ecosystem during 1983 to 2001. The proportion of these human-caused mortalities was 17% in Yellowstone National Park, 33% in adjacent national forest areas inside the Grizzly Bear Recovery Zone, and 85% in areas outside the Recovery Zone. In other words, vulnerability to human-caused mortality generally increases from the core to the periphery of the ecosystem. (Schwartz et al. 2006c, Schwartz et al. 2006d)

## Population Growth and Density

Although population estimates from the 1970s are suspect, the Yellowstone grizzly bear population was small, with perhaps fewer than 250 bears. The population began a path towards recovery with the protections of the Endangered Species Act starting in 1975 and the implementation of conservation measures in the early 1980s (see Chapter 2). Conservative population estimates have been relatively constant since the early 2000s, currently indicating a population of at least 690 grizzly bears. The population has a sex ratio among adults and subadults that is approximately equal, and the sex ratio at birth is also equal. Adults comprise approximately 59% of the population, subadults about 11%, and cubs and yearlings about 30%. (Cowan et al. 1974, Craighead et al. 1974, U.S. Fish and Wildlife Service 1975, Knight and Eberhardt 1985, Craighead et al. 1988, Craighead et al. 1995, Interagency Grizzly Bear Study Team 2012, Haroldson et al. 2016)

The annual growth rate of the Yellowstone grizzly bear population was between 4.2% and 7.6% from 1983 through 2001, but slowed to between 0.3% and 2.2% during 2002 to 2011. The slowing of population growth was due to lower survival of cubs and yearlings and a moderate decrease in reproduction. The decrease of cub survival beginning around 2000 was most apparent where densities of grizzly bears were high. Similarly, the decrease in reproduction was most pronounced in areas with high bear densities. As the density of a population increases, some factors may start influencing population dynamics. These are referred to as density-dependent factors and tend to follow a predictable sequence among long-lived vertebrates: juvenile survival decreases first, followed by lower reproduction and, ultimately, a decrease in adult survival. Studies in Scandinavia and Alaska have shown cub survival is a density-dependent factor contributing to population regulation among bear populations. Small, inexperienced cubs are particularly vulnerable to killing by other bears (intraspecific killing) when densities are higher, which may reduce cub survival. Studies in Scandinavia support the notion of sexually-selected infanticide, whereby immigrant male bears kill cubs they did not sire to create a new mating opportunity. Similarly, studies in North America indicate greater vulnerability of cubs to various sources of mortality, including intraspecific killings, when populations are at a high density. Males are primarily responsible for these intraspecific killings, and in the Greater Yellowstone Ecosystem there may be a connection between the increased survival of males and increased mortality of cubs since the early 2000s. Field observations of males killing cubs have increased during the last 10 years compared with previous decades, supporting this hypothesis. Such killings may reflect an evolutionary strategy among bears, in which densities beyond carrying capacity are avoided through high offspring mortality, rather than reductions in adult survival. Because bear mothers present a formidable defense, offspring are most vulnerable to killing by other bears, and larger males in particular. (Swenson et al. 1997, Swenson et al. 2001, Eberhardt 2002, Miller et al. 2003, Gunther and Smith 2004, Harris et al. 2006, Interagency Grizzly Bear Study Team 2012, Interagency Grizzly Bear Study Team 2013, van Manen et al. 2016a)

Alternative explanations for the higher cub mortality rate and lower reproduction have been evaluated, but so far have little support. For example, an overall decrease in food resources could have increased competition among bears for access to nutritious foods, thereby reducing cub survival and reproduction in areas with higher bear densities. However, changes in juvenile survival and reproduction, were not associated with a decrease in healthy whitebark pine trees. Additionally, with a drop in habitat productivity, one would expect bears to respond with larger home ranges and movements, more reliance on lower-energy food resources, and decreased body condition. However, female home ranges have actually decreased in size and are least variable in areas with greater bear densities. Also, daily movement rates and activity have not changed during fall, bears continue to use high-quality foods, and body mass and percent body fat have not decreased. These combined findings indicate carrying capacity may have been reached in portions of the ecosystem because of population growth and high bear densities, rather than a decrease in food resources. The relatively constant population size since the early 2000s may be a reflection of this, which will be an important consideration for future management of the Yellowstone grizzly bear population. (Caughley 1977, Miller 1990, McLoughlin et al. 2000, Rode et al. 2001, Miller et al. 2003, Robbins et al. 2004, Haroldson et al. 2005, Schwartz et al. 2006d, Zedrosser et al. 2006, McLellan 2011, Fortin et al. 2013, Interagency Grizzly Bear Study Team 2013, Bjornlie et al. 2014b, Costello et al. 2014, Schwartz et al. 2014, Teisberg et al. 2014, van Manen et al. 2016a)

## Conclusions

Scientific data, exceptional in terms of study duration, sample size, and depth, have provided valuable insights into the reproduction, survival, and population growth of Yellowstone grizzly bears. A crucial conservation decision that likely changed the growth trajectory for the population and started the path towards recovery was the recognition that adult female survival was insufficient for sustained population growth. Management changes were implemented within the Grizzly Bear Recovery Zone to limit access to human foods through the use of food storage orders, limit motorized access, retire livestock allotments, and set standards to prevent the loss of secure habitat. Annual survival of independent-age females started to increase in the early 1980s and has remained at 95% for 3 decades and population growth increased accordingly through the late 1990s. Maintaining this level of female survival will be a key aspect for the long-term persistence of the population.

Lower survival of cubs and yearlings and a moderate decrease in reproduction lessened population growth in the early 2000s, and the population has been relatively constant ever since. Evidence to date suggests the recent change in the trajectory was more likely associated with the population reaching high bear densities in portions of the ecosystem, rather than a decrease in food resources. These findings suggest that the biological goal of population recovery has been accomplished. Finally, with substantial range expansion, we have observed shifts in the primary causes of mortality. Those shifts happen because bears are increasingly occupying areas outside protected zones where human influence and the potential for management conflicts are greater. For managers, the challenge is to adapt and respond to ever-changing conditions that lead to human-bear conflicts. For the public, the challenge is even greater and may require citizens to transcend focusing on their immediate concerns, which may represent opposing views such as economic impacts and safety versus concerns about grizzly bear population viability, and accept both grizzly bears and differing social values. (Schwartz et al. 2006d)

Photograph by Jake Davis

*A grizzly bear feeds on verdant springtime vegetation. In the Greater Yellowstone Ecosystem, grizzly bear diets include more than 260 plant and animal species, with plants making up nearly 70% of that number.*

# Chapter 4

## NUTRITIONAL ECOLOGY

*Charles T. Robbins and Jennifer K. Fortin-Noreus*

### Introduction

UNDERSTANDING THE NUTRITIONAL ecology of grizzly bears begins with a basic knowledge of their anatomy, physiology, and evolution. The digestive tract of grizzly bears is similar to humans, with an esophagus, acidic stomach, and small and large intestine. Like humans, grizzly bears are omnivores or generalist feeders in which anything that is palatable and nutritious may be part of their diet. Because of their relatively simple, carnivore-type digestive system and lack of specialized areas for fiber digestion, food moves through the digestive tract in as little as 6 to 8 hours. This quick rate of passage is adequate to digest many of the sugars, starches, fats, and proteins found in plants and animals, but too fast to digest plant fiber. Meat in the form of elk or cutthroat trout consumed by grizzly bears is 90% digestible, whereas early season forbs such as dandelions and clover might be only 40% digestible even though such plants might be 75% digestible for an elk or deer that can digest plant fiber. To make up for this reduced efficiency, grizzly bears eat larger volumes of food, particularly if plant matter such as roots and leaves are being consumed. Bears also eat more digestible and nutrient-dense foods such as high-fat nuts and high-carbohydrate berries when they are available. (Pritchard and Robbins 1990)

The grizzly bear's inefficiency in using plant-based foods is amplified by their overwhelming focus on gaining body mass and fat storage. Bears need to accumulate fat that will sustain them during hibernation, but there are also many other important selective factors that drive this process. For example, larger males do most of the breeding and females with better body condition are more successful at producing cubs that survive. The drive for females to accumulate fat is particularly intense because they will give birth to 2 to 3 cubs in January or early February, which is at least 1 to 2 months after the mother has stopped consuming food and another 4 or 5 months before she will exit the den and eat again. Thus, the expectant mother has to retain enough resources in her body prior to entering hibernation to sustain her for 6 to 7 months and produce the milk that will allow her new cubs to grow for their first 4 or 5 months. Grizzly bear milk is particularly concentrated, enabling cubs that weigh 1.1 pounds (0.5 kilograms) at birth to grow to 10 to 20 pounds (4.5 to 9.1 kilograms) by the time they emerge from the den. When compared to human milk that averages 4% fat and less than 1% protein, grizzly bear milk averages 18% fat and more than 6% protein during hibernation. Each cub consumes an average of three-quarters of a pint per day of this very rich milk. Even though the mother is hibernating, the cubs are not hibernating and must be fed, cleaned, and kept warm because they are growing, vocalizing, learning to walk, and even playing as they get bigger. Because of these demands, pregnant females must have at least 20% body fat going into hibernation to have a chance of producing cubs, and more than 30% body fat is even better. Accordingly, all bears have an innate desire to be obese, if not morbidly obese in human terms. Remarkably, grizzly bears do not suffer from the harmful health effects associated with obesity in humans such as high blood pressure, heart disease, and Type 2 diabetes.

Consequently, grizzly bears spend their entire life in a quest for the most nutritious and abundant foods and consume them at some of the highest levels measured in any animal. (Robbins 1993, Farley and Robbins 1995, Kovach and Powell 2003, Dahle et al. 2006a, McLellan 2011, Robbins et al. 2012, Erlenbach et al. 2014, Nelson and Robbins 2015, Rigano et al. 2016)

## Seasonal Diets, Dietary Breadth, and Resiliency

Grizzly bears are omnivores, meaning they consume both plants and animals. Because they seek the most nutritious foods, their diets will change as different plants and animals vary in abundance and nutritional value (Figure 4.1). Even though elk numbers have decreased in some portions of the Greater Yellowstone Ecosystem in recent years, ungulates continue to be an important part of the spring, early summer, and fall diets of grizzly bears. The energy, fat, and protein in meat are over 90% digestible, which is approximately double that of most plant matter. Elk calves are the predominant food for many grizzly bears during spring and early summer. For example, in the Lamar Valley in the northern portion of Yellowstone National Park both male and female grizzly bears kill an elk calf about every 2 days during June. The kill rate decreases to 1 elk calf every 4 to 5 days in the Yellowstone Lake area, where elk arrive later in the spring after significant snow melt. As a result, the calves are larger and less vulnerable to bear predation. Seventy percent of these elk calf kills occur at dusk or during the night. Calves become much less vulnerable to bear predation by July, although adult elk continue to be an important part of bear diets. Male grizzly bears tend to be more carnivorous than females because of their larger size. For example, in the Yellowstone Lake area male grizzly bears feed on an adult elk carcass about every 4 days, and female grizzly bears every 14 days. Some of these elk were killed by wolves and subsequently usurped by more dominant grizzly bears. Almost one-half of the adult elk carcasses and all of the bison carcasses consumed by grizzly bears in the Lake area had wolf sign

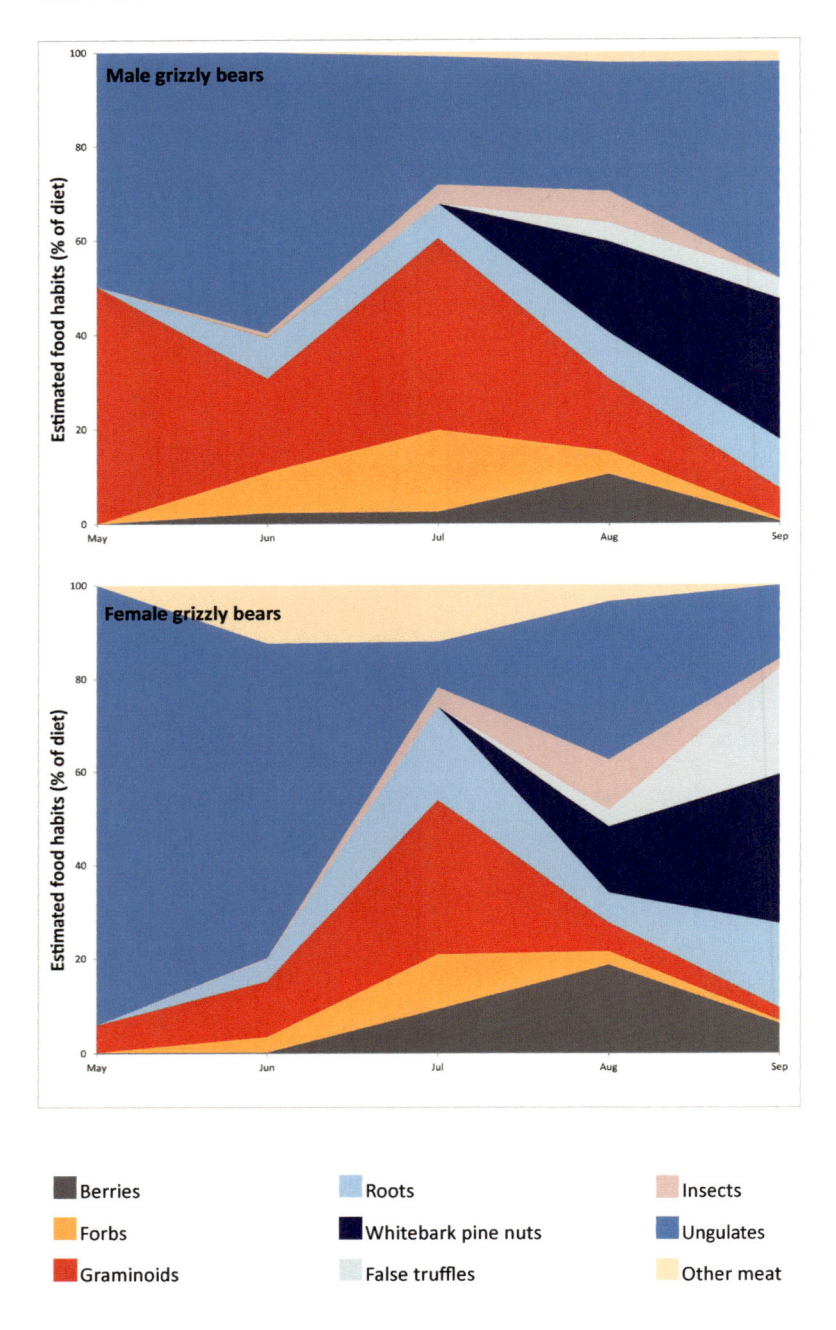

*Figure 4.1. Estimated food habits of male and female grizzly bears in the vicinity of Yellowstone Lake, 2007-2009. (Fortin et al. 2013)*

present. (Gunther and Renkin 1990, Barber-Meyer et al. 2008, Fortin et al. 2013)

Because killing or scavenging ungulates is quite opportunistic, grizzly bears must also feed on a wide range of other plant and animal matter. Historically, cutthroat trout spawning in the shallow streams flowing into Yellowstone Lake were an important spring and early summer food. Grizzly bears with home ranges in the vicinity of Yellowstone Lake used cutthroat trout as recently as the late 1990s. However, as numbers of cutthroat trout decreased precipitously in response to predation by introduced lake trout, whirling disease, and other factors, the number of grizzly bears visiting spawning streams decreased by 63% between 1997 to 2000 and 2007 to 2009. In turn, the amount of trout consumed by grizzly bears decreased by 70%. Thus, cutthroat trout are no longer an important food, though the bears would readily consume them if their numbers increase. Interestingly, the decrease in cutthroat trout may have increased predation on elk calves as grizzly bears that once patrolled spawning streams searched for other high-quality foods. This dietary flexibility, or diet switching, as foods increase or decrease is an important characteristic of grizzly bears that allows them to adapt to changes in food resources and occupy a wide range of habitats. (Haroldson et al. 2005, Fortin et al. 2013, Middleton et al. 2013, Teisberg et al. 2014)

Because the non-fiber components of young grasses and forbs can be digested, they represent the bulk of the remaining diet during spring and summer. Whereas grasses are more abundant than forbs, they are also less nourishing. For example, the protein content and digestibility of early season grasses are one-third or less than clover and other forbs. Mature grasses and forbs with much less nutritional value are not consumed, although the roots and seeds of forbs that store starch may be consumed at any time. Other spring and summer foods include biscuitroot, clover, cowparsnip, dandelion, fireweed, oniongrass bulbs, spring beauty, horsetail, and thistle. Ants are also a consistently used summer food, particularly during July and August. Ants are obtained primarily by excavating worker ants and pupae from nests in logs and

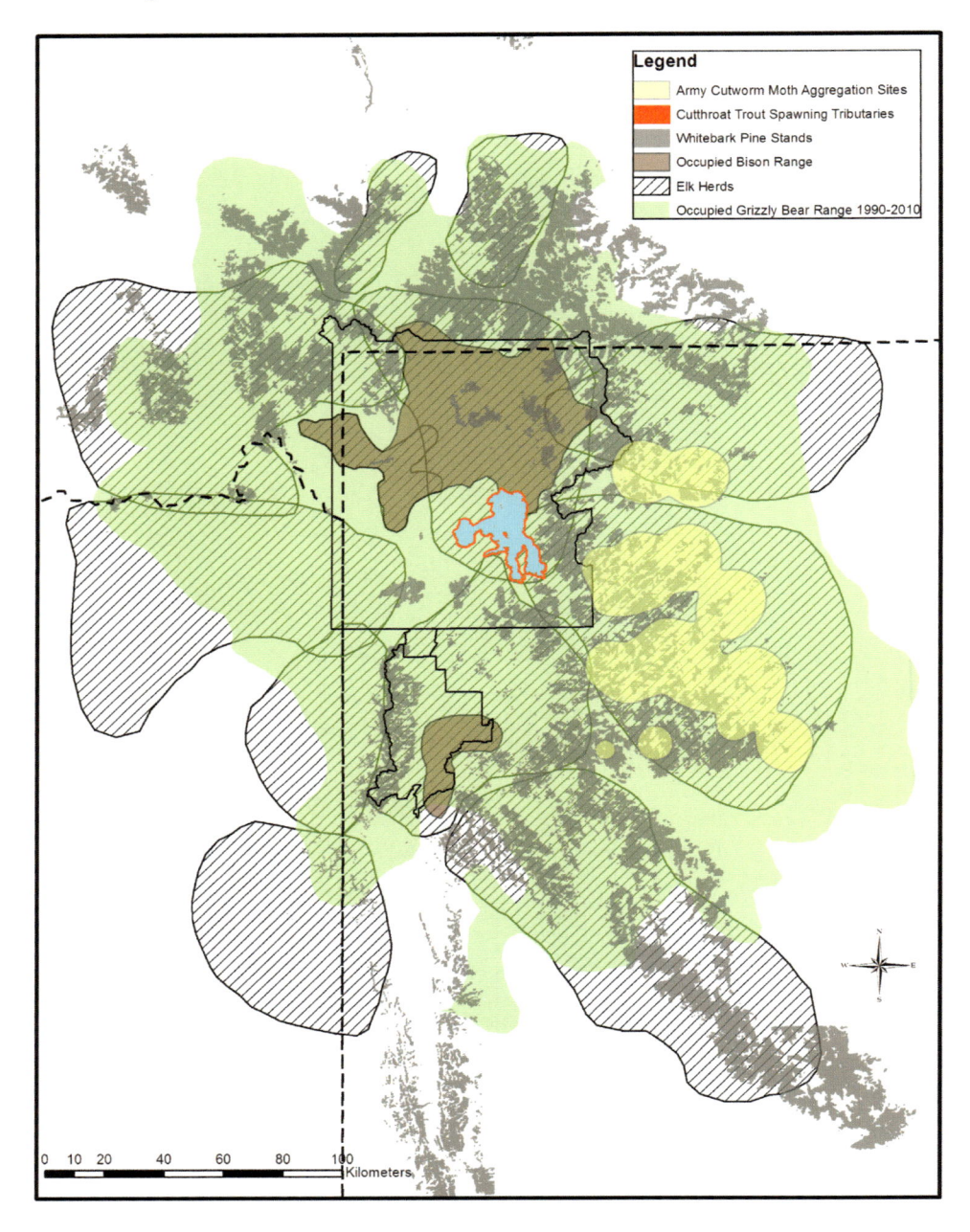

*Figure 4.2. Distribution of concentrated high-caloric grizzly bear foods (army cutworm moths, bison, elk, cutthroat trout, and whitebark pine) within occupied grizzly bear range in the Greater Yellowstone Ecosystem. (Gunther et al. 2014)*

debris hills. In late summer, primarily male bison that were gored and died during the breeding season (known as the rut) are scavenged. The rut occurs from mid-July through mid-August, although some bulls do not die from goring-related injuries and infection until early to mid-September. Bison carcasses generally attract multiple grizzly bears for several days. As many as 23 grizzly bears have been observed feeding on a single bison carcass in the Hayden Valley. (Mattson et al. 1991a, McLellan and Hovey 1995, Rode et al. 2001, Gunther et al. 2014)

Fall is a time for seeking foods that enable grizzly bears to store excess energy as fat that can be metabolized during hibernation. These foods are often particularly high in available fat, carbohydrates, or protein and include whitebark pine nuts (seeds), berries, false truffles, and ungulates. Ungulate meat comes from adult elk that are killed by wolves and those weakened or injured during the fall breeding season, gut piles left by hunters that killed ungulates outside preserves, or animals that were wounded by hunters but not found and later died. Whitebark pine trees have experienced substantial mortality throughout the Greater Yellowstone Ecosystem since the early 2000s, but continue to be an important fall food during years of seed abundance. For example in 2009, 25% of the annual diet of grizzly bears living in the Yellowstone Lake area was pine nuts. With 52% fat and 20% protein, the nuts are a substantial source of nourishment and eagerly sought when abundant. However, about one-third of grizzly bears in the Yellowstone area do not have whitebark pine habitat within their home ranges (Figure 4.2). Other fall food items include ants, bistort roots, buffaloberry, clover, dandelion, false truffles, horsetail, pondweed roots, strawberry, sweet cicely roots, vaccinium berries, and yampa roots. (Kendall 1983, Mattson et al. 1991a, Lanner and Gilbert 1994, Ruth et al. 2003, Haroldson et al. 2004, Fortin et al. 2013, Costello et al. 2014, Mahalovich et al. 2016)

False truffles are the underground fruiting structure of a fungus that grows at the base of lodgepole pine trees. They are similar in size and coloration to the black truffles of Europe, famous for their culinary properties, but are not edible to humans. Although male grizzly bears make little use of them, virtually all females use them during years of

*Even though many public lands are protected in the Greater Yellowstone Ecosystem, human activities both within and far outside of Yellowstone remain a major force influencing the nutrition of its grizzly bears.*

poor whitebark pine nut production. Like dogs and pigs that are trained to find true truffles, bears are apparently able to smell the false truffles; all one sees when bears are eating them is a small scrape at the base of trees where the bears removed the dead needles to expose the truffle. (Fortin et al. 2013)

Berries and fleshy fruits such as grouse whortleberry, huckleberry, and soapberry are eaten in the fall, but comprise a relatively small part of the diet because of their limited availability in Yellowstone. In areas where elk numbers and, as a result, browsing have decreased substantially in recent decades, berry-producing shrubs may begin to proliferate. The importance of berries as a fall food is greater than merely providing a rich carbohydrate food source. While not appreciated until recently, grizzly bears are like people in needing and, if given the chance, selecting a diet composed of foods rich in a mixture of proteins, carbohydrates, and fats. The mixing of high protein foods, such as ungulate carcasses, with high carbohydrate berries maximizes the efficiency of growth and fat storage in grizzly bears. Thus, fall berries may become an important replacement for whitebark pine nuts as the Yellowstone ecosystem changes. Something similar occurred in the Northern Continental Divide Ecosystem (Glacier National Park and surrounding national forests and Native American Reservations) where whitebark pine disappeared decades ago and fruits and berries now compose more than 85% of the summer-fall diet. (Mattson et al. 1991a, McLellan 2011, Fortin et al. 2013, Erlenbach et al. 2014, Ripple et al. 2014, Ripple et al. 2015, Costello et al. 2016a)

Grizzly bears in the Yellowstone ecosystem continue to adapt to ever-changing food resources. From the 1890s through the late 1960s, when food scraps from the hotels were being fed at organized bear viewing sites and in open-pit garbage dumps, animal matter or meat contributed 98% of the nourishment for the male bears and 72% for females in Yellowstone National Park. The remaining portion came from plants, which included natural foods as well as human-provided foods such as garbage. Meat contribution to nourishment decreased to 79% for adult males and 45% for adult females when human-provided foods were no longer available during 1977 to 1996, but prior to wolf and grizzly bear recovery and the decrease in elk abundance. After predator populations increased, and elk and cutthroat trout numbers decreased, meat now provides 45% of the nourishment for male grizzly bears and 38% for females. Surprisingly, these most recent values are approaching estimates for the importance of meat (32%) to the nourishment of grizzly bears that lived in Yellowstone about 1,000 years ago when large predators were likely common and humans had an insignificant impact. (Jacoby et al. 1999, Felicetti et al. 2003, Fortin et al. 2013, Schwartz et al. 2014)

All of the above values were determined at the atomic level, which is why scientists could estimate the diet of the grizzly bears 1,000 years ago. Growing hair and bones lock in an atomic signature that reflects the dietary proportion of meat to plant matter that provided the nourishment for their growth. This atomic signature can be measured using a technique called stable isotope analysis. Luckily, a packrat encountered a few grizzly bear bones 1,000 years ago and stashed them in a cave. Because the bones were protected from the weather, they remained largely unchanged until excavated and analyzed during the 1990s. Noteworthy, all these values that cover 1,000 years of Yellowstone history indicate one striking characteristic of grizzly bear diets in the Yellowstone area compared with most other interior ecosystems, which is the importance of meat, large ungulates in particular. For comparison, meat provides as little as 3% of a grizzly bear's nourishment in Glacier National Park in Montana and Denali National Park in Alaska. (Hadley et al. 1998, Hilderbrand et al. 1999b, Jacoby et al. 1999, Schwartz et al. 2013)

## Body Mass Gain and Body Condition

Body mass and fat content of bears are often good indicators of the integrated value of an ecosystem's food resources. Because of the long-term grizzly bear research program in the Greater Yellowstone Ecosystem, many bears have been weighed and their body fat content determined over the years. During the days when bears were feeding extensively on human-provided foods, adult females averaged 301 pounds (137 kilograms) prior to August 15 and 377 pounds (171 kilograms) after August 15. Corresponding weights for adult males were 532 pounds (242 kilograms) and 739 pounds (336 kilograms), respectively. Now that those foods are gone and grizzly bears are feeding on natural foods that are more dispersed and often of lower quality, adult females average 257 pounds (117 kilograms) and adult males average 416 pounds (189 kilograms) from June to September. Adult females in September and October average 296 pounds (135 kilograms) and adult males 457 pounds (208 kilograms). Adult males are typically much larger than adult females and, therefore, tend to seek higher-quality foods than females. The increased weights in the fall are due to the innate drive that dramatically increases appetite (hyperphagia) to accumulate the fat necessary for hibernation. (Craighead et al. 1995, Schwartz et al. 2014)

Bears are generally leanest in the early spring after hibernation and before other nutritious foods become available (Figure 4.3). As snow melts and early season vegetation, elk calves, and other plant and animal foods become available, grizzly bears are able to eat enough food to start replenishing their body protein and fat content. These spring and early summer foods are generally higher in protein than foods consumed in the late summer and fall. Fortunately, this also corresponds to the time when older bears selectively replenish their protein reserves, or lean mass, and when younger bears must rapidly gain muscle mass. (Hilderbrand et al. 1999a)

Growth continues through the late summer and fall as berries, whitebark pine nuts, truffles, and various types of meat are consumed. Feeding is especially intense in autumn and bears may gain as much as 3 pounds (1.4 kilograms) of body mass each day at this time of year. The weight added in the fall is preferentially fat. Since 2000, the body fat content of adult females has averaged 23% throughout the year and 24% for adult males. The substantial mortality of whitebark pine trees due to mountain pine beetle infestations, blister rust, and fire is of concern because it may reduce a major fall food resource for many

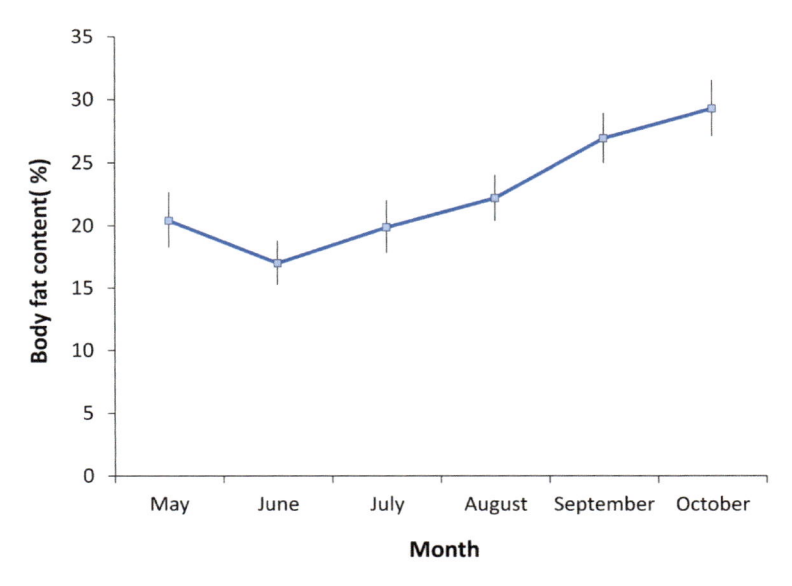

*Figure 4.3. Average percent body fat (±1 standard error) for male and female grizzly bears 2 years or older by month in the Greater Yellowstone Ecosystem, 2000-2010. (Schwartz et al. 2014)*

grizzly bears. Thus far, bears have been able to compensate for poor whitebark pine seed production by increasing the amount of meat and berries in their fall diets, which has prevented a reduction in body condition of both males and females and maintained the ability of females to produce cubs. (Hilderbrand et al. 1999a, Felicetti et al. 2003, Interagency Grizzly Bear Study Team 2013, Schwartz et al. 2014, Ripple et al. 2015, van Manen et al. 2016a)

While we typically think about grizzly bears preying on other large mammals, army cutworm moths that weigh less than 0.007 ounces (0.2 grams) each are the most concentrated source of fat for grizzly bears in the Greater Yellowstone Ecosystem. Each year, millions of moths migrate hundreds of miles in June from the farms, yards, and prairies of the Great Plains to feed at night on the nectar of flowering alpine plants in the Rocky Mountains. They return to the plains in late summer and early autumn to reproduce. Although the geographic source of the moths summering in the Greater Yellowstone Ecosystem is unknown, they could be coming from as far away as Nebraska and North and South Dakota. While feeding in the alpine, the moths are able to almost double their weight and increase their total body fat content up to 65%. During the day, the moths hide under rocks in high-elevation talus slopes (over 10,500 feet or 3,200 meters), reaching densities as high as 178 moths per square meter. Many Yellowstone grizzly bears living on the east side of the ecosystem travel to these steep talus slopes in late summer to consume moths and obtain the dietary energy needed to synthesize the fat that will be used for hibernation and reproduction. Starting in early morning, these bears turn over rocks to expose and consume as many as 40,000 moths per day, or more than 20,000 Calories (compared to the human daily caloric need of 1,500 to 2,500 Calories). Since 1986, when this foraging behavior was first documented, the number of moth sites used by grizzly bears and the number of bears observed has increased, with range expansion as a contributing factor. So far, 31 feeding complexes have been identified, with the highest use occurring in 2014 when 220 individual grizzly bears were counted during aerial surveys. (Mattson et al. 1991b, French et al. 1994, White et al. 1998, Bjornlie and Haroldson 2015a)

Army cutworm moths can be agricultural and lawn pests and are killed with a wide variety of pesticides. Consequently, well-meaning agriculturalists and homeowners living hundreds of miles from the Greater Yellowstone Ecosystem who use pesticides to kill the larval stages of the moth may affect the foods available to Yellowstone grizzly bears and, depending on the importance of the moths to individual bears, their nutritional well-being. Such challenges, both within and outside the ecosystem, will always drive the need to monitor the nutritional health, well-being, and productivity of the bears. (White et al. 1998, Robison et al. 2006)

## Hibernation

Much of a bear's active season is spent eating as much nutritious food as possible to gain enough fat to survive the winter without eating. Yellowstone grizzly bears spend approximately 5 months inactive in

Photograph by Drew Rush

*A large male grizzly bear enters a red squirrel midden looking for whitebark pine nuts in the Beartooth Mountains, Wyoming. Grizzly bears often take advantage of industrious red squirrels who cache the calorie-rich seeds by the thousands.*

winter dens. Becoming inactive during winter is an adaptive strategy that conserves energy during a period when food is scarce. While denning, grizzly bears enter a state of lethargy, called hibernation, during which they do not eat, drink, urinate, or defecate. They metabolize primarily stored fat to provide the energy used during hibernation. Hibernation reduces energy expenditure relative to remaining active by over 70%. Protein is also metabolized, although 99.7% of the protein that is broken down is resynthesized back into protein by bears that are not nursing cubs. This extreme efficiency is why bears do not need to urinate during hibernation. The body temperature of hibernating grizzly bears decreases from about 100 degrees Fahrenheit (38 degrees Celsius) to 91 degrees Fahrenheit (33 degrees Celsius), which conserves energy but enables them to quickly awaken and react to danger. Heart rate decreases from 80 to 90 beats per minute during the active season to 8 to 19 beats per minute during hibernation, while respiration decreases from 6 to 10 breaths per minute to about 1 breath per minute. Surprisingly, the heart rate of a hibernating grizzly bear can increase from the hibernation rate of 8 to 19 beats per minute to over 100 beats per minute within 1 second of being disturbed. Thus, hibernating grizzly bears are very capable of defending their dens and themselves from either humans or predatory wolves. When Frank and John Craighead were studying Yellowstone grizzly bears (see Chapter 2), they attempted to dig into the den of a hibernating grizzly bear, as is often done with black bears. However, as soon as they started digging, they heard a low growl and quickly left the area, a very wise decision. Female grizzly bears can lose 15 to 30% of their body weight during hibernation, depending on body condition, pregnancy status, and duration of hibernation. Gestation, birth, and lactation impose substantial energetic demands on pregnant bears during this period of lethargy. (Craighead and Craighead 1972, Craighead and Mitchell 1982, Bagget 1984, Judd et al. 1986, Wickelgren 1988, Barboza et al. 1997, Hilderbrand et al. 2000, Podruzny et al. 2002, Schwartz et al. 2003b, Robbins et al. 2012, Nelson and Robbins 2015, Evans et al. 2016, Gunther 2016)

## Conclusions

Due to their need to fast in winter dens for 4 to 5 months, Yellowstone bears are a very food-driven species. The food resources consumed by Yellowstone grizzly bears will always be changing, and the bears will do their best to adapt. Even though many public lands are protected in the Greater Yellowstone Ecosystem, human activities both within and far outside of Yellowstone remain a major force influencing the nutrition of its grizzly bears. If climate change or other factors result in fewer of the high-calorie foods bears currently eat (such as whitebark pine nuts), bears may switch to less nutritious and more widely scattered foods, particularly less digestible plant matter. The consumption of less nutritious or more dispersed plant foods could potentially lead to a reduction in the body size of Yellowstone's grizzly bears, as was observed in the 1970s when bears compensated for the dump closures by eating more plant matter. While decreasing body size reduces the overall energy and nutrient requirements and allows the bears to adapt to poorer quality foods, it also increases their competition with resident American black bears that are better adapted for using less nutritious and more dispersed foods. Thus, there are undoubtedly limits to the ability of Yellowstone's grizzly bears to adapt to changing food resources, and the effects of those limits may be very subtle but critically important over generations to the perpetuation of this population of bears. (Mattson et al. 2005, Fortin et al. 2013)

Photograph by Jake Davis

*A female grizzly bear on the move with her young cubs near Dunraven Pass, Yellowstone National Park. Females with cubs traverse annual home ranges that average 62 square miles (161 square kilometers).*

# Chapter 5

## MOVEMENTS AND OCCUPIED RANGE

*Daniel D. Bjornlie and Mark A. Haroldson*

### Introduction

THE ABILITY TO move great distances and use diverse habitats in search of resources needed to survive and reproduce is fundamental to grizzly bear ecology. These movements allow grizzly bears to locate a wide variety of locally and seasonally available food resources, find receptive mates for breeding, avoid threats such as more dominant grizzly bears and human disturbance, and disperse from natal home ranges and expand into unexploited habitats. Their mobility and inherent adaptability are factors that have contributed to the recovery of Yellowstone grizzly bears from low numbers in the 1970s and expand into areas of the Greater Yellowstone Ecosystem uninhabited by grizzly bears for nearly 100 years. (Schwartz et al. 2003b, Bjornlie et al. 2014a, Costello et al. 2014)

Movements of Yellowstone grizzly bears vary seasonally, annually, and throughout the lifetimes of individuals. The sizes of home ranges used by brown bears are related to habitat productivity, with bears in highly productive coastal habitats having much smaller ranges than bears in less productive inland habitats such as the Greater Yellowstone Ecosystem. Population density also influences grizzly bear movements, particularly subordinate bears such as females and subadults. Given similar food resources, in areas of high population density the sizes of ranges used by female bears are smaller than in lower density areas, likely due to competition for space and avoidance of large males at foraging sites. (Blanchard and Knight 1991, Dahle and Swenson 2003b, Schwartz et al. 2003b, Dahle et al. 2006b, Edwards et al. 2013, Bjornlie et al. 2014b)

## Seasonal Movements and Strategies

Yellowstone grizzly bears are not considered migratory, but they do make recurring seasonal movements to access available resources within their home ranges. Upon emergence from their winter dens, grizzly bears often move to lower-elevation, snow-free areas where they are more likely to find spring foods such as newly-emergent vegetation or carcasses of ungulates killed during the previous winter. This is a period of relatively low food availability so movement rates tend to be the lowest of the active season (Figure 5.1). Females with cubs move even less during this period due to the limited mobility of young cubs and the need to protect young from potential predation by adult male bears. Thus, females with cubs tend to remain at higher elevations and in closer proximity to their dens. (Blanchard and Knight 1991, Haroldson et al. 2002, Schwartz et al. 2003b, Fortin 2012, Costello et al. 2014)

As spring progresses to early summer, the increased availability of foods such as newborn elk calves and the greening of vegetation at progressively higher elevations results in increased movements. This continues through the summer and into the fall as bears increase their food consumption, until bears localize around prospective dens in the fall. Movements of male grizzly bears peak in May and June

*The sizes of home ranges used by brown bears are related to habitat productivity, with bears in highly productive coastal habitats having much smaller ranges than bears in less productive inland habitats such as the Greater Yellowstone Ecosystem.*

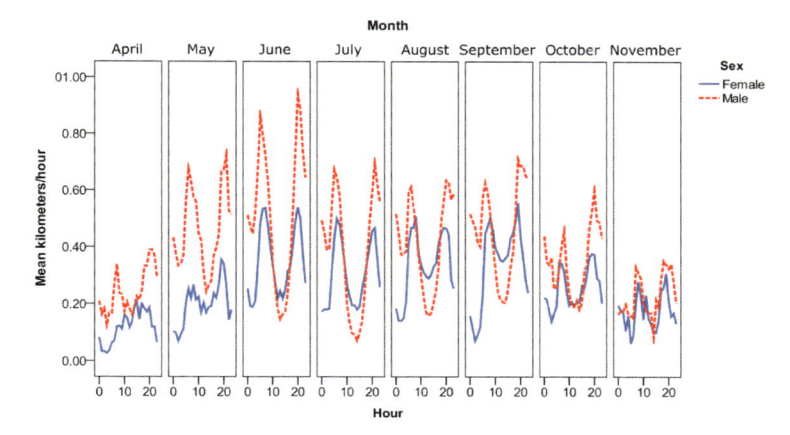

*Figure 5.1. Average movement rate (kilometers per hour) by month and hour (0 = midnight; 20 = 8 p.m.) of day for male and female grizzly bears 2 years or older in the Greater Yellowstone Ecosystem, 2000-2008.*

as they search for breeding opportunities. In contrast to seasonal movements, the daily movements of grizzly bears show a much more consistent pattern. Movement rates and activity levels for both sexes peak during dusk and dawn periods (crepuscular activity pattern), with male grizzly bears moving slightly more. During hyperphagia, a period of increased food consumption in late summer and fall to store fat and protein for hibernation, females become more active during midday as they intensify their search for food (Figure 5.1).

Grizzly bear movements are often a reflection of available resources; where grizzly bears have access to rich and localized foods, ranges may be contracted while bears concentrate on these feeding sites. In the Greater Yellowstone Ecosystem, grizzly bears feeding on army cutworm moth sites are an example of this phenomenon. The focus on these resources can result in very small seasonal ranges during the period of army cutworm moth abundance. Movements of some grizzly bears can be limited to less than 0.6 miles (1 kilometer) for weeks while they are actively exploiting a plentiful and spatially dense resource. However, like most brown bears worldwide, Yellowstone grizzly bears have an exceptionally diverse diet consisting of hundreds

Table 5.1. Annual home-range size (square miles/square kilometers; 95% minimum convex polygon method) for grizzly bears in the Greater Yellowstone Ecosystem, 1980-2012.

| Sex and age group | Number of ranges | Home-range size in square miles (square kilometers) Average | Standard deviation |
|---|---|---|---|
| Subadult female | 38 | 59 (153) | 51 (131) |
| Females with cubs | 64 | 62 (161) | 66 (170) |
| Adult females[b] | 145 | 66 (170) | 111 (287) |
| Subadult males[a] | 54 | 197 (509) | 225 (582) |
| Adult males | 125 | 154 (399) | 146 (379) |

[a] 2 to 4 years old.
[b] Females without cubs, includes females with yearlings or older offspring and lone adult females.

of species, including mammals, fish, birds, plants, invertebrates, and fungi. Consequently, although Yellowstone grizzly bears may focus on certain food items during periods of great abundance, when these foods are seasonally decreased or unavailable, grizzly bears are able to locate other food resources that allow them to meet their caloric requirements without greatly increasing their movements. (Blanchard and Knight 1991, Dahle and Swenson 2003b, Schwartz et al. 2003b, Edwards et al. 2013, Costello et al. 2014, Gunther et al. 2014, Bjornlie and Haroldson 2015b)

## Annual and Lifetime Home Ranges

A home range is often defined as the "area traversed by the individual in its normal activities of food gathering, mating, and caring for young." Annual home ranges are the accumulation of all seasonal movements within each year that allow animals to meet their ecological needs. The sizes and locations of annual home ranges may vary over the lives of individuals based on factors such as sex, age, presence and age of young, availability of resources, and population density. Male grizzly bears in the Greater Yellowstone Ecosystem have annual home ranges that average more than twice the area of females (Table 5.1). Bears are not strictly territorial and home ranges often overlap. The home ranges of male bears typically overlap ranges of several female bears, thus enhancing breeding opportunities. However, even within sex and age classes, annual home ranges can be quite variable, ranging from less than 3.9 square miles (10 square kilometers) to more than 772 square miles (2,000 square kilometers). The ranges of females with cubs are smaller than those of lone females or females with yearlings. Subadult males have the largest annual home ranges of Yellowstone grizzly bears, even when large movements related to dispersal are excluded, whereas subadult females have the smallest ranges. A possible reason for the large home ranges of subadult males is avoidance of, or displacement by, resident adult males. Compared with other areas of North America, ranges used by Yellowstone grizzly bears tend to be intermediate in size; larger than those of coastal brown bears in Alaska and Canada, but much smaller than those of interior grizzly bears found in less productive areas of the Alaskan and Canadian arctic. Annual home ranges of Yellowstone grizzly bears are similar in size to the nearest grizzly bear populations in northwestern Montana. (Burt 1943, Blanchard and Knight 1991, Dahle and Swenson 2003b, Schwartz et al. 2003b, Dahle et al. 2006b, Bjornlie et al. 2014b)

The aggregation of annual ranges of an individual represents its lifetime home range. The lifetime home range incorporates all the movements of an animal as it ages from subadult to adult and, for females, includes years with and without young. Lifetime ranges of female grizzly bears in the Greater Yellowstone Ecosystem tend to increase as annual home ranges shift, but eventually plateau around 193 square miles (500 square kilometers) and do not change much

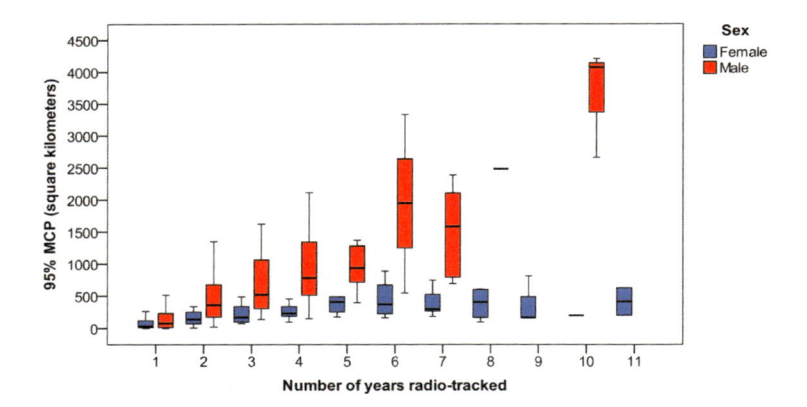

*Figure 5.2. Box plots of 95% minimum convex polygon (MCP) home-range sizes for grizzly bears 2 years or older in the Greater Yellowstone Ecosystem based on the number of years individual bears were radio-tracked to obtain locations, 1975-2012. Horizontal bold bar = median (middle value); box = middle 50% of data and whiskers indicate upper and lower 25% of data. Outliers (values beyond whiskers) and data from 4 individual bears located for more than 12 years using radio-tracking are not shown.*

after approximately 6 years (Figure 5.2). Lifetime ranges of adult males may reach 1,544 square miles (4,000 square kilometers) in size and typically continue to increase over time. Lifetime ranges for male and female Yellowstone grizzly bears did not change between the periods 1975-1993 and 1994-2012, indicating these patterns have remained consistent despite substantial changes in availability and distribution of food resources and habitats. (Blanchard and Knight 1991, Schwartz et al. 2003b, Bjornlie et al. 2014b)

## Dispersal and Range Expansion

For most young grizzly bears in the Greater Yellowstone Ecosystem, separation from their mother begins at 2 years of age, typically in June during the breeding season. Similar to grizzly or brown bears around the world, male dispersal patterns are different from those of females. When young females separate from their mothers, they tend to establish home ranges next to, or overlapping, their maternal home ranges. In contrast, when young males disperse, they may travel considerable distances in search of suitable habitats within which they can establish a home range. This behavior is thought to be a means of selection against inbreeding and may also allow young female grizzly bears the advantage of familiarity with their home range. The result is much larger ranges for subadult males than for subadult females. (Blanchard and Knight 1991, McLellan and Hovey 2001, Schwartz et al. 2003b, Dahle et al. 2006b, Støen et al. 2006a)

The search for new habitat brings young male grizzly bears into areas of the Greater Yellowstone Ecosystem that are potentially unexploited by grizzly bears for many decades. It is this exploration that results in the establishment of new home ranges on the periphery of the population and the expansion of grizzly bears into unoccupied areas. A subadult male grizzly bear captured and radio-collared as a 2-year-old late in 2014 provides an illustration (Figure 5.3). In 2015, upon den emergence, he circumnavigated the Wind River mountain range in the southeastern portion of the ecosystem before denning that fall. In early 2016, at the age of 4, he traveled north across the Wind River Range and Wind River basin and entered the southern Absaroka mountains before returning to the southern Wind River Range later that summer, a total movement of over 310 miles (500 kilometers). This movement is typical of young males in search of food resources, breeding opportunities, and potential areas to establish residency. (Bjornlie et al. 2014a)

As dispersing males make excursions into areas of the Greater Yellowstone Ecosystem that have not been occupied by grizzly bears since the early 1900s, the range of Yellowstone grizzly bears has more than doubled from the early 1980s to 2014, now occupying over 14.3 million acres (5.8 million hectares; Figure 5.4). Because males disperse further and have larger home ranges, they make up the majority of the periphery of the grizzly bear range in the ecosystem. On average, the area of occupied range of females is about 75% of that occupied

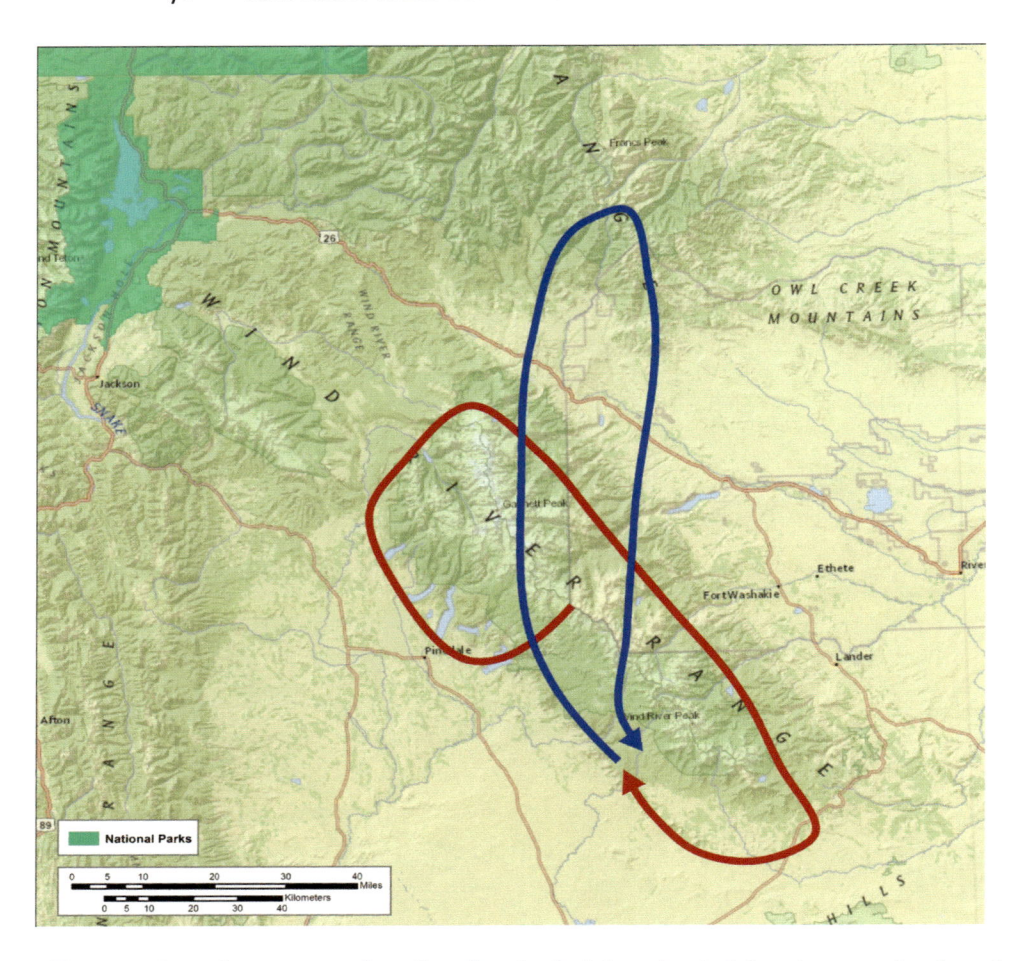

*Figure 5.3. General movements of a radio-collared, subadult, male grizzly bear in 2015 and early 2016 in the Greater Yellowstone Ecosystem. The red arrow represents movements during 2015; the blue arrow represents movements during early 2016. Base map source: National Geographic World Map, ESRI, Redlands, California.*

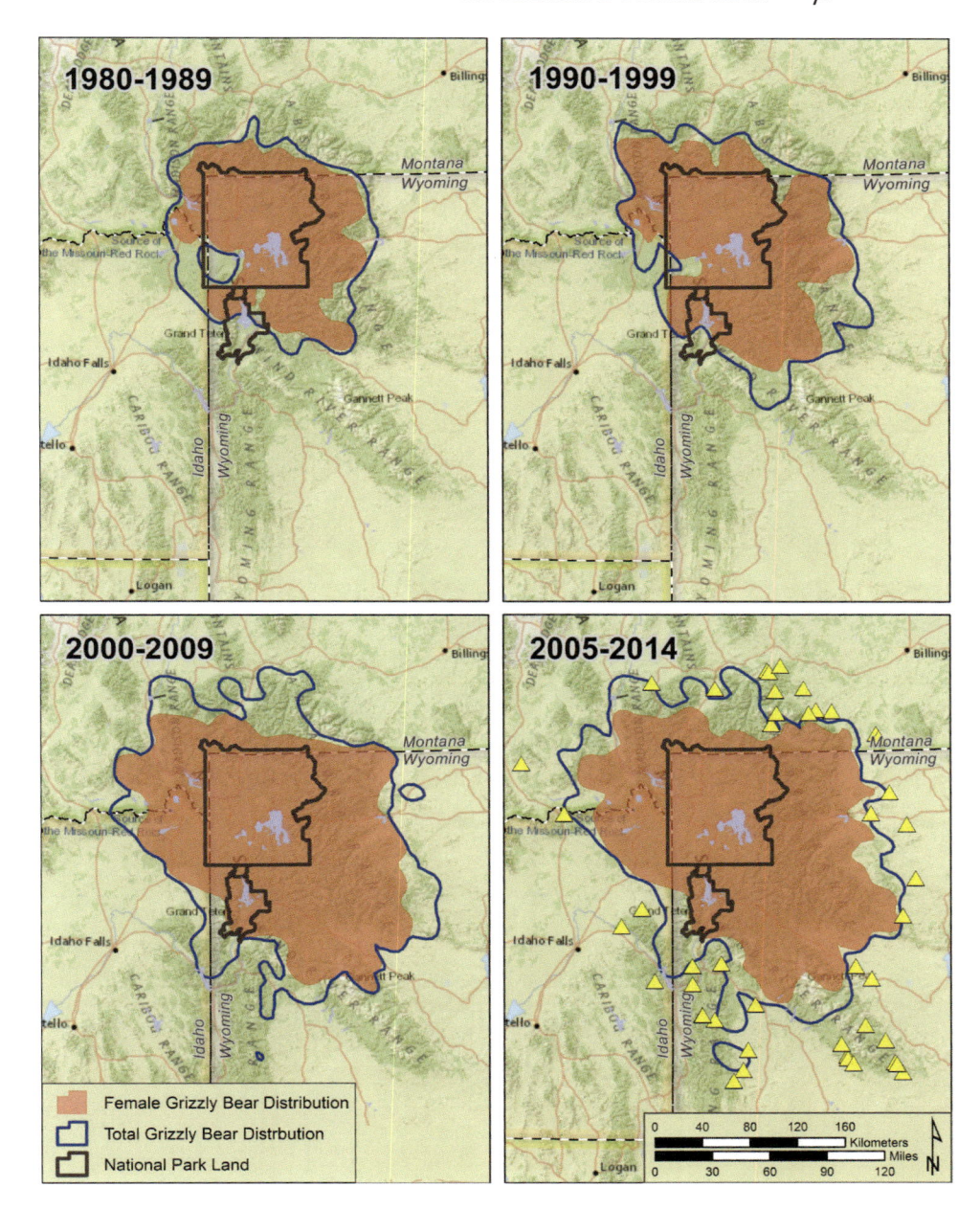

*Figure 5.4. Total (blue solid line) and female (red shaded area) grizzly bear distribution during 4 decades in the Greater Yellowstone Ecosystem, 1980-2014. Yellow triangles represent confirmed locations of grizzly bears outside the defined distribution during the period 2005-2014. Base map source: National Geographic World Map, ESRI, Redlands, California.*

by males. Because female grizzly bears do not disperse as far as male bears, their area of occupied range can be used to identify the core area used by Yellowstone grizzly bears. Perhaps even more notable than the increase in area of grizzly bear range during recent decades are the many confirmed locations of grizzly bears well beyond the boundary of occupied range (Figure 5.4, panel 2005-2014). The farthest southeast of these locations, near South Pass at the terminus of the Wind River Range, are closer to the town of Boulder, Colorado, than they are to the most northwesterly confirmed grizzly bear location on the opposite side of the Greater Yellowstone Ecosystem. To the north and west, confirmed grizzly bear locations in the Big Hole valley and Pioneer Mountains of Montana during 2016 are approximately 56 miles (90 kilometers) from the most northwesterly edge of occupied range in the Greater Yellowstone Ecosystem. Although these observations are likely from a bear, or bears, that originated from the Northern Continental Divide population, there is a possibility of origins in the Greater Yellowstone Ecosystem. These outliers do not necessarily constitute occupied range, but they reveal the leading edges of expansion and the potential for future connectivity between the ecosystems as dispersing grizzly bears search for new areas.

## Conclusions

The ability to move vast distances is one characteristic that makes grizzly bears the quintessence of remote and wild places. However, with the expansion of grizzly bears into long-unoccupied areas, there will be some inevitable conflicts with humans. Some grizzly bears are moving into areas with greater human influence than the more remote core of the Greater Yellowstone Ecosystem. In the 1970s, approximately 108 square miles (280 square kilometers) of occupied grizzly bear range encompassed private lands, less than 2% of the total area. Today, the area of private land is over 3,475 square miles (9,000 square kilometers), more than 16% of total occupied range. A consequence of range expansion is the potential for increases in human-bear conflicts and possibly human-caused bear mortality on private lands. Indeed, documented grizzly bear mortalities from human causes for independent-age bears (2 or more years old) on private lands increased from 4 during the decade of the 1970s to 41 during the decade of the 2000s.

People living, working, and recreating in these areas of expansion must now consider the presence of grizzly bears in various ways, whether it be in wildlife and land management practices, storage of food or other attractants for backcountry users and homeowners, or changes in techniques for hunting ungulates to avoid conflicts with grizzly bears. The arrival of grizzly bears in these areas creates new challenges for wildlife managers, and requires new and innovative approaches. As grizzly bears again occupy areas where they have long been absent, the dedicated management that has allowed the population to recover will continue to be important to maintain a place for one of the most iconic species of the American West.

Photograph by Ronan Donovan

*A grizzly bear, having just emerged from hibernation, guards a drowned bison carcass alongside the Yellowstone River in Hayden Valley, Yellowstone National Park.*

# Chapter 6

## ECOLOGICAL NICHE

*Frank T. van Manen, Mark A. Haroldson, and Kerry A. Gunther*

### Introduction

MANY BOOKS AND articles have been written on bears in human culture and their relationships with humans, but ecological processes associated with grizzly bears and their effects on other species and the ecosystem have not been widely documented. One reason is that grizzly bears are generalists with broad ecological niches compared with other large members of the taxonomic Order of Carnivora, such as mountain lions or wolves. Consequently, grizzly bears exhibit many flexible behaviors and relationships with other species that are difficult to study. In this chapter, we explore the varied and dynamic relationships of grizzly bears with other species, recognizing that many aspects remain poorly understood.

## Predation

Predation represents one of the most direct interactions grizzly bears have with other species. Grizzly bears are formidable predators and take advantage of large ungulate herds in the Greater Yellowstone Ecosystem. Field investigations of telemetry locations from the late 1970s through early 1990s indicated about 30% of meat consumed was obtained through predation, with highest proportions for moose (46%) and elk (43%). In contrast, only 4% of bison meat was from predation, with the rest being obtained through scavenging (see below). One of the most vulnerable prey for grizzly bears are elk calves. Bears are most successful preying on elk calves within about 15 to 30 days after their birth, generally from late May to mid-June. During this period, the primary strategy of calves to avoid predators is to remain hidden and motionless. Once discovered, however, they are easy prey for bears. By early July calves are bigger and stronger so their behavior changes. They flee when discovered by bears and are no longer easy prey. (Gunther and Renkin 1990, Mattson 1997a)

Grizzly bears residing near tributary streams to Yellowstone Lake were effective predators on spawning cutthroat trout from mid-May through July. However, the use of this resource is now much reduced because cutthroat trout populations decreased substantially following the illegal introduction of predatory, nonnative lake trout in the 1980s, with whirling disease and prolonged droughts as contributing factors. Today, the cutthroat trout population is estimated to be less than 10% of historical numbers. The biomass of cutthroat trout consumed by grizzly bears in this region decreased by 70% between 1997 and 2007 and, in turn, the number of grizzly bears using these stream corridors decreased by 63%. However, efforts to suppress the lake trout population have increased substantially over the past decade, and there are indications of a gradual rebound of cutthroat trout numbers in Yellowstone Lake. (Koel et al. 2003, Haroldson et al. 2005, Koel et al. 2005, Fortin et al. 2013, Teisberg et al. 2014, Gunther et al. 2016)

Predation on small mammals is common, involving 14 documented species, mostly rodents ranging in size from beavers and porcupines to voles. Grizzly bears may also consume food caches of species such as pocket gophers and red squirrels. Voles and pocket gophers are particularly vulnerable to predation in spring, when population densities are high and snowmelt in subalpine meadows allows grizzly bears to excavate them from their burrows. Although small mammals do not compose a large proportion of grizzly bear diets, they are widely distributed throughout the ecosystem. Also, based on food abundance surveys conducted in Yellowstone National Park from 1960 to 1971, there is less annual variation in this food resource compared with berries, carrion, or whitebark pine seeds. Indeed, one of the feeding economies, or strategies, for Yellowstone grizzly bears is in grasslands of the valley-plateau regions where intensive digging for rodents is common. (Mealey 1980, Craighead et al. 1995, Mattson 2004, Gunther et al. 2014)

There is substantial variation among grizzly bears in hunting strategies and the level of predation. One factor is body size because, similar to many other predators, larger bears can kill larger prey. For example, a radio-collared, male grizzly bear in the vicinity of Old Faithful was proficient at killing adult bison and did so for several springs. Similarly, we have recently documented 2 instances of predation on denning black bears by a male grizzly bear. Some bears may be more successful during a specific season, such as the fall rut when breeding occurs and bull elk may be less vigilant. When given the opportunity, some grizzly bears kill livestock. Because this is a specialized behavior, targeting the offending bear for relocation or removal is usually effective at reducing livestock depredations. (Knight and Judd 1983, Schleyer 1983, Cohen et al. 1993)

Of all foraging activities, predation likely has the greatest potential to impact other species in the ecosystem. To our knowledge, no studies have demonstrated grizzly bear predation on adults affected the population growth of an ungulate population. However, grizzly bear and black bear predation on newly born elk can affect recruitment and growth of elk populations. During 2003 to 2005, grizzly bear predation accounted for 38% of all elk calf mortality during the first 30 days after birth in the northern range of Yellowstone National Park. Based on the estimated number of grizzly bears in the study area, this translated to a predation rate of 0.55 calf kills per day. Grizzly bear predation rates were 0.23 calf kills per day in the vicinity of Yellowstone Lake during 2007 to 2009, after the decrease in cutthroat trout.

Prior to the reintroduction of gray wolves in 1995 and 1996, numbers of northern Yellowstone elk were high (around 17,000), but fluctuated widely, primarily due to winter severity. The number of grizzly bears in this area was not large enough at the time to affect the number of elk, particularly given the short, 3-week period that elk calves are vulnerable to bear predation. Once wolves were established, however, northern Yellowstone elk numbers began a steady decrease due to the combined effects of predation, hunting, and other factors. With a substantially smaller elk population and multiple carnivores on the landscape, we speculate that grizzly bear predation on elk calves contributed to this decrease. (Zager and Beecham 2006, Barber-Meyer et al. 2008, Griffin et al. 2011, Yarkovich et al. 2011, Fortin et al. 2013)

## Scavenging

A sizeable proportion of animal matter consumed by grizzly bears comes from scavenging carcasses. Grizzly bears have a remarkable ability to locate carcasses. In bears, nasal passages are very complex and well developed so grizzly bears typically locate carcasses by smell. Telemetry data show instances of direct movements towards a carcass from as far as 9 miles (15 kilometers) away. Carcasses, especially larger ones, are often visited by multiple bears. Observations of 4 or 5 individual bears near a single carcass are common, with occasional records of more than 20 bears near a large bison carcass.

Grizzly bears commonly scavenge the viscera or other remains of hunter-killed ungulates, as well as the carcasses of ungulates that succumb to wounding loss. The value of this resource for bears is high because it coincides with the period of hyperphagia. Telemetry studies from the 1980s and 1990s showed grizzly bears moving outside Yellowstone National Park once elk hunting began near the park's northern and southern boundaries. Even when whitebark pine cone production

*Two grizzly bears fight over a wolf-killed carcass near the Firehole River in Yellowstone National Park.*

was good, grizzly bears were 2.4 times more likely to be outside the park during the hunt, suggesting that scavenging carcasses was a good trade-off. Of course, this response brings grizzly bears in closer proximity to people and increases the potential for hunter-bear conflicts. (Ruth et al. 2003, Haroldson et al. 2004)

Grizzly bears are capable of usurping carcasses from other predators or scavengers. For example, grizzly and black bears in the northern region of the Greater Yellowstone Ecosystem visited 19 of 58 documented mountain lion kills and displaced them in 7 instances, providing an average of 4.2 pounds (1.9 kilograms) of biomass per day. Similarly, a grizzly bear was observed usurping and killing a bison calf captured by 5 wolves. This may lead to an indirect effect of increased kill rates by other carnivores, which may impact their prey populations. For mountain lions, the loss of ungulate biomass represented approximately 17% to 26% of their daily energy requirements. The ability to effectively locate and obtain carrion is a basic component of the foraging strategy of grizzly bears in the Greater Yellowstone Ecosystem. Increasing global temperatures could result in reduced availability of carrion for species that show seasonal patterns in resource use such as grizzly bears. However, the amount of carrion is probably regulated more by the full suite of large carnivores in the ecosystem rather than factors such as snow depth and starvation. Consequently, scavengers in the Greater Yellowstone Ecosystem may be less vulnerable to effects of climate change compared with ecosystems lacking a complete suite of predators. (Murphy et al. 1998, MacNulty et al. 2001, Wilmers and Post 2006)

## Interactions and Competition

Yellowstone grizzly bears consume a wide variety of animals and plants, but given that bear densities are low relative to other species, competition with other wildlife is likely limited. Many of the same plants are consumed by tens of thousands of ungulates in the Greater Yellowstone Ecosystem, including bison, deer, elk, and pronghorn. However, bears are not dependent on plants for nourishment and primarily consume young, succulent plants that are nutritious and easily digested. Conversely, ungulates digest plants with much higher fiber throughout the summer, which may limit competition. In addition, grizzly bears have substantial diet overlap with mountain lions and wolves because a large portion of their diets consists of meat from ungulates. Whereas grizzly bears are a primary predator of young elk calves, wolves and other predators kill more ungulate calves later in summer and winter, thereby possibly limiting competition. Also, mountain lions and wolves are dependent on meat for sustenance, whereas carnivory by grizzly bears is much more opportunistic. (Gunther and Renkin 1990, Singer and Norland 1994, Barber-Meyer et al. 2008, Metz et al. 2012, Fortin et al. 2013, Schwartz et al. 2013)

Interactions and competition among grizzly bears and black bears have been studied in more detail than those with other species. Black bears are numerous throughout much of the Greater Yellowstone Ecosystem. Grizzly bears occasionally prey on black bears, and large males of both species sometimes kill smaller bears. Black bears may compete with grizzly bears for food, especially in spring when both species are attracted to succulent new plant growth and ungulate carcasses. Their diets diverge during summer and autumn, with black bears eating more berries and grizzly bears more meat and plant roots. Because of their smaller size, black bears can gain body mass by acquiring smaller, scattered foods such as berries, whereas grizzly bears can defend concentrated food sources such as clover patches and ungulate carcasses. As grizzly bears in the Greater Yellowstone Ecosystem expanded their range, it afforded a unique opportunity to study whether black bears responded differently when their range overlapped with grizzly bears (sympatric) or not (allopatric). Studies in Grand Teton National Park during 2004 to 2006 showed black bears altered their activity patterns when they occurred together with grizzly bears, but not in areas where grizzly bears were still absent. The presence of grizzly bears resulted in black bears being more active during daylight hours than either male or female grizzly bears, presumably to avoid encounters. (Herrero 1978, Gunther et al. 2002,

Schwartz et al. 2003b, Mattson et al. 2005, Belant et al. 2006, Schwartz et al. 2010a, Schwartz et al. 2013, Costello et al. 2016a)

As research technologies advance, data on social interactions among grizzly bears are providing new and intriguing insights. For example, genetic data are offering new evidence of kinship recognition; in 2 cases, we were able to confirm cub adoptions that involved offspring from a mother and daughter. Continuing advances in telemetry technology and the use of remote cameras add to our understanding of male and female movements associated with mating behaviors, movement and activity patterns of multiple bears at ungulate carcasses, interactions among members of family groups, and visits by numerous bears to unique areas such as natural seeps . (Haroldson et al. 2008a, Gunther et al. 2015a, Haroldson et al. 2015a, Ebinger et al. 2016)

Similar to other areas with abundant resources, such as salmon streams in Alaska, grizzly bears competing for nutritious foods in the Greater Yellowstone Ecosystem form a dominance hierarchy in which access to the highest-quality food resources is contingent on social status. Large males, by virtue of their body size, typically have the greatest access, followed by females with older offspring, solitary females, and smaller males. Sibling groups and lone subadults are lowest in the hierarchy. Although females with cubs or yearlings often avoid other bears to lessen threats to their offspring, they can be aggressive and stand their ground with dominant males. Occasionally, this may increase the vulnerability of their offspring to male aggression. Indeed, greater losses of dependent young have been documented for females in areas where grizzly bears aggregated to feed on spawning cutthroat trout. In contrast to areas where nutritious foods are somewhat dispersed, such as cutthroat trout and army cutworm moths, a carcass provides a high-quality resource at a single location. Therefore, dominance hierarchies at carcasses are more pronounced and access may be more temporally regulated. Data from GPS telemetry collars collected since the early 2000s show some bears stay with a carcass almost continuously, whereas others have repeated movements to a nearby daybed (Figure 6.1). Additionally, we have observed "looping movements" of bears at carcass sites, possibly

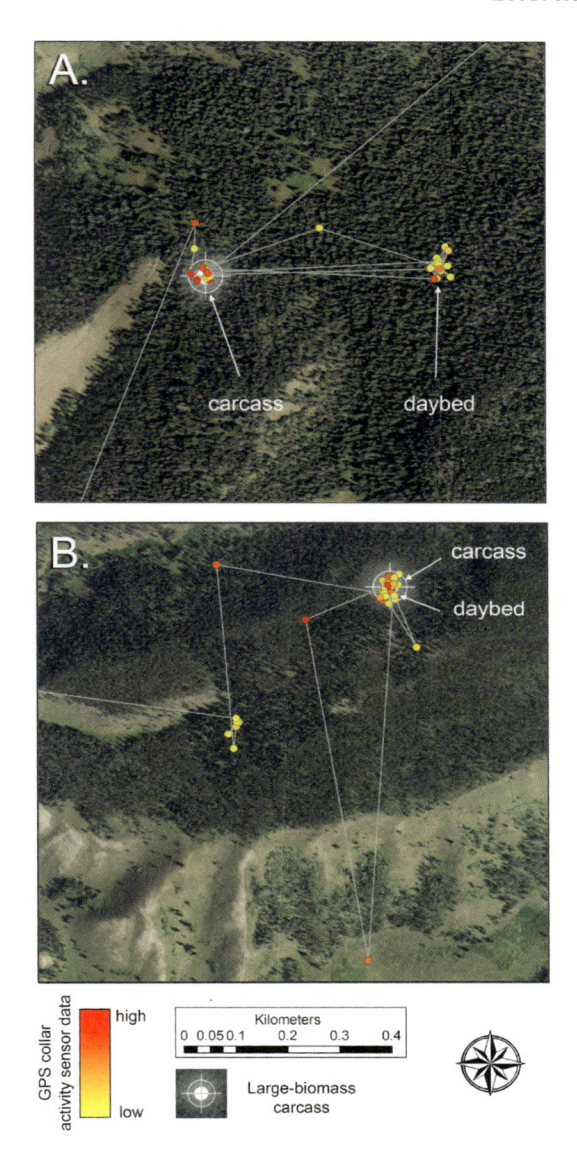

*Figure 6.1. Examples of grizzly bear GPS telemetry locations, activity sensor data (yellow to red), and cluster patterns associated with ungulate carcass visitation, Greater Yellowstone Ecosystem, 2005. A) Bedding site occurs about 492 yards (450 meters) away from a carcass site; carcass locations are primarily high activity (orange and red) and daybeds show low activity (yellow), with multiple visits to the daybed and carcass. B) Bedding site is at a carcass location with a mixture of activity levels represented in the cluster of GPS locations. (Ebinger et al. 2016)*

*Grizzly bear food webs are complex and dynamic, involving relatively weak connections with many food resources and a few stronger associations with high-calorie foods such as whitebark pine seeds, ungulates, and army cutworm moths.*

indicating repeated displacements from, and returns to, a carcass. The reason bears congregate near carcasses becomes clear when we examine the energetic rewards a carcass can provide. Studies on captive bears (see Chapter 4) suggest an elk carcass with approximately 300 pounds (136 kilograms) of edible meat would last 8.5 days for a male grizzly bear weighing 425 pounds (195 kilograms) and he would gain about 49 pounds (22 kilograms) of body mass. The same male would be able to feed on the carcass of a 1,000-pound (454-kilogram) bison for 28 days and gain 160 pounds (73 kilograms) of body mass. Clearly, if a carcass can be defended, the benefits to an individual bear are considerable. If a bear cannot defend a carcass, however, even a brief opportunity to gain access may provide energetic rewards, which likely explains why we generally observe more bears near larger carcasses. (Stonorov and Stokes 1972, Mattson and Reinhart 1995, Ben-David et al. 2004, Ebinger et al. 2016)

Food competition among grizzly bears can take several basic forms. One form of competition occurs when bears deplete a food resource to the point that other bears cannot efficiently use it anymore. Another form is when some bears exclude other bears from accessing a resource, which may reduce the feeding efficiency of subordinates, even when foods are plentiful. Both forms of competition increase with bear density, but the second is probably most common. At higher densities, social behaviors may lead to displacement, increased vigilance, and increased energy expenditure from social stress. Such behaviors can incur a nutritional cost. For example, females with cubs reduced energy intake by 37% when selecting sub-optimal habitats in a salmon-rich environment in British Columbia. The presence of black bears further complicates how competition may affect grizzly bear diets and body condition. However, analyses of percent body fat and assimilation of animal matter in the diet suggest grizzly bears in the Greater Yellowstone Ecosystem have a competitive advantage over black bears, and adult male grizzly bears tend to outcompete subadult male and female grizzly bears. Stable isotope signatures of nitrogen from hair samples, which estimate the proportion of animal matter assimilated into the diet over the previous year (see Chapter 4), indicated grizzly bear diets contained more meat than black bear diets, and adult male grizzly bears showed greater use of meat resources than females or subadult males. Studies in Alaska also support the notion that the proportion of animal matter assimilated into the diet was greater for grizzly bears compared with black bears. (McLellan 1994, Gende and Quinn 2004, Nevin and Gilbert 2005a, Nevin and Gilbert 2005b, Belant et al. 2006, Schwartz et al. 2014, Costello et al. 2016a)

## Food Webs

In the context of food webs, or who eats who in an ecosystem, omnivory is highly relevant to grizzly bears given their adaptable diets. An omnivore can be defined as a species that consumes food at more than one trophic (feeding) level such as plants, plant eaters, meat eaters, and decomposers. Recent studies show that omnivory is ubiquitous in the natural world and it may have a stabilizing effect on food webs. Grizzly bear food webs are complex and dynamic, involving relatively weak connections with many food resources and a few stronger associations with high-calorie foods such as whitebark pine seeds, ungulates, and army cutworm moths. (Pimm and Lawton 1978, Pimm 1982, Thompson et al. 2007, Kratina et al. 2012, Fortin et al. 2013, Interagency Grizzly Bear Study Team 2013, Gunther et al. 2014)

As an example of the complexity and dynamic aspects of grizzly bear food webs, the consumption of whitebark pine seeds is noteworthy. Red squirrels are a key link in the ability of grizzly bears to access whitebark pine seeds because more than 90% of seeds consumed by grizzly bears involves excavation of cone caches (middens) made by squirrels. With high mortality of whitebark pine trees, these relationships have likely changed as bears reduced their selection of whitebark pine habitats. However, ecological factors influencing midden formation by red squirrels, as well as the potential effects of whitebark pine decline on squirrel populations, are poorly understood. The connections among these species demonstrate the need to understand the ecology of the larger system. Indeed, in response to the decrease in whitebark pine, we documented that grizzly bears have shifted fall diets towards other foods. Stable isotope analyses of bear tissue samples and analyses of fall carcass use suggest an increase in consumption of animal matter during 2000 to 2010. Such diet shifts reveal a key benefit of being an opportunistic omnivore. (Kendall 1983, Stirling and Derocher 1990, Mattson and Reinhart 1997, Podruzny et al. 1999, Schwartz et al. 2003a, Van Daele et al. 2012, Yeakel et al. 2013, Costello et al. 2014, Gunther et al. 2014, Schwartz et al. 2014, Ebinger et al. 2016)

Extensive movements and the large home ranges of bears potentially make them ideal dispersers of plant seeds they ingest while feeding on soft mast (fruits). With the exception of studies on American black bears and Asiatic black bears, the role of bears as seed dispersers has not been investigated in detail. These studies indicated bears can be effective dispersers, especially of seeds that may be too large for consumption by fruit-eating birds. An important prerequisite for effective seed dispersal is that the digestive process in the gastrointestinal tract of bears does not negatively affect seed viability and germination. Studies showed this was the case for soft mast consumed by American black bears. Given that grizzly bear diets in the Greater Yellowstone Ecosystem include a soft mast component, they likely play a role in seed dispersal. However, the importance of seed dispersal by bears compared with other dispersers remains largely unclear, as are the potential effects of bear density, habitat types, and seed predators. (Auger et al. 2002, Takahashi et al. 2008, Enders and Vander Wall 2012, Naoe et al. 2016)

Finally, several foraging activities of grizzly bears involve digging, such as for small mammals or plant roots, which can cover extensive areas. The tilling of soils can result in increasing ammonium-N and nitrate-N concentrations and differences in plant composition compared with patches undisturbed by bears. Moreover, bear digging in Glacier National Park was associated with increased seed production among mature glacier lilies and may benefit more deeply seated plants that survive digging and reproduce. Easier digging conditions and more nutritious plant bulbs may also attract bears to the same patches in subsequent years and influence short- and long-term community structure. Since grizzly bears in the Greater Yellowstone Ecosystem consume the roots, bulbs, corms, or tubers of at least 10 species of plants, we speculate the effect of grizzly bears on community structure may be substantial, but data are generally lacking. Clearly, these topics provide a fertile area for future research. (Tardiff and Stanford 1998, Gunther et al. 2014)

**Trophic Interactions**

Interactions among species at different trophic levels are a topic of considerable interest in ecology, and Yellowstone grizzly bears have been at the center of several recent studies. Because of their extensive movements and varied diets, grizzly bears redistribute energy and nutrients across the landscape. For example, historically, as many as 60 grizzly bears annually transferred energy and nutrients from aquatic to terrestrial systems during spring foraging on spawning cutthroat trout in tributaries of Yellowstone Lake. Studies of brown bears feeding on salmon in Alaska indicated the importance of large, mobile consumers contributing to landscape heterogeneity through such nutrient transfers. (Haroldson et al. 2005, Holtgrieve et al. 2009)

A "trophic cascade" occurs when a change in the abundance of one or more species changes the survival of species in another trophic level through predation or herbivory. For example, scientists hypothesized that with the reintroduction of wolves and a reduced elk population, lower browsing pressure enhanced the reestablishment of berry-producing shrubs, such as serviceberry. They suggested this led to an increase in the proportion of fruit in grizzly bear diets. However, serviceberry is not a common grizzly bear food and an alternative explanation is that increased berry consumption by grizzly bears, if it indeed occurred, could simply be the result of decreases in more nutritious foods such as whitebark pine seeds and cutthroat trout, as well as increased competition due to a larger grizzly bear population. (Ripple et al. 2014, Barber-Meyer 2015)

Similarly, the decrease in native cutthroat trout due to predation by lake trout, and subsequent reduction of grizzly bear consumption of spawning cutthroat trout along tributary streams, has been well documented. Scientists investigated whether this could have indirectly affected elk populations as grizzly bears searched for alternative foods. They concluded that newborn elk calves in some areas of the ecosystem indeed became more vulnerable to predation by grizzly bears. Model simulations indicated elk population growth decreased 2% to 11% due to lower calf recruitment. Although this presents an intriguing hypothesis, we caution against interpretation of a cause and effect; cutthroat trout are localized around Yellowstone Lake and were historically used only by grizzly bears with home ranges in the vicinity of the lake. Additionally, grizzly bear predation on elk calves was common throughout the ecosystem prior to the decrease in cutthroat trout, but those predation rates may have been underestimated due to different data and methods. (Gunther and Renkin 1990, Koel et al. 2003, Haroldson et al. 2005, Koel et al. 2005, Middleton et al. 2013, Teisberg et al. 2014)

As one of the largest nearly intact temperate ecosystems in the world, the Greater Yellowstone Ecosystem provides excellent opportunities to test these fascinating hypotheses and the allure to demonstrate the existence of these ecological concepts is great. However, the probability of trophic cascades decreases with increasing levels of omnivory. Indeed, trophic cascades appear to be most evident where food chains are relatively short. As food chains lengthen, omnivory becomes increasingly prevalent, potentially spreading the effects of changes in top predators across trophic levels. We suggest grizzly bear food webs fit the latter scenario best. Thus, conclusions regarding trophic cascades involving grizzly bears in the Greater Yellowstone Ecosystem will require further testing with more rigid experimental designs and better consideration of alternative explanations. (Bascompte et al. 2005, Thompson et al. 2007, Barber-Meyer 2015)

## Conclusions

Many aspects of the ecological niche of grizzly bears have not been studied extensively and their exact role and importance remains unclear.

The potential effects of nutrient transfer, digging activities on plant communities, and the role of grizzly bears as possible plant seed dispersers are particularly fascinating. The role of grizzly bear predation is better defined, particularly with regard to elk populations. Grizzly bears are effective predators of elk calves, which can affect the growth of elk populations through reduced calf recruitment. However, whether predation on elk calves increased among grizzly bears near Yellowstone Lake as a consequence of the decrease in cutthroat trout remains unclear. Grizzly bears effectively exploit carrion as a food resource and frequently usurp kills from other carnivores, such as wolves and mountain lions. Data are incomplete to assess the impact this may have on these other carnivores or their prey. Finally, due to the omnivorous diets of grizzly bears, their food webs are complex and dynamic. Future research may provide valuable insights into how this ecological plasticity may allow grizzly bears to adapt to a changing landscape and how it may affect other species. The Greater Yellowstone Ecosystem provides a unique field laboratory to examine these relationships.

Photograph by Jake Davis

*A grizzly yearling in midsummer. The Yellowstone grizzly bear population is currently at the most southeastern extreme of the species' distribution in North America. Although the population remains isolated, the prospects of bears immigrating from other ecosystems have substantially improved in recent years.*

# Chapter 7

## GENETICS AND ADAPTIVE CAPABILITIES

*Mark A. Haroldson, Pauline L. Kamath, and Frank T. van Manen*

### Introduction

THE HISTORIC DISTRIBUTION of grizzly bears in North America extended west from the Mississippi River to California and from northern Mexico to the Arctic Ocean. With settlement of the western portions of the continental United States by Euro-Americans in the late 1800s, and the livestock husbandry they brought with them, the grizzly bear's vast range in North America began to decline. Without question, human-caused mortality was the driving factor behind the grizzly bear's population decline and range contraction. Settlers viewed the bear's presence as a threat to themselves and their livelihoods. By the early 1900s, grizzly bear numbers and the extent of their range in the lower 48 states were dramatically reduced and, by the 1920s, the Yellowstone grizzly bear population was most likely isolated. This genetic isolation is a concern for the long-term health of the population because inbreeding and genetic drift can reduce genetic diversity and affect fitness of individuals, particularly in small populations. (Servheen 1990, Franklin and Frankham 1998, Mattson and Merrill 2002)

Reductions in the number of Yellowstone grizzly bears also occurred after the closure of the open-pit garbage dumps in Yellowstone National Park and surrounding communities during the late 1960s and early 1970s. During these dump closures, and for several years after, a substantial number of food-conditioned grizzly bears became involved in conflicts. Many of those bears were killed and some estimates put the Yellowstone grizzly population lower than 250 individuals after the dump closures (see Chapter 2). Such large-scale removals can reduce genetic diversity and compromise a population's ability to adapt to changing environmental conditions. (Cowan et al. 1974, Servheen 1990, Craighead et al. 1995)

The Yellowstone grizzly bear population is currently at the most southeastern extreme of the species' distribution in North America and evidence from available data indicates it remains isolated. Despite this isolation, concerns for the genetic health of the Yellowstone grizzly bear have lessened with recent findings indicating no significant loss in genetic diversity, low levels of inbreeding, and a considerable increase in the effective population size (the number of individuals contributing offspring to the next generation) since the population was listed as threatened under the Endangered Species Act in 1975. (Miller and Waits 2003, Haroldson et al. 2010, Kamath et al. 2015)

## Genetic Diversity

When populations become small, genetic factors may accelerate further decline through what is called inbreeding depression. Therefore, monitoring of genetic diversity can provide key insights into the genetic health and viability of isolated populations. Genetic material (DNA) obtained from museum specimens and more recently sampled bears were used to investigate whether the Yellowstone population declined in the early 20th century and whether the dump closures resulted in subsequent loss of genetic diversity. Alleles represent alternative forms of a gene and their variability, or allelic richness, is a useful index of genetic diversity. Similarly, heterozygosity is a metric used to estimate the proportion of genes with different alleles in a population. Heterozygosity and allelic richness were estimated at 8 microsatellite loci which are short, non-coding segments of DNA. Such non-coding segments do not have any specific function and are not selected against, which allows them to accumulate mutations and increase in variability over time. A comparison for 2 time periods, early in the century (1912 to 1920) and just before and during the dump closures (1959 to 1981), indicated only a gradual decline in genetic diversity in the Yellowstone population over the century. Additionally, there was no support for a bottleneck or an acute drop in genetic diversity after closures of open-pit garbage dumps in Yellowstone National Park and surrounding communities. This finding might be due to the long generation time for brown bears (more than 10 years), the short time period during which the population was below several hundred individuals, or because the population was actually larger than estimated after the dump closures and subsequent mortality. Regarding the latter point, although some population estimates after dump closures were as low as 136 individuals, these estimates were contested. It is possible that a relatively large segment of grizzly bears in Yellowstone remained in more remote areas and were not counted or affected by the dump closures. (Barnes and Bray 1967, Miller and Waits 2003)

More recent (1985 to 2010) estimates of heterozygosity and allelic richness from a larger sample of Yellowstone grizzly bears suggested little change in genetic diversity at microsatellite loci. The apparent stability in genetic diversity in the Yellowstone grizzly population since the 1980s was further corroborated when the genotyping effort was expanded to 20 microsatellite loci. Heterozygosity varied from 0.615 in 1985 to 0.612 in 2010, suggesting a low rate of inbreeding (the loss of heterozygosity over time) of 0.2% over the 1985 to 2010 period (Table 7.1). (Kamath et al. 2015)

Table 7.1. Genetic diversity indices (A = allelic richness, $H_O$ = observed heterozygosity, $H_E$ = expected heterozygosity) across 20 common microsatellite loci for the Yellowstone grizzly bear population over time. Standard errors (se) of estimates are in parentheses. (Kamath et al. 2015)

| Year | Number of gene copies | A (se) | $H_O$ (se) | $H_E$ (se) |
|------|----------------------|--------|------------|------------|
| 1985 | 132 | 4.65 (0.31) | 0.611 (0.042) | 0.615 (0.038) |
| 1990 | 228 | 4.60 (0.30) | 0.618 (0.040) | 0.609 (0.037) |
| 1995 | 422 | 4.59 (0.30) | 0.621 (0.038) | 0.616 (0.036) |
| 2000 | 654 | 4.55 (0.30) | 0.617 (0.036) | 0.614 (0.036) |
| 2005 | 740 | 4.56 (0.29) | 0.610 (0.037) | 0.612 (0.036) |
| 2010 | 576 | 4.52 (0.29) | 0.610 (0.038) | 0.612 (0.037) |

Although only a slight decline in genetic diversity has been observed in the Yellowstone population over the past century, diversity remains lower than brown bear populations to the north and in Europe. Genetic diversity for the geographically closest populations was greater in the Northern Continental Divide Ecosystem (heterozygosity = 0.68), but lower in the United States portion of the Selkirk Mountains (heterozygosity = 0.54; Figure 7.1). (Paetkau et al. 1998, Waits et al. 1998a, Waits et al. 2000, De Barba et al. 2010, Proctor et al. 2012, Skrbinšek et al. 2012)

## Gene Flow and Population Structure

Gene flow occurs when individuals from one population immigrate to another population and reproduce, thus introducing new genes that may help maintain or increase genetic diversity. Gene flow can occur through natural dispersal or human-mediated translocations. There is no genetic or observational evidence for recent immigration of grizzly bears from the geographically closest population in the Northern Continental Divide Ecosystem to the Greater Yellowstone Ecosystem. Indirect estimates of gene flow based on a fixation index, a measure of the amount of genetic material shared between two populations,

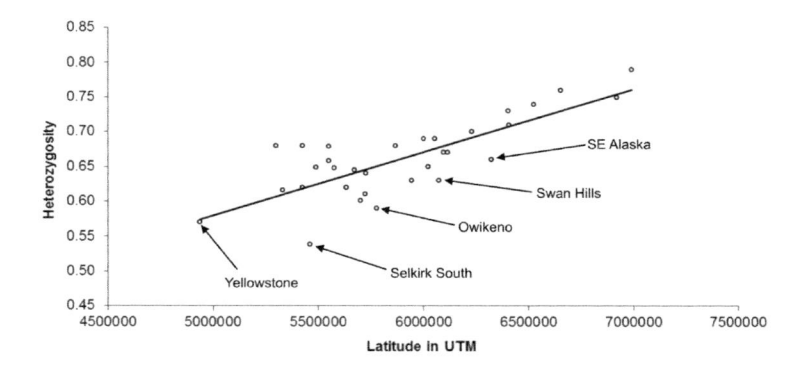

*Figure 7.1. Expected heterozygosity (an index of genetic diversity) of grizzly bears in sample areas (1983-2007) across western North America in relation to latitude as measured in Universal Transverse Mercator (UTM) units. Several study areas below the expected line are identified. (Proctor et al. 2012)*

indicates genetic differentiation of these two populations (Wright's $F_{ST}$ = 0.096) and lack of evidence of dispersal. This conclusion is further supported by over 5 decades of monitoring radio-collared bears, from which there has never been a movement detected between the Greater Yellowstone Ecosystem and neighboring populations. Although the Northern Continental Divide Ecosystem is geographically the nearest population, grizzly bears in the Yaak Mountains in northwestern Montana may be genetically more closely related to the Yellowstone population than bears in the Northern Continental Divide Ecosystem. (Haroldson et al. 2010; Proctor et al. 2012; D. Paetkau, Wildlife Genetics International, personal communication)

Studies of genetic structure among grizzly bear populations in western North America indicate there are genetic differences among populations related to natural features such as mountain ranges and ice fields at northern latitudes and human development at southern latitudes. Within this large geographic region, genetic differences between the Greater Yellowstone Ecosystem and the Northern Continental Divide Ecosystem were relatively large compared with other areas, likely due to barriers posed by human development and interstate highways. However, the prospect for natural immigration may be greater now than

*By the 1920s, the Yellowstone grizzly bear population was most likely isolated. This genetic isolation is a concern for the long-term health of the population because inbreeding and genetic drift can reduce genetic diversity and affect fitness of individuals, particularly in small populations.*

in the past. The Northern Continental Divide Ecosystem and Greater Yellowstone Ecosystem populations are increasing in numbers and expanding occupied range. These populations are now only separated by approximately 68 miles (110 kilometers; Figure 7.2), with confirmed grizzly bear locations in 2016 as far away from occupied range as the Big Hole Valley and Pioneer Mountains. (Proctor et al. 2012, Bjornlie et al. 2014a, Costello et al. 2016b)

Within the Greater Yellowstone Ecosystem there are no known barriers to grizzly bear movement, either natural or human-related. Evidence from radio-collared grizzly bears reveals they routinely cross two-lane highways with relatively high traffic volumes. For example, 12 grizzly bears whose home ranges overlapped U.S. Highway 20 in Idaho crossed the road at least 146 times during 2001 to 2011. Seven of those bears also crossed State Highway 47 a total of 96 times. Bears typically crossed these highways in early morning and late evening. Because there are no distinct human-made or natural barriers to gene flow, there is no evidence of area-specific genetic differentiation within the Greater Yellowstone Ecosystem. This may also be due to historic and ongoing use of translocation as a management tool to address human-bear conflicts. Although there is no evidence of genetic structure within the Yellowstone grizzly bear population, preliminary findings indicate a slight northwest to southeast gradient of allele frequencies. This spatial pattern may be suggestive of broader gene flow patterns. For example, given that Yaak grizzly bears may be genetically closest to the Yellowstone population, one hypothesis is that historic gene flow occurred from the Yaak Mountains to the south and then east into the Yellowstone area. Alternatively, this spatial pattern may reflect the directionality of range expansion. (Paetkau et al. 1998; Interagency Grizzly Bear Study Team, unpublished data)

## Genetic Structure of Brown Bears Worldwide

Mitochondrial DNA is inherited from mothers and accumulates mutations relatively quickly. Therefore, mitochondrial DNA sequence

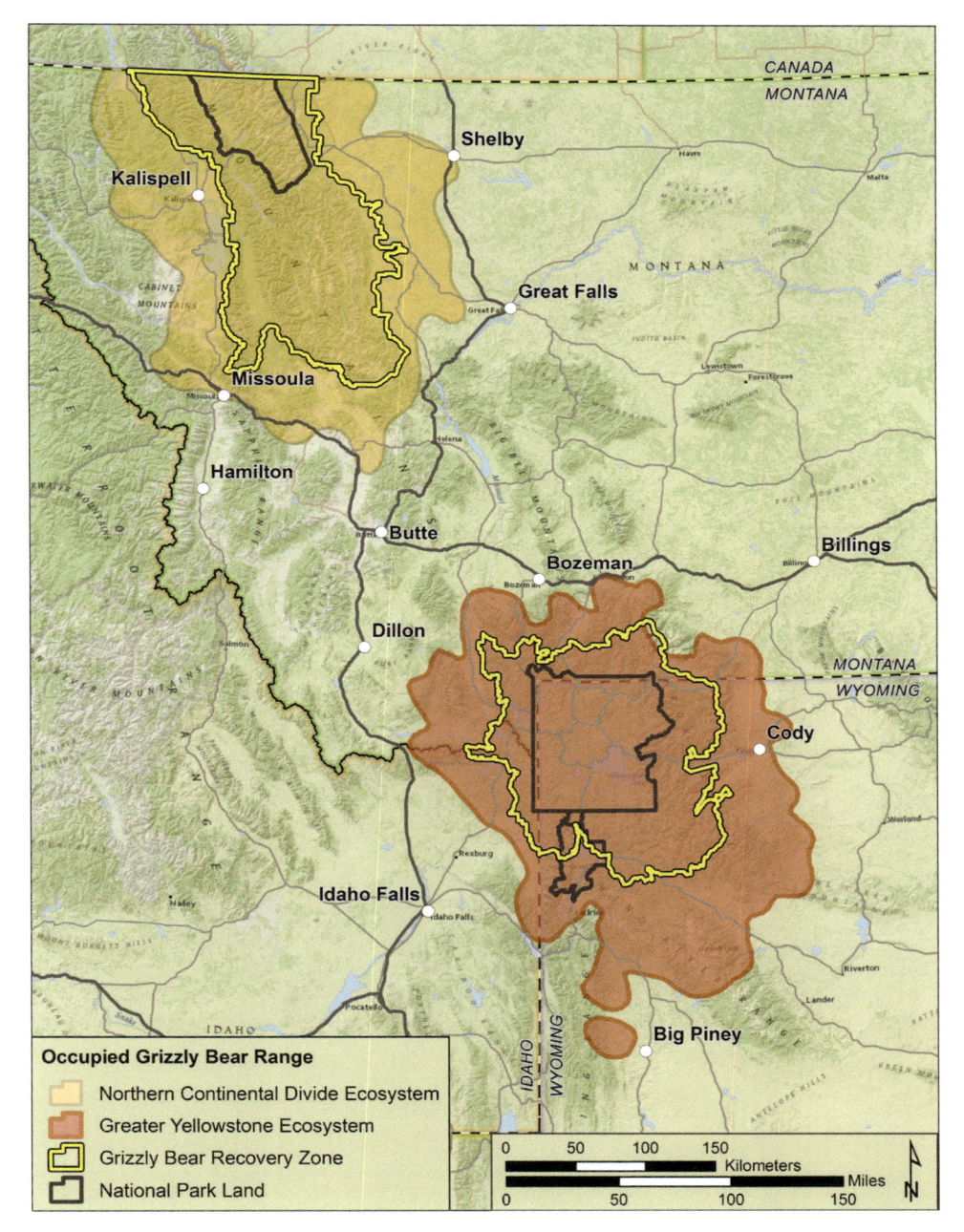

*Figure 7.2. Occupied range of grizzly bears in the Greater Yellowstone Ecosystem (2000-2014) and the Northern Continental Divide Ecosystem (2004-2014). (Bjornlie et al. 2014a, Costello et al. 2016) Confirmed occurrences of grizzly bears have been documented between the two areas of occupied range since 2005. Base map source: National Geographic World Map, ESRI, Redlands, California.*

Grizzly bear in springtime near Swan Lake, Yellowstone National Park.

analysis can be a powerful means for resolving the evolutionary relationships among populations and species, particularly when females exhibit more limited dispersal from their natal range than males. Groups of individuals that can be traced to a common ancestor, such that they are more closely related to one another than to members of another group, are referred to as clades. Mitochondrial DNA analyses of brown bears from across their Palearctic (Europe and Asia) and Nearctic (North America) distribution have revealed a number of different clades and subclades. (Randi et al. 1994, Taberlet and Bouvet 1994, Waits et al. 1998b, Matsuhashi et al. 1999, Matsuhashi et al. 2001, Miller et al. 2006, Korsten et al. 2009, Davison et al. 2011)

To date, researchers have identified 6 well-defined brown bear clades worldwide that are widely distributed. Clade I is restricted to southern Scandinavia and western Europe. Clade II occurs on Admiralty-Baranof-Chichagof islands off the southeastern coast of Alaska; this clade also clusters with polar bears. Clade III occurs in eastern Europe, Asia, and Alaska. Clade IV is found in Japan, southern Canada, and the lower 48 states, including the Yellowstone population. Clade V occurs in Tibet and clade VI occurs in Pakistan and the Gobi desert. A recent study found bears from Iran form another distinct group outside of these designated clades. (Miller et al. 2006, Davison et al. 2011, Ashrafzadeh et al. 2016)

## Genetic Viability

Effective population size, or $Ne$, is the fraction of the gene pool passed on by reproducing individuals to the next generation, and influences the level of inbreeding and rate of genetic drift. Genetic drift is the change in gene types in a population due to the random nature of reproduction, resulting in a reduction of genetic variation. As effective population size increases, the rate of genetic drift and loss of genetic diversity decreases. Effective population size can provide valuable information on the long-term viability of a population under current conditions and the ability to adapt to future environmental changes. The effective population

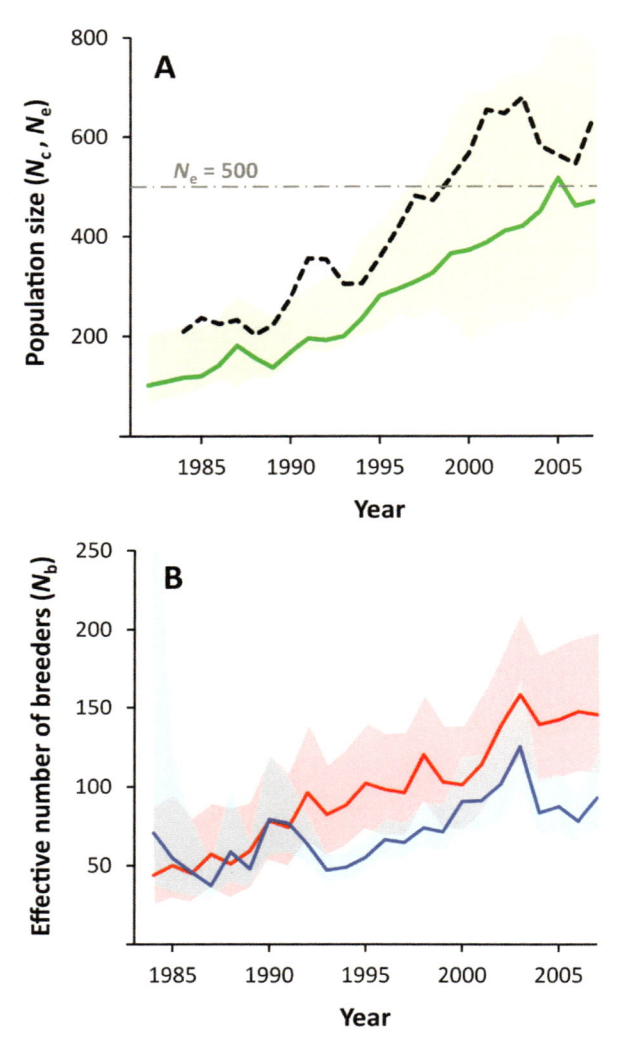

Figure 7.3. Population size indices of Yellowstone grizzly bears during 1982-2007. A) Estimates of population size ($N_c$; dashed black line), including bears of all ages, compared with estimates of effective population size ($N_e$; green line); estimator by parentage assignment method. The gray dash-dotted line indicates the $N_e$ criterion for long-term ($N_e = 500$) genetic viability. B) Estimates of the effective number of breeders ($N_b$) based on cohorts using the Linkage Disequilibrium (blue) and Sibship Analysis (red) methods. For all $N_e$ and $N_b$ indices, annual point estimates and 95% confidence intervals are indicated by the lines and shading, respectively. (Franklin 1980, Kamath et al. 2015)

size is generally smaller than the total number of animals in a population because not all individuals breed. The effective population size of Yellowstone grizzly bears increased from approximately 100 in 1982 to 450 in 2007 (Figure 7.3), suggesting the current effective population size of Yellowstone bears is approaching established recommended criteria of 500 for long-term genetic viability. The observed increase in effective population size corresponded with changes in the effective number of breeders producing offspring, as well as the increasing trend in population size (Figure 7.3). (Franklin 1980, Waples 1989, Keating et al. 2002, Miller and Waits 2003, Cherry et al. 2007, Wang et al. 2010, Kamath et al. 2015)

## Conclusions

Findings of increasing effective population size and stable genetic diversity are promising for the persistence of the Yellowstone bear population. Although the population remains isolated, the prospects of bears immigrating from other ecosystems have substantially improved in recent years. Studies to date have used neutral markers, such as microsatellites, to examine genetic variation in Yellowstone bears. However, because these markers do not code for functional proteins, they are not likely to represent genetic material that undergoes natural selection. Future studies based on genomic approaches, particularly those targeting functional coding genes (expression of genes that ultimately leads to observable traits), will be important to better understand the ability of grizzly bears to genetically adapt and respond to environmental changes. By taking advantage of the increasing feasibility and decreasing costs of sophisticated genetic analyses, future studies may be able to directly identify functional genes distributed across the bear genome that are effective indicators of genetic health of bear populations. (Paetkau et al. 1998, Miller and Waits 2003, Kamath et al. 2015)

Photograph by Jake Davis

*Who's investigating whom? A curious black bear, quite unfazed by this long line of cars (likely previously fed by visitors), examines a visitor through the windshield, Craig Pass, Yellowstone National Park.*

# Chapter 8

## HUMAN-BEAR INTERACTIONS—INCREASING VISITATION AND DECREASING AWARENESS

*Kerry A. Gunther, Katharine R. Wilmot, Travis C. Wyman, and Eric G. Reinertson*

**Introduction**

MOST VISITATION TO Yellowstone and Grand Teton national parks occurs from May through October, the same period when grizzly bears are out of their winter dens and active on the landscape. Visitation to Yellowstone National Park has set new record highs almost every decade, with 9 of the 10 highest years recorded between 2007 and 2016. Grand Teton National Park and other public lands in the Greater Yellowstone Ecosystem have also experienced significant increases in visitation in recent years. The majority of today's visitors come from urban areas, including from many foreign countries, where they have little exposure to wild, free-ranging, large predators capable of damaging personal property or inflicting serious injury to people. With more bears and a greater number of inexperienced visitors recreating in the ecosystem, more human-bear interactions will occur. As a result, it is necessary to increase safety infrastructure, education, and staff to avoid substantial increases in human-bear conflicts. (Haroldson et al. 2002, Gunther 2015c)

**Human-Bear Conflicts**

Grizzly bears in the Greater Yellowstone Ecosystem spend up to 6 months hibernating in winter dens. Due to this long period of fasting and the need to accumulate large reserves of fat prior to hibernation, grizzly bears are very food-motivated during the 3 to 4 months before entering their dens. This motivation, combined with their behavioral adaptability, intelligence, and diet flexibility, allows bears to quickly learn to exploit new food resources, particularly high-calorie foods associated with people. Shortly after the establishment of Yellowstone National Park and the settlement of surrounding areas by Euro-Americans, bears learned that people and their camps, developments, and garbage piles provided easy sources of concentrated, energy-rich foods. Once conditioned to human foods, many bears learned to break into buildings, tents, and vehicles to obtain human foods, often causing considerable property damage and sometimes injuring people. Due to the propensity for bears to seek human foods, human-bear conflicts are a management challenge wherever people and bears share habitat. These conflicts typically increase during late summer and fall, and during years when natural bear foods are less available. (Schullery 1992, Haroldson et al. 2002)

Human-bear conflicts occur when bears obtain human foods, garbage, or pet and livestock feed; kill or injure livestock, pets, or people; or damage property such as buildings, vehicles, camping equipment, gardens, fruit trees, or beehives. From 2002 through 2014, there were 2,497 conflicts reported in the Greater Yellowstone Ecosystem, an average of approximately 200 each year. Reported conflicts included bears killing livestock (43%); damaging property while obtaining human foods (34%); damaging property without obtaining human foods (14%); damaging gardens, fruit trees, and beehives (6%); and attacking people and causing injury (3%) or death (0.2%). Conflicts were approximately equally distributed on private (52%) and public (48%) lands. On private lands, 72% of 1,287 conflicts involved bears damaging property or obtaining human-related foods. On national forest lands, 68% of 1,062 conflicts involved bear depredations of livestock, primarily cattle and sheep. There were relatively few conflicts on National Park Service, state-owned, and Bureau of Land Management lands, with 84% of 146 conflicts involving bears damaging property or obtaining human foods or garbage. (Gunther et al. 2004a)

Most incidents where bears damage property to obtain human foods occur during late summer and fall when bears are attempting to gain weight to support hibernation, and during years with below-average abundance of natural foods. However, grizzly bears often kill livestock regardless of the abundance of natural foods, typically during mid-summer when cattle and sheep are grazed on national forest lands. Human-bear conflicts are relatively infrequent on public lands where bear-resistant garbage cans, dumpsters, and food storage boxes are provided to recreational users. Conflicts are more prevalent on private lands, where many land owners are unable or reluctant to incur the financial costs and life-style changes required to make human foods, garbage, gardens, orchards, beehives, livestock and their feed, and pet foods unavailable to bears. Currently, many human-bear conflicts occur on the periphery of the ecosystem, where bears have expanded into long-unoccupied habitats that are now occupied by people. Bear-resistant infrastructure was not initially in place in these areas, and people were not accustomed to living, working, or recreating in habitats occupied by grizzly bears. (Gunther et al. 2004a)

Human-bear conflicts do not just negatively impact people. Approximately 85% of grizzly bear deaths in the Greater Yellowstone Ecosystem are caused by people and most are a direct result of human-bear

*Compliance with bear spray recommendations among all backcountry recreationalists was low. Only 52% of backpackers, 14% of day-hikers, and less than 1% of boardwalk hikers carried bear spray.*

conflicts. From 2002 to 2014, 311 grizzly bears died from human causes in the ecosystem. Two-hundred and twenty-six deaths occurred on federal lands, 77 on private lands, 7 on state lands, and 1 on tribal land. Causes included self-defense shootings by ungulate hunters and misidentification by black bear hunters (37%), removals for conflicts at developed sites (21%), removals for livestock depredations (14%), vehicle strikes (8%), poaching (6%), and various other causes (14%). Although human-caused deaths have been low enough to allow the grizzly bear population to increase in numbers and expand in range, continued efforts to reduce conflicts are warranted to enhance public support for their conservation and protect their habitats. (Gunther et al. 2004a, Schwartz et al. 2006c, Schwartz et al. 2006d, Bjornlie et al. 2014a)

The larger the area of social tolerance for grizzly bears, the less vulnerable the population will be to long-term changes in climate, habitat, and human occupation, and the greater the probability bears will be able to successfully move between the Greater Yellowstone and other ecosystems. Bear managers have developed many effective methods for preventing human-bear conflicts, such as bear-resistant garbage cans, dumpsters, and campsite food storage boxes, as well as electric fencing to protect gardens, orchards, beehives, and chicken coops. However, it is a continual challenge to maintain bear-resistant infrastructure and bear-wise community efforts on a long-term basis. Many non-profit bear advocacy groups have contributed toward these efforts, including the purchase and distribution of bear-resistant garbage cans and electric fence materials, testing of bear-resistant products, promotion of bear spray and bear safety practices, protection of bear habitat and linkage zones, and retiring livestock grazing leases on public lands. More details on methods to manage bear habitat and the human-bear interface are provided in Chapter 10. (Gunther et al. 2004a, Lasseter 2015)

**Human-Bear Encounters**

Many people wonder about the risk of being attacked by a grizzly bear in the Greater Yellowstone Ecosystem. From 1991 through 2015, grizzly bears in Yellowstone National Park reacted with neutral behaviors (57%) or by fleeing (35%) during 5,578 reported encounters with visitors. Much less common were curious behaviors such as approaching people (3%) and stress, bluster, or warning behaviors such as jutting out their lips, blowing, teeth clacking, or slapping a paw to the ground (1%; Table 8.1). Grizzly bears reacted by bluff charging without contacting people in 4% of encounters, and actually attacked in less than 1% of encounters. All of the attacks during 1991 through 2015 were in the backcountry though, historically, some attacks occurred within developments. The relative frequency of attacks was slightly greater when people were hiking off maintained trails (2%; 7 attacks in 381 reported encounters) than on trails (1%; 14 attacks in 1,340 encounters). Since 1991, there have been no attacks during 2,103 encounters in areas of the park where human presence was consistent and predictable, such as along primary roads, within developments, and in designated backcountry campsites. (Gunther and Wyman 2016)

**Grizzly Bear Attacks**

Although grizzly bear attacks on people in Yellowstone and Grand Teton national parks are extremely rare, they draw worldwide media coverage when they occur. Managers strive to make the parks as safe for visitors as possible, while still maintaining their wilderness character and protecting the resources therein. The parks have extensive bear safety messaging programs that use face-to-face interactions, social media, web pages, video, printed handouts, newspaper articles, and roadside and trailhead signs to convey information to visitors. Documenting trends in bear attacks is one method managers use to gauge the efficacy of these programs.

The first grizzly bear mauling documented in Grand Teton National Park occurred in 1994, with another 6 people injured by grizzly bears over the next 21 years; an average of about 1 attack every 3 years. Five of the 7 attacks occurred in the park's backcountry. During the same 22-year period, the park recorded more than 57 million visits. To date,

Table 8.1. Grizzly bear reactions to people in 5,578 interactions that occurred in developments, roadside corridors, backcountry campsites, backcountry trails, and off-trail backcountry areas in Yellowstone National Park, 1991-2015.

### Reaction of bear

| Location of encounter | Flee Number | Flee Percent | Neutral behavior Number | Neutral behavior Percent | Curious Number | Curious Percent | Stress/agitation Number | Stress/agitation Percent | Aggression without contact Number | Aggression without contact Percent | Attack Number | Attack Percent |
|---|---|---|---|---|---|---|---|---|---|---|---|---|
| Park development | 280 | 48% | 275 | 47% | 16 | 3% | 2 | <1% | 8 | 1% | 0 | 0% |
| Roadside corridor | 685 | 22% | 2,297 | 74% | 47 | 2% | 9 | <1% | 56 | 2% | 0 | 0% |
| Backcountry campsite | 78 | 43% | 83 | 46% | 15 | 8% | 1 | 1% | 5 | 3% | 0 | 0% |
| Backcountry trail | 675 | 50% | 412 | 31% | 101 | 8% | 19 | 1% | 119 | 9% | 14 | 1% |
| Backcountry off-trail | 211 | 55% | 125 | 33% | 12 | 3% | 1 | <1% | 25 | 7% | 7 | 2% |
| Total | 1,929 | 35% | 3,192 | 57% | 191 | 3% | 32 | 1% | 213 | 4% | 21 | <1% |

Bears are not exclusively found off-trail or in remote areas. Here, a female grizzly bear and her cub make use of the boardwalks near Old Faithful, Yellowstone National Park.

Table 8.2. Odds of a grizzly bear attack during different recreational activities in Yellowstone National Park, 1980-2014.

| Type of recreational activity | Odds of grizzly bear attack |
|---|---|
| In developments or on roadsides and boardwalks | 1 in 25.1 million visits |
| Camping in a roadside campground | 1 in 22.8 million overnight stays |
| Camping in a backcountry campsite | 1 in 1.4 million overnight stays |
| Traveling during a multiple-day backcountry trip | 1 in 232 thousand person-travel days |
| All activities combined | 1 in 2.7 million visits |

there have been no grizzly-caused human fatalities in the park. Many grizzly bear encounters are chance events during non-hunting, recreational activities. However, mounting evidence suggests fall elk hunting increases the probability of human-bear conflicts as grizzly bears exploit resources provided by wounding loss and gut piles left behind by successful hunters. Grand Teton National Park has a program to reduce numbers of elk in the Jackson herd, which was established through legislation in 1950 when the park was expanded to its present size. Since 1951, elk hunts have occurred in Grand Teton National Park in all but 2 years. Three of the 5 grizzly bear attacks that occurred in the backcountry involved hunters. As a result, elk hunters have been required to carry bear spray in areas of the park occupied by grizzly bears since 2001.

In Yellowstone National Park, 37 people were injured by grizzly bears from 1980 through 2014, an average of 1.1 attacks per year. During that period, the park recorded over 100 million visits. For all visitors combined, the odds of being attacked by a grizzly bear were 1 in 2.7 million visits. The odds of a bear attack were significantly less for visitors who did not leave developments or roadsides, but greater for those hiking in backcountry areas (Table 8.2). There were 100,436,902 visits to Yellowstone during 1980 to 2014 and 4 people were injured in frontcountry areas such as developments, roadside campgrounds, road corridors, and roadside boardwalk trails. Therefore, the odds of being injured by a grizzly bear while in frontcountry areas of Yellowstone were 1 in 25.1

million visits. Of the 4 people injured in frontcountry areas, 1 occurred in a roadside campground. There were 22,824,762 overnight stays in roadside campgrounds during 1980 to 2014, where the odds of being injured by a grizzly bear were 1 in 22.8 million overnight stays. Of the 33 people attacked in backcountry areas since 1980, 7 were on multiple-day overnight trips (1 in a campsite; 6 traveling) and 26 were on day-trips. With 1,393,299 multiple-day overnight stays in the backcountry during 1980 to 2014, the odds of being injured in a campsite were 1 in 1.4 million, while the odds of being attacked while traveling were approximately 1 in 232,000 person-travel days. There are no statistics on how many visitors hike during the day in the backcountry without staying overnight but, on average, less than 1 day-hiker per year is attacked. (Gunther and Hoekstra 1998, Gunther 2015b)

During the 145-year (1872-2016) history of Yellowstone National Park, 7 people have been killed by grizzly bears inside the park (Table 8.3), and another was killed by either a black bear or a grizzly bear. More people have died in the park from drowning (119), falling (36), suicide (24), airplane crashes (22), thermal burns after falling into boiling thermal pools (20), horse-related accidents (19), freezing (10), and murder (9) than have been killed by grizzly bears. In fact, the number of people killed by grizzly bears in the park is only slightly higher than being killed by a falling tree (6), an avalanche (6), or lightning (5) while visiting the park. Fatal bear attacks are also rare outside of the national parks. From 1890 through 2016, 8 people were killed by bears on national forest and private lands in the Greater Yellowstone Ecosystem. (Whittlesey 2014)

## Visitor Compliance with Bear Safety Recommendations

Although the consequences of a bear attack can be quite severe (mauling or death), bear safety messaging is especially challenging because the odds of an attack for most park visitors are extremely small. Bear managers are challenged with convincing people to willingly take proactive measures to reduce the risk of bear attack, without unduly scaring them from supporting grizzly bear conservation or recreating on public lands.

Table 8.3. Known human fatalities caused by bears in Yellowstone National Park since 1872.

| Date | Species of bear | Incident description |
| --- | --- | --- |
| September 8, 1916 | Grizzly bear | A teamster sleeping under a wagon was killed by a grizzly bear at Ten Mile Spring near Turbid Lake at the southern end of Pelican Valley. |
| August 22, 1942 | Undetermined | A woman was attacked at night while walking to the restroom in the Old Faithful Campground. The woman died of her wounds five days later. The species of bear responsible for the attack was never determined. |
| June 23, 1972 | Grizzly bear | A man camping in an illegal camp near Grand Geyser was killed by an adult female grizzly bear when he returned to the camp at night and surprised the bear while she was feeding on improperly stored food. |
| July 30, 1984 | Grizzly bear | A woman was pulled from her tent and killed by a grizzly bear at a backcountry campsite at the southern end of White Lake near Pelican Valley. |
| October 4, 1986 | Grizzly bear | A photographer was killed by an adult female grizzly bear near Otter Creek in Hayden Valley. |
| July 6, 2011 | Grizzly bear | A man hiking with his wife on the Wapiti Lake Trail in Hayden Valley was killed by an adult female grizzly bear accompanied by 2 cubs. |
| August 25, 2011 | Grizzly bear | A man hiking alone was killed by a grizzly bear while hiking on the Mary Mountain Trail in Hayden Valley. |
| August 6, 2015 | Grizzly bear | A man hiking alone and off-trail on Elephant Back Mountain was killed by an adult female grizzly bear accompanied by 2 cubs. |

To reduce the risk of bear attack in national parks, safety information distributed to visitors recommends recreationalists carry bear spray and know how to use it, hike in groups of 3 or more people, stay at least 100 yards (91 meters) away from bears, stay alert and on established trails, and make noise in areas with limited visibility. (Herrero and Higgins 1998, Herrero 2002, Smith et al. 2008)

During 2011 to 2015, summer visitors at Yellowstone National Park were monitored to evaluate compliance with these recommendations, including 11,395 people in 4,012 groups on 64 different backcountry trails and 5 boardwalk trails. Observations included 7,770 backcountry day-hikers, 3,238 people walking on boardwalk trails, and 387 overnight backpackers. The most common group sizes for these types of recreationalists was only 2 people per party, fewer than the recommended group size of 3 or more for hiking in bear country. Also, compliance with bear spray recommendations among all backcountry recreationalists was low. Only 52% of backpackers, 14% of day-hikers, and less than 1% of boardwalk hikers carried bear spray. The reasons for the low rate of compliance are not known, but may be due to the park's reliance on inexpensive but impersonal signs, printed material, and web sites for conveying safety information. Research indicates that park visitors retain verbal information given by uniformed park staff better than written information. Indeed, backpackers had the highest compliance with bear spray recommendations and were the only recreationalists that always received face-to-face bear safety information from park staff. (Taylor et al. 2014, Gunther and Reinertson 2016)

## Conclusions

Despite numerous human-bear encounters on public lands every year, grizzly bears are remarkably tolerant and rarely attack people. Most attacks involve females with cubs responding with defensive aggression to surprise encounters with recreationalists at relatively close distances in backcountry areas. Visitor compliance with bear safety recommendations could prevent most encounters and diffuse most

*Studies show bear spray is successful at deterring unwanted behavior in bears. Bear spray can be rented or purchased in Yellowstone National Park.*

confrontations. Occasionally, bear-resistant food and garbage storage devices fail, visitors do not comply with food storage regulations, education efforts fail to change visitor behavior, or food storage violations are not detected by park patrols. In such instances, bears may obtain human food rewards. Once conditioned to human foods, bears are more likely to damage property or injure people in subsequent efforts to obtain human attractants and, as a result, pose a significant threat to visitor safety. In addition, although extremely rare, grizzly bears sometimes kill and consume people during surprise or predatory encounters. As a general rule, bears conditioned to human foods that become a distinct threat to human safety, or bears that kill and consume people, are captured and killed or sent to zoos. People should remember their actions affect not only themselves and their families, but could result in the death of a bear. Therefore, it is imperative that people adhere to food storage regulations and bear safety guidelines such as carrying bear spray, not only for personal safety, but also for the conservation of bears. (Herrero 2002)

Photograph by Michael Nichols courtesy of National Geographic

*Excitement builds at a "bear jam," Yellowstone National Park. Nearly all visitors expect to see a bear and about two-thirds actually do.*

# Chapter 9

## BEAR VIEWING IN YELLOWSTONE AND GRAND TETON NATIONAL PARKS—HABITUATION, VISITOR EXPECTATIONS, AND ECONOMICS

*Kerry A. Gunther, Katharine R. Wilmot, Steven L. Cain, Travis C. Wyman, Eric G. Reinertson, and Amanda M. Bramblett*

### Introduction

IN THE PREVIOUS chapter, we discussed human-bear interactions including conflicts, encounters, and attacks. Although the potential for attack is a serious safety consideration, bears are also very adaptable animals capable of living in proximity to high densities of people with relatively few conflicts if bear-resistant infrastructure is provided and people are willing to incur some lifestyle changes. For example, grizzly bears flourish in national parks with high levels of visitors and recreational activities as long as development is minimized, food storage regulations are strictly enforced, and sources of human-caused mortality are reduced. This is especially apparent with grizzly bears in Yellowstone and Grand Teton national parks (including the John D. Rockefeller, Jr. Memorial Parkway) where millions of tourists visit each year and new record highs for visitation are set almost every decade. In this chapter, we provide information on the adaptability of bears as expressed through habituation to people, the bear viewing opportunities habituation provides, and the challenges of managing millions of visitors that want to view and take close-up photographs of wild grizzly bears that frequent roadside habitats. (Chapron et al. 2014, Gunther et al. 2015d)

## Habituation

The ability of grizzly bears and black bears to survive in habitats with relatively high levels of human activity can be attributed to their intelligence, behavioral plasticity, and opportunistic use of resources. Habituation to human presence is a behavioral expression of that adaptability. The responses of bears to people are shaped by the predictability of human activities. When bears experience a non-threatening human activity frequently enough that it becomes expected, they learn to show little overt response. The waning of a bear's flight response to people is an example of habituation, which is adaptive and conserves energy by reducing unnecessary behaviors such as fleeing from people that are not a threat. Habituation allows bears to access and use habitats near areas with high levels of human activity, thereby increasing the availability of resources. Habituation is most commonly observed in national parks where exposure to humans is frequent, benign, predictable, and does not result in negative consequences for bears. In these circumstances, bears readily acclimate to predictable human activities such as road traffic, structures, and associated human activities. (McCullough 1982, Jope 1985, Knight and Cole 1995, Herrero et al. 2005, Smith et al. 2005)

Habituation differs markedly from food conditioning, whereby bears learn to seek people for rewards such as food, garbage, and livestock and pet feed. Food conditioning usually results in bear conflicts with humans and, ultimately, the death of the bear. National parks have been successful in decreasing the presence of food-conditioned bears because of strict food storage regulations, relatively high compliance from visitors, and staff to patrol developed areas and campgrounds on a daily basis. In contrast to the negative aspects associated with conditioning to human foods, under certain circumstances habituation can reduce the energy expended in response to stimuli that have no adverse consequences and allow bears to access natural food resources avoided by human-wary bears. Evidence suggests habituation is commonly site-specific. A bear that displays highly habituated behavior along park roads, for example, may be more wary or intolerant of people in backcountry areas where it does not expect to encounter them. (Gunther et al. 2004a, Herrero et al. 2005, Hopkins et al. 2010)

## Yellowstone National Park

The first roadside bear jams were reported in 1910, when a black bear began approaching tourists along a road and begging for food handouts. By the 1920s, bear jams caused by panhandling were common at many points along Yellowstone's grand loop road. Traffic jams involving these food-conditioned bears were common until 1970, when biologists and rangers implemented a new management plan. As part of this plan, visitors were no longer allowed to feed bears along roads or anywhere else in the park. Bears that persisted in trying to obtain human foods and garbage were captured and killed or sent to zoos. By 1979, most bears conditioned to human foods had been removed from the park. In the early 1980s, bear jams resurfaced as a management concern, although the bears involved were not conditioned to human foods. As visitation and numbers of grizzly and black bears increased following the high mortality associated with the closing of the park's garbage dumps, bears that were habituated to people, but not conditioned to human foods, began to appear in roadside meadows foraging for natural foods. Initially, these roadside bears were not tolerated and were hazed, relocated,

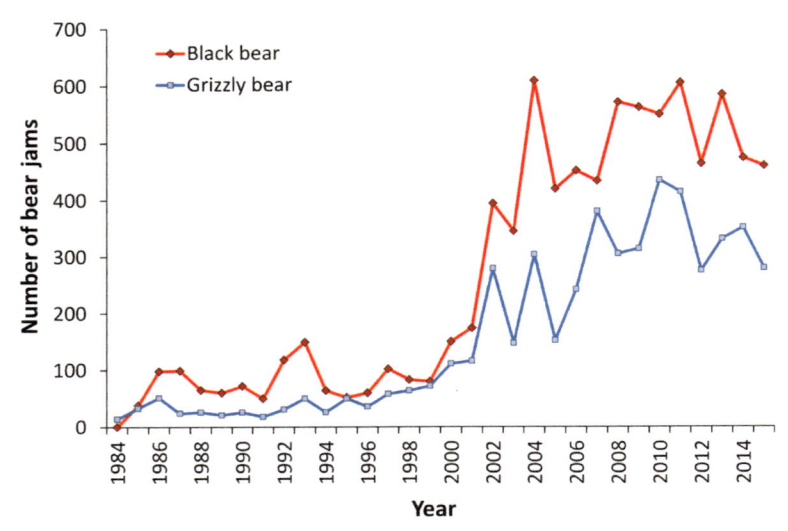

*Figure 9.1. Annual number of traffic jams caused by people stopping their vehicles to view grizzly bears and black bears in Yellowstone National Park, 1984-2015.*

or removed by park officials out of concern they would eventually get fed by visitors, damage property, attack people, or get hit by cars. When these tactics failed to prevent habituation, managers adopted an entirely different management strategy that was quite controversial at the time. Beginning in 1990, management efforts focused on humans instead of bears. Rather than trapping or hazing bears, rangers were dispatched to bear jams to ensure visitors parked their vehicles safely, did not approach or feed bears, and behaved in a predictable manner. (Meagher and Phillips 1983, Schullery 1992, Gunther and Wyman 2008, Haroldson and Gunther 2013)

During 1990 to 2014, a total of 12,386 bear jams were reported, including 4,587 with grizzly bears, 7,618 with black bears, and 181 with the species of bear not recorded (Figure 9.1). There were no bear attacks on visitors that stopped to view and photograph bears, and bear-caused property damage, management removals of bears, and bear mortality from vehicle strikes all remained low or decreased (Table 9.1). Thus, the concern that tolerating habituated bears along roadways would lead to increases in human-bear conflicts was unfounded. Interestingly,

Table 9.1. Numbers of human-bear conflicts, bear attacks, bear removals, and vehicle strike mortalities of grizzly bears and black bears occurring during two different habituated bear management eras in Yellowstone National Park, 1979-2014.

|  |  |  | Number per 1 million visits |  |  |  |  |  |  |  |
| --- | --- | --- | --- | --- | --- | --- | --- | --- | --- | --- |
|  |  |  | Property damage[a] |  | Bear attacks |  | Bear removals |  | Vehicle strike mortality |  |
| Time period | Habituated bear management strategy | Mean annual visitation | Grizzly | Black | Grizzly | Black | Grizzly | Black | Grizzly | Black |
| 1979-1989 | Prevent habituation | 2,303,894 | 3.9 | 2.5 | 0.6 | 0.1 | 0.4 | 0.1 | 0.1 | 0.4 |
| 1990-2014 | Tolerate habituation | 3,079,479 | 1.6 | 1.4 | 0.3 | <0.1 | 0.1 | 0.1 | 0.1 | 0.3 |

[a] Includes incidents where bears damaged property or obtained anthropogenic foods.

humans and vehicles turned out to be more dangerous than roadside bears due to several vehicle accidents and at least 5 people struck by vehicles at bear jams. Also, the strategy of focusing management on people instead of bears presents challenges for managers because it is labor-intensive and expensive. Approximately 2,500 to 3,000 personnel hours are spent annually managing bear jams, yet personnel are only able to respond and manage approximately 80% of the bear jams reported. (Gunther et al. 2015d)

The number of bear jams occurring annually is influenced by the availability of bear foods. For example, in years when whitebark pine produces abundant cones, bears move away from roadside meadows to high-elevation whitebark pine stands to feed on the nutritious seeds. However, during years of poor whitebark pine seed production, the number of bears foraging in roadside meadows and the number of bear jams increase significantly. Therefore, natural foods found in roadside meadows may be important to the survival of some individual bears during years exhibiting poor whitebark pine cone crops. (Haroldson and Gunther 2013)

Given adequate staff, habituated bears can be managed along roads in a manner that is relatively safe for both park visitors and bears. As a result, hundreds of thousands of visitors are able to view, photograph, and appreciate roadside bears while visiting the park each year. The opportunity to view bears not only provides a positive visitor experience, it contributes millions of dollars to the local economies of gateway communities. Positive bear viewing experiences also help build an important appreciation and conservation ethic for bears among people that visit national parks. (Herrero et al. 2005, Gunther and Wyman 2008, Haroldson and Gunther 2013, Richardson et al. 2014, Taylor et al. 2014, Gunther et al. 2015c)

*By itself, bear viewing contributes about 10 million dollars to the economies of park gateway communities and supports about 155 local jobs.*

## Grand Teton National Park

Prior to the early 2000s, grizzly bears were rarely observed outside the northern canyons of the park. However, observations increased steadily as grizzly bears expanded their range to the south boundary near Jackson, Wyoming. Observations of habituated grizzly bears followed this trend, first in high visitor-use areas such as Jackson Lake Lodge, Oxbow Bend, and Colter Bay and, eventually, to the Moose developed area and the Moose-Wilson Road corridor. (Gunther et al. 2015d)

The first documented observation of a habituated grizzly bear foraging naturally along roadside habitat occurred in 2004. Recognizing the success of Yellowstone's bear management program, Grand Teton adopted a similar strategy of managing humans at bear jams and tolerating habituated, but non-food conditioned, bears near roads. In 2007, as demands for managing bear jams escalated, the park created a *Wildlife Brigade* of paid and volunteer staff to manage visitors at the human-bear interface and provide food storage patrols and public education in frontcountry campgrounds. (Gunther et al. 2015d)

Since 2008, the first year for which reliable bear jam statistics are available, personnel in Grand Teton have managed at least 1,266 black bear jams, 1,099 grizzly bear jams, and 301 jams where the species of bear was not recorded (Figure 9.2). To date, grizzly bear jams have been dominated by family groups and subadults, classes of bears generally considered to be lowest in the bear dominance hierarchy. This finding has led to speculation that these bears are using roadside habitats to avoid more dominant adult males that sometimes kill cubs and smaller bears. The number of grizzly bear jams doubled from 2010 to 2011 due to the presence of 2 related adult females with cubs that foraged naturally along roadside habitats. To date, it appears annual grizzly bear jam numbers fluctuate based on the habituated bears' reproductive status, such as the presence or absence of cubs or yearlings, and survival of a small number of resident females. Not surprisingly, bear jam numbers also seem to reflect the condition of natural foods that occur near roads. For example, years with high numbers of black bear jams corresponded with years of excellent huckleberry, black hawthorne, or chokecherry crops along the Signal Mountain Summit and Moose-Wilson roads. (Gunther et al. 2015d)

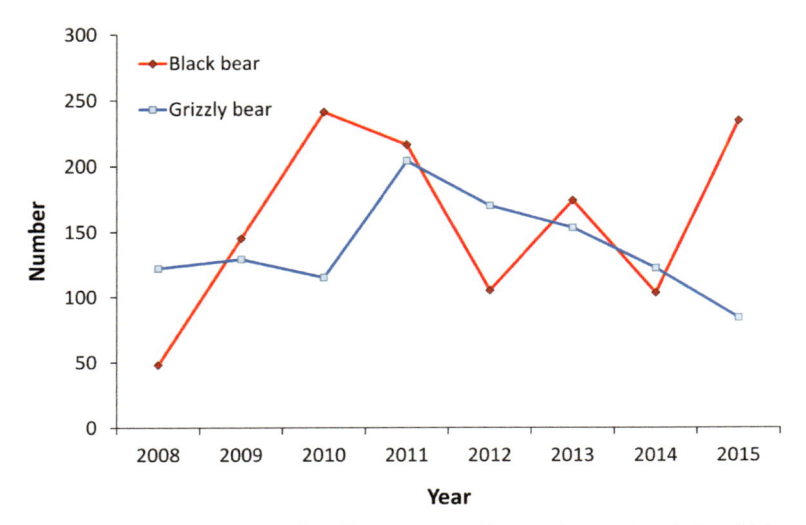

*Figure 9.2. Annual number of traffic jams caused by people stopping their vehicles to view grizzly bears and black bears in Grand Teton National Park and the John D. Rockefeller, Jr. Memorial Parkway, 2008-2015.*

Although Grand Teton National Park's history with habituated bear management is still relatively short, human-bear conflicts have remained very low (Figure 9.3). There have been no bear-inflicted human injuries associated with bear jams, and no increase in bears killed by vehicle strikes. However, several offspring produced by habituated female grizzly bears have died as a result of circumstances possibly exacerbated by habituation. A 3-year-old bear was illegally killed by a hunter at close range on national forest lands just outside the park and her comfort with close human proximity may have been a contributing factor. A yearling weaned in 2012 by a habituated female was killed by a vehicle strike later that year. Four years later, a male cub-of-the-year from the same habituated female was killed by a vehicle strike. A male offspring of a different habituated grizzly bear was removed after a history of frequenting human developments outside the park. Another offspring of a habituated bear was removed at 7 years old for repeated cattle depredation, although he did not exhibit habituated behavior as an adult. In contrast to Yellowstone National Park, which

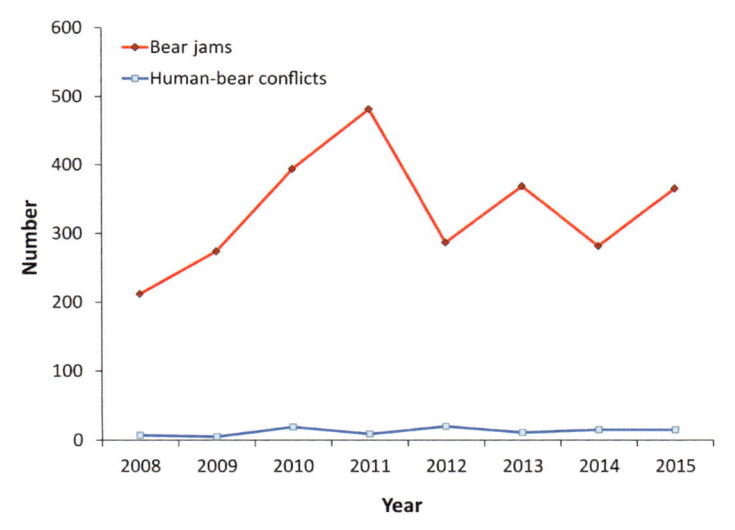

*Figure 9.3. Number of bear jams and human-bear conflicts (human food rewards, property damage, and human injury) in Grand Teton National Park and the John D. Rockefeller, Jr. Memorial Parkway, 2008-2015.*

is approximately 7 times larger and positioned in the center of the Grizzly Bear Recovery Zone, habituated bears in Grand Teton may be more likely to leave the protected confines of the park and be more susceptible to human-caused mortality associated with inadequate bear-attractant storage or attempts to use habitats in close proximity to people. (Gunther et al. 2015d)

Bear viewing opportunities are popular with local residents and visitors. Some bears are so popular they have their own Facebook pages. A program large enough to adequately manage the human-bear interface using paid employees is cost prohibitive and the *Wildlife Brigade* has been supported largely by volunteers since its inception. In 2016, the *Wildlife Brigade* consisted of 3 paid seasonal park rangers, 22 volunteers, and 1 intern, whom together provided human-bear interface coverage 7 days a week for over 7 months of the year. While the program has been successful, this level of commitment will require substantial financial support into the future. (Gunther et al. 2015d)

## Positive and Negative Aspects of Bear Habituation

In determining the extent to which bear habituation is tolerated, managers must weigh several factors. Habituation can benefit some bears by allowing them to access high-quality food resources adjacent to roads and developments, areas that are avoided and underutilized by human-wary bears. Therefore, the tolerance of habituated bears may allow national parks to support a higher density of bears. In addition, since habituation increases bear exposure to park visitors, it may increase public appreciation of bears and build support for conservation and habitat protection. (Herrero et al. 2005)

The habituation of some bears also benefits people by providing enjoyment and offering opportunities for bear viewing, photography, and filming, which can promote an appreciation of bears in people that never have a chance to visit a park with bears. Habituated bears also provide excellent opportunities for teaching park visitors about bears, their ecology, and conservation. Public viewing of habituated bears also provides economic benefits to gateway communities, park concessions operations, and the wildlife tour industry. Habituated bears are also less likely to respond with defensive aggression and attack and injure people during surprise encounters. (Herrero et al. 2005)

However, there are negative aspects of bear habituation to people. When habituated bears are foraging near roads or developments they often create traffic congestion that leads to angry and frustrated drivers, accidents and, potentially, bear injuries and fatalities. Although habituated bears may be less prone to react aggressively during encounters with people, the number of human-bear encounters and, therefore, the cumulative odds of a bear attack may increase. In addition, habituation increases the odds people might feed, approach, or otherwise behave inappropriately around bears, which could lead to injury or death of people and bears. Habituated bears may also be more likely to encounter unsecured human foods and become food conditioned. (Jope 1985, Mattson et al. 1987, Herrero et al. 2005, Gunther and Wyman 2008, Richardson et al. 2014)

## Managing Habituation Depends on the Circumstances

How wildlife managers deal with habituated bears depends on the location and situation. In some national parks, where humans are temporary visitors and their activities and developments are highly controlled, habituated bears have been managed to reduce human-bear conflicts, allow for popular recreational bear viewing, and maximize the effectiveness of available habitat by reducing human-caused displacement from prime food sources. Public lands managed under this philosophy include the McNeil River State Game Sanctuary, as well as Grand Teton, Katmai, and Yellowstone national parks. On other public and private lands, human activities are less strictly regulated and habituation can greatly increase the probability of bears becoming conditioned to human foods, struck by vehicles, or being involved in other types of conflicts that put both humans and bears at risk. Habituation is not tolerated by managers in these areas, with examples including Glacier National Park and private lands in Idaho, Montana, and Wyoming. (Aumiller and Matt 1994, Gunther et al. 2004a, Herrero et al. 2005, Smith et al. 2005, Gunther et al 2015c)

## Visitor Expectations and Economics of Bear Viewing

Yellowstone, Grand Teton (including the John D. Rockefeller, Jr. Memorial Parkway), and Glacier are the only national parks in the contiguous United States with grizzly bear viewing opportunities, providing not simply an opportunity to see an iconic carnivore, but also a wilderness experience. Many visitors feel a sense of kinship with the first human explorers to these areas, with their awareness of nature heightened by viewing wild predators up close and personal. As a result, bear viewing can be a valuable addition to family life, lore, and vacation memories. (Taylor et al. 2014)

Visitation to Yellowstone National Park exceeded 4.2 million visits during 2016 and is expected to increase in the future. The majority of visitors participated in geyser viewing (97%), sightseeing (88%), and wildlife viewing (81%). Bears are the wildlife species visitors most want to see. Nearly all visitors expect to see a bear and about two-thirds actually do. Surveys indicate most visitors that see a bear are inspired to support the conservation of bears and protection of their habitats. Nearly one-half of surveyed visitors conveyed the level of habituation or wariness of a bear did not matter to them, and 59% conveyed radio collars or other tagging devices did not detract from their viewing experience. Ten percent of visitors indicated they would take fewer trips to the park if management changed and bears were no longer readily visible from roads. (Richardson et al. 2014, Richardson et al. 2015, Cullinane Thomas and Koontz 2016)

Spending by visitors to Yellowstone National Park contributes significantly to the economies of gateway communities and the states of Idaho, Montana, and Wyoming. Visitors spent an estimated $524.3 million dollars during 2016 in communities surrounding the park and their expenditures supported approximately 8,156 local jobs. By itself, bear viewing contributes about 10 million dollars to the economies of park gateway communities and supports about 155 local jobs. Surveys indicated visitors were willing to pay about $40 more in park entrance fees to support the management of roadside bear viewing opportunities. (Richardson et al. 2014, Richardson et al. 2015, Cullinane Thomas and Koontz 2016)

## Conclusions

The habituation of some bears to people in Yellowstone and Grand Teton national parks is inevitable and may increase with more visitors in the future. Thus, the safety of visitors and habituated bears along roadways is a growing concern for managers. To be successful, strategies need to consider not only human and bear safety, but also the energetic needs and nutritional state of habituated bears, their contribution to population viability, the aesthetic value of public bear viewing and the conservation awareness this brings, and the economic value of bear viewing to gateway communities. (Gunther et al. 2004b, Robbins et al.

2004, Herrero et al. 2005, Haroldson and Gunther 2013, Richardson et al. 2014, Gunther et al. 2015c)

Although the ability of grizzly bears to adapt to increasing visitation undoubtedly has some limits, their behavioral flexibility allows them to exist across a broad continuum of human presence and activities. As a general rule, when human activities in bear habitat increase, staff time and budgets dedicated toward human-bear management require a commensurate increase. Based on our experience, the key components of a successful program to manage habituated bears include preventing bears from becoming conditioned to human foods and garbage, making human activities as predictable as possible, and setting certain boundaries for both bears and people. Appropriate boundaries for habituated bears include teaching them not to enter park developments and campsites or to approach people too closely. Appropriate boundaries for people include teaching them to store attractants such as food in a bear-resistant manner, not to feed bears, and to maintain a minimum distance of at least 100 yards (91 meters) when viewing bears. Although signs, printed material, and website posts are the least expensive media for teaching bear safety and viewing etiquette to visitors, research shows that retention of safety messages is highest from face-to-face interactions with uniformed park staff. The most formidable challenge for managing habituated bears in national parks is not managing the bears, but sustaining and expanding as necessary the people management programs that have made bear management successful to date. Managing visitors around habituated bears is a long-term commitment. Habituation is a relatively new challenge faced by bear managers throughout the world, and many of these managers are considering the management approaches used in Yellowstone and Grand Teton national parks while formulating their own strategies. (Taylor et al. 2014, Gunther et al. 2015c)

Photograph by Ronan Donovan

A Yellowstone National Park Bear Management Technician retraces the steps of a collared grizzly bear to record foraging behavior.

## Chapter 10

CURRENT MANAGEMENT STRATEGY

*Kerry A. Gunther, Daniel B. Tyers, Tyler H. Coleman, Katharine R. Wilmot, and P. J. White*

**Introduction**

PUBLIC LANDS IN the Greater Yellowstone Ecosystem are administered by the U.S. Forest Service, National Park Service, Bureau of Land Management, U.S. Fish and Wildlife Service, and the states of Idaho, Montana, and Wyoming. The respective mandates of these agencies determine what activities can occur on these lands. Therefore, the array of human activities that can affect grizzly bears varies considerably among agency jurisdictions. For example, the National Park Service's mandate is to preserve cultural and natural resources unharmed for the benefit and enjoyment of future generations, which requires providing access, accommodations, and recreational experiences for large numbers of visitors on a landscape shared with grizzly bears. In comparison, the U.S. Forest Service has a mandate to wisely manage resources for a variety of sustainable practices, allowing for multiple uses of public land for the greatest good for the greatest number of people. In other words, renewable resources can be used in ways that best meet the needs of the American people, including resource extraction for commercial and other purposes, provided these actions do not impair the productivity of the land.

Visitors to the Greater Yellowstone Ecosystem are most familiar with the experiences and landscapes provided in Yellowstone and Grand Teton national parks, where grizzly bears and recreating humans coexist in a relatively natural environment. In this context, the activities of people are carefully regulated to ensure minimal effects to the environment, including free-ranging grizzly bears. However, beyond the borders of the parks, other more diverse human activities on federal and state public lands affect grizzly bears because they involve recreational activities and the removal of natural resources in keeping with a multiple-use approach. Grizzly bears adjust to many of these activities by modifying their behavior. For example, bears are quick to take advantage of changes that provide new foraging opportunities, which some human-caused habitat modifications provide. However, the interjection of human activities in grizzly bear habitat has inherent risks. Grizzly bear survival in the Greater Yellowstone Ecosystem decreases where there are increases in road density and development, and in areas where hunting is permitted. As a result, survival has been highest in the national parks, somewhat lower in wilderness areas surrounding the parks, and lower elsewhere; corresponding directly to the level of restrictions on human activities. (Schwartz et al. 2010b)

## Management of Grizzly Bears in National Parks

Yellowstone and Grand Teton national parks, the core of occupied grizzly bear range in the Greater Yellowstone Ecosystem, are managed in 3 broad zones: developed areas, road corridors, and backcountry/wilderness. Each zone has differing strategies for managing the human-bear interface (Table 10.1). Human activities are prioritized in developed areas, road corridors are managed for both people and bears, and bears are given priority in backcountry areas.

Table 10.1. Management of the visitor-bear interface in Yellowstone and Grand Teton national parks is divided into broad zones, each with specific management strategies for interactions.

| Management zones | Area | Management prescription |
|---|---|---|
| Developments | Yellowstone: 5,467 acres or 2,212 hectares (<1% of park)<br>Grand Teton: 2,652 acres or 1,073 hectares (1% of park) | • Managed for people to the exclusion of bears when conflicts occur<br>• Human-food conditioned bears are removed<br>• Visitors are given priority when visitor and bear activities are not compatible |
| Road corridors | Yellowstone: 1,617 acres or 654 hectares (<1%)<br>Grand Teton: 13,469 acres or 5,451 hectares (4%) | • Managed for transportation and bear viewing<br>• Bears are allowed to use roadside habitats for foraging and other natural behaviors<br>• Habituation of bears to people and people to bears is expected<br>• Human-food conditioned bears are removed |
| Wilderness and undeveloped lands | Yellowstone: 2,190,718 acres or 886,552 hectares (99%)<br>Grand Teton: 317,254 acres or 128,388 hectares (95%) | • Managed primarily for bears and other wildlife<br>• Overnight visitation is capped by a limited number of designated backcountry campsites<br>• Most human day-use is <3 miles from roads<br>• Implementation of seasonal recreational use closures for high use bear areas<br>• Bears generally given priority in recreation management decisions where bear and human activities are not compatible<br>• Human-food conditioned bears are removed |

Food and Garbage—Preventing bears from obtaining human foods, garbage, and other human attractants is the foundation of the bear management programs in Yellowstone and Grand Teton national parks. Successful prevention reduces human-bear conflicts and the removal of these bears from the ecosystem. It is rare for bears to obtain human food or garbage in either park due to bear-resistant receptacles, education programs, and enforcement efforts. Both parks use bear-resistant food storage boxes, garbage cans, and dumpsters, combined with diligent enforcement of food storage regulations, nightly patrols of campgrounds, and extensive information and educational efforts designed to increase visitor awareness and compliance and prevent food rewards. Because of the low number of human-bear conflicts, few bears are captured, relocated, or removed from the parks.

Backcountry Camping—Yellowstone National Park contains 301 designated backcountry campsites distributed along more than 1,000 miles (1,609 kilometers) of hiking trails that can be accessed from 92 trailheads. These campsites accommodate up to 3,112 people each night during the peak camping season. Each designated campsite provides a food-hanging pole or steel food storage box. Campsites designed for large parties guided by commercial outfitters have multiple food storage devices to accommodate larger volumes of food. Dispersed camping, or camping in non-designated backcountry sites, is allowed in some areas of the park, but accounts for less than 2% of total over-night stays. When camping in non-designated sites, visitors are required to rig their own food-hanging device or carry a bear-resistant food storage container approved by the Interagency Grizzly Bear Committee (http://igbconline.org/bear-resistant-products/).

Approximately 70% of visitors that camp in the backcountry of Yellowstone National Park travel by foot, 17% use stock (horses, mules, and llamas), and 13% travel by boat. Although total recreational visits to the park have increased significantly in recent years, overnight stays in the backcountry have been relatively stable, ranging from 39,280 to 45,615 per year. The number of overnight stays is limited by the number and capacity of the designated backcountry campsites. A permit is required to stay overnight in the backcountry and campers are given face-to-face, verbal information about bear encounters, bear spray, and food storage by the ranger issuing the permit. Campers are also required to watch a safety video containing bear safety information and given a booklet containing further bear safety guidelines. These bear safety messages, the convenience of the provided food storage devices, and the requirement that all parties camping in undesignated campsites carry an approved bear-resistant container, have kept backcountry campers remarkably free of conflicts with bears. There were about 1.3 million overnight stays in the backcountry during 1984 to 2015, but only 1 camper was attacked by a grizzly bear in a campsite and there were only 24 incidents where grizzly bears damaged property or obtained human foods in backcountry campsites. Due to the low number of conflicts in the backcountry, few bears are captured and killed in management actions.

Grand Teton National Park has approximately 250 miles (402 kilometers) of maintained hiking trails and 264 backcountry campsites that can accommodate up to 1,072 people each night. Recreational visits have increased significantly in recent years, but overnight stays in the backcountry have been relatively stable, ranging from 26,858 to 33,798 during the past 10 years. The majority of backcountry camping is managed as zone camping, which allows visitors to camp almost anywhere within an indicated zone provided they are at least 200 feet (60 meters) from trails and water sources. All backcountry campers are required to carry and use a bear-resistant container approved by the Interagency Grizzly Bear Committee because food storage infrastructure is not provided and hanging food is prohibited. Dispersed camping is allowed in some areas of the park, though this type of camping comprises a minor percentage of total backcountry over-night use. The remaining backcountry camping occurs at designated campsites where food-hanging poles or storage boxes are provided.

A permit is required for all overnight stays in the backcountry of Grand Teton National Park. Information about bear safety and food storage regulations is provided to campers by the ranger issuing the permit. Campers are also required to watch a backcountry safety video containing bear safety information. The park provides approved bear-resistant food storage containers to campers and a sticker is affixed to each container to remind backcountry campers of their proper use. The number of campers in each zone is limited based on the size of the zone and the availability of good campsites within the zone, while the number of campers in designated sites is limited by the availability and capacity of designated campsites.

Bear Management Areas—In 1982, Yellowstone National Park instituted a program to increase the protection of habitat for grizzly bears. The program restricts human access to 16 backcountry areas of the park deemed critical for grizzly bear recovery and conservation. Known as Bear Management Areas, these areas restrict off-trail travel and/or seasonally restrict camping or hiking in defined areas. Bear Management Areas currently cover 464,637 acres (188,032 hectares), which equates to 21% of the park. Each of the 16 areas have unique guidelines, but share the following primary goals: (1) minimize human-bear interactions that may lead to the habituation of bears to people, (2) prevent human-caused displacement of bears from prime food sources, and (3) decrease the risk of bear attack in areas with high levels of bear activity. (National Park Service 1982, Gunther 2003)

Research during the mid-1980s indicated Bear Management Area closures, time of day restrictions, and backcountry campsite closures were effective at limiting human-bear interactions and helped achieve the primary goals outlined for the program. Also, a recent 3-year study found bear movements changed throughout the year depending on the presence and activity of people. Human use of 6 Bear Management Areas was documented during summer and autumn by giving people Global Positioning System (GPS) units to track their movements and identify areas commonly used by both humans and radio-collared grizzly bears. Bear movements were also monitored from early spring until early July when these areas were closed to humans. When the Bear Management Areas were closed, grizzly bears were twice as likely to be in areas commonly used by humans at other times of the year. Also, the study found radio-collared bear locations were, on average, between 0.9 and 2.4 miles (1.5 and 3.8 kilometers) from areas of common human use. When the Bear Management Areas were open to humans, grizzly bears were 2.6 to 4.0 miles (4.2 to 6.4 kilometers) away from areas of common human use. In addition, the daily activity patterns of bears changed, with twice as much activity in common use areas at times of the day when people were no longer active. These findings suggest that if Bear Management Area restrictions were not in place, people would be in closer proximity to places frequented by bears during certain times of the year. In turn, bears would be forced to adjust their activity patterns and, consequently, could miss important foraging opportunities. Seasonal restrictions on human access provide unhindered foraging opportunities for bears and increase safety for people. (Gunther 1990, Schwartz et al. 2010a, Coleman et al. 2013a)

Bear Management Areas were established, in part, to decrease potential disturbances to bears caused by overnight, backcountry, camping groups. During 2007 to 2009, radio-collared bears avoided areas within 437 yards (400 meters) of occupied backcountry camps, but this response lessened at greater distances. The converse was true when backcountry camps were unoccupied and bears frequented these areas, possibly due to the proximity of the campsites to travel corridors or natural herbaceous foods. Also, grizzly bears occasionally investigate fire rings in unoccupied campsites because some campers burn their unconsumed food. The avoidance of occupied backcountry campsites by bears suggests Bear Management Area restrictions that close campsites during certain times of the year or within about 550 yards (503 meters) of seasonal food sources are effective at preventing human-caused displacement of bears from food sources. (Mealey 1980, Jope 1985, Gunther 1990, Kasworm and Manley 1990, Mattson et al. 1991a, Coleman et al. 2013b)

Bear Safety Messaging—Visitors are targeted for bear safety messages both before and after they arrive at the parks. These safety messages appear to be working because there have been very few bear attacks during the last 30 years. In addition, surveys indicate visitors are receiving and understanding the parks' bear safety messages.

Since 2011, however, 3 hikers have been killed by grizzly bears in separate incidents on backcountry trails in Yellowstone National Park. The circumstances of these fatalities suggested some people may be underestimating the risks of hiking in bear country and knowingly not following the park's bear safety advice. For example, surveys of backcountry hikers conducted after these well-publicized fatalities, when visitors would be expected to use high vigilance, indicated few (14%) day-hikers carried bear spray. Bear spray has been proven effective at deterring unwanted behavior in bears and its use is promoted in bear safety literature. These survey findings prompted park managers to examine current bear safety messages and delivery methods to ensure messages are conveyed to the public in an effective manner. The parks are attempting to improve compliance with bear safety recommendations through the use of branding, message layering, and behavioral systems that make it easy for visitors to comply. For example, providing visitors in campgrounds with bear-resistant boxes makes compliance with food storage regulations easy for visitors and, therefore, promotes passive adoption of bear-safe behavior. (Schwartz et al. 2002, Schwartz et al. 2006c, Nelson et al. 2011, Austin and Kohring 2013)

## Management of Grizzly Bears on National Forests

The removal of natural resources in keeping with a multiple-use approach includes harvesting wood products, livestock grazing, mining, and hunting, with associated effects from building roads, vegetation and surface disturbance, employee camps, moving machinery, constructing fences, distributing livestock, and allowing humans considerable access for state-regulated hunting seasons. Many of these actions potentially affect grizzly bear habitat. Before being implemented, these activities are evaluated to assess environmental effects, with potential effects on grizzly bears and their habitats weighed against the value of resource

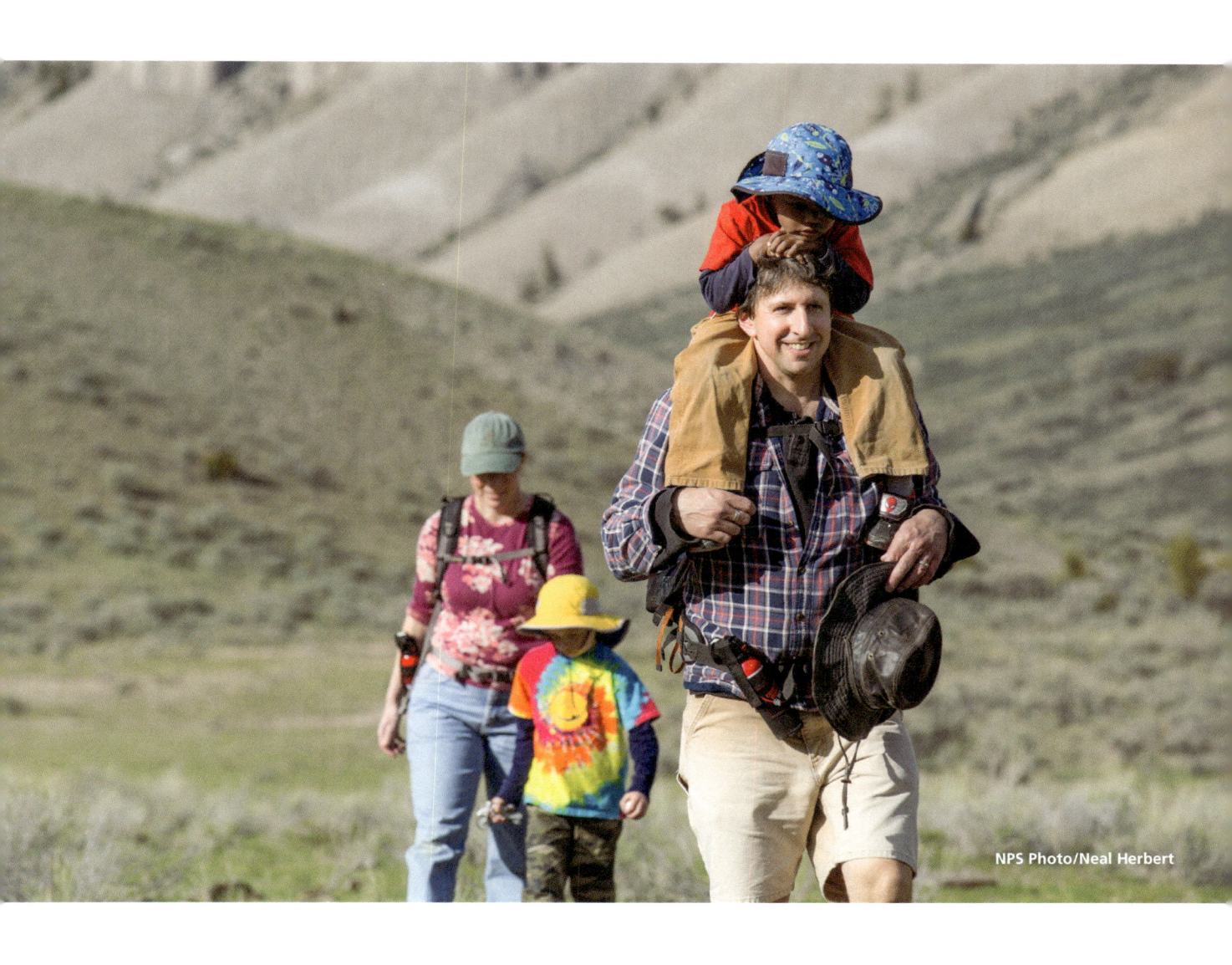

*A bear-aware family hiking with bear spray in Yellowstone National Park. Surveys indicate that only 14% of day-hikers in the park carry bear spray.*

NPS Photo/Neal Herbert

extraction. Managers make adjustments to proposed projects to lessen potential negative effects on bears and their habitats.

Timber Harvest—Research generally supports a link between intact mature forests and grizzly bear habitat use in the Greater Yellowstone Ecosystem. Undisturbed lodgepole pine stands in Yellowstone National Park were neither selected for nor avoided. However, forested areas with wetter environments or mature whitebark pine were favored by bears. Radio-collared grizzly bears spent substantial time in habitats containing timber, particularly areas where openings were less than 110 yards (100 meters) away. This implies the importance of forest cover for Yellowstone grizzly bears, particularly when interspersed with small meadows. (Blanchard 1983, Mattson 1997b)

Forests in the Greater Yellowstone Ecosystem are characterized by low species diversity, slow regrowth, and high variability in terms of commercial value. The most economically efficient harvest method for most commercial forest types involves building a spur road from an existing road and clear-cutting the unit. Areas are generally checked for regrowth at 3 and 5 years post-harvest. If needed, replanting usually occurs about 8 years after logging with thinning after 20-25 years. All of these activities have the potential to affect grizzly bears, including negative impacts from a loss of cover and beneficial impacts from enhancing foraging opportunities. The production of grasses, herbaceous plants, and berry-producing shrubs is stimulated by opening forest canopies to allow more light to reach the ground. However, the reduction in security for bears is generally more significant than increases in food plants because grass and forb production wanes as new trees establish. In addition, roads represent a significant hazard to grizzly bears and are a conduit for human-bear conflicts because they provide access for people into bear habitat. Managers attempt to lessen these effects by limiting the duration of road use and road density. (Mattson and Knight 1991, Anderson 1994, McLellan and Hovey 1995, Schwartz et al. 2010b)

Livestock Grazing—Homesteading and the development of the livestock industry in the late 19th and early 20th century led to a decrease in grizzly bear foraging opportunities through agricultural cultivation and a reduction in ungulate numbers from hunting. During the same period, grizzly bear mortalities increased from humans protecting livestock and crops from bears. Livestock grazing may negatively impact grizzly bear habitat by reducing the vigor or abundance of bear foods such as grasses, forbs, and berry-producing shrubs or by reducing the amount of security cover such as riparian shrubs and trees. Impacts to vegetation depend on the season, duration, and intensity of livestock grazing. With modern management, livestock likely have minimal effects on the amount and structure of vegetation used by grizzly bears. (Mattson 1990)

National forests within the Greater Yellowstone Ecosystem use a variety of strategies to minimize livestock-related habitat deterioration and livestock depredation (killing) by bears. Stocking rates and the timing and duration of grazing are manipulated to reduce the loss of forage for wildlife species. The U.S. Forest Service has not permitted any new grazing allotments within the Grizzly Bear Recovery Zone, and with financial assistance from non-governmental organizations such as the National Wildlife Federation, cattle and sheep allotments are being phased out. Despite these efforts, grizzly bear depredation on livestock has increased during the last decade, with many of these conflicts occurring on national forest allotments. As a result, management removals of grizzly bears due to livestock depredation have increased from 4% of the average annual mortalities during 1993-2003 to 13% during 2004-2014. Furthermore, as grizzly bears expanded to the periphery of the ecosystem, they occupied large tracts of relatively undisturbed, high-quality habitat on public lands. Many of these areas have permitted livestock allotments, which contributed to the increase in bear-livestock conflicts. From 1992 to 2000, 69% of livestock depredations by grizzly bears occurred in the periphery of the ecosystem and 80% occurred on public lands. (Schwartz et al. 2002, Gunther et al. 2004a, U.S. Fish and Wildlife Service 2007b, DeBolt et al. 2015, Frey 2015)

Grizzly bear depredation on livestock increases through the summer season and most incidents are caused by adult males. However, adult female and subordinate grizzly bears are sometimes displaced by larger

*The Yellowstone grizzly bear population will likely always need to be closely monitored and carefully managed, including efforts to control human-caused mortality.*

males into marginal habitats such as grazing allotments where human activity is greater. The result may be an increase in depredations by a few bears that habitually kill livestock or a number of bears that kill livestock opportunistically. Grizzly bears can occupy the same areas as livestock without conflicts occurring, but there is also evidence grizzly bears opportunistically take advantage of livestock already in their foraging area. Selective removal has been used by management agencies to contend with grizzly bears responsible for livestock depredations. Also, carcasses are removed to avoid concentrating grizzly bears in areas used by livestock. Hazing and relocations may provide temporary or local relief from grizzly bear-livestock conflicts, but these bears generally soon return to their original range. Although expensive and logistically difficult, electric or traditional fencing can isolate livestock from grizzly bears. Furthermore, livestock losses to grizzly bears can be reduced by limiting grazing in riparian areas to late autumn and winter, when seasonal overlap with bears would be minimal. (Mattson 1990, Anderson et al. 2002, Gunther et al. 2004a, Wilson et al. 2005)

Mineral Extraction—Prospectors searching for precious metals were a driving force in Euro-American settlement of the Greater Yellowstone Ecosystem. A number of significant gold and silver strikes were made in the last half of the 19th century. Some played out quickly and others were worked for decades, such as the mining districts near Gardiner and Cooke City, Montana. Palladium and platinum deposits in south-central Montana were developed in the 1940s and are still active today. Less valuable materials, such as coal, have also been exploited in the Gardiner and Red Lodge, Montana, areas. Exploration for low- and high-value minerals continues today. (Picton and Lonner 2010)

Although usually spatially limited by the nature of access to minerals, mining can cause significant environmental alteration. Impacts from mining include exploration activities, surface disturbance, disruption of aquifers, toxic compounds in tailings ponds and waste/overburden storage areas, road construction and use, and infrastructure development to support miners and processors. Toxic runoff and habitat disturbance from abandoned mines can create as big or bigger problems than extant mines. Also, roads facilitate human access into bear habitat, thereby increasing the potential for human-bear conflicts and mortality risks. Moreover, the increased presence of people on the landscape can generate human-bear conflicts by increasing the availability of foods and other attractants. Depending on the location of the mining activity, the destruction of bear habitat and displacement of bears is also a concern. (Horejsi 1985, U.S. Environmental Protection Agency 2004, Johnson et al. 2005)

The role of the U.S. Forest Service in regulating mining in the Greater Yellowstone Ecosystem is limited by the provisions of the General Mining Act of 1872. Under this law, an individual or corporation can claim minerals and the right to mine those minerals, as well as fee title ownership of national forest land above the minerals, by staking a claim, paying a fee, and working the claim in an economically plausible manner. Permit restrictions can be used to lessen the adverse effects of these human activities on grizzly bears. Examples include limiting road density and directing road placement, restricting camping and employee camp arrangements, prohibiting the harassment of bears, and enforcing the proper storage of food and other attractants. Also, habitat restoration can be secured through bonds with the respective states.

Sport Hunting—State-regulated hunting seasons periodically bring an influx of people into bear habitat. Hunters move quietly and often early in the morning or evening, which increases their chances of encountering a bear. Also, hunters may mimic their prey, such as an elk, which can attract a bear. If game is harvested, grizzly bears may contest hunters for the carcass. Given these circumstances, hunters shooting grizzly bears in self-defense is one of the primary causes of grizzly bear deaths in the Greater Yellowstone Ecosystem. In fact, defensive shootings by primarily elk hunters contributed to 43% of grizzly bear mortalities on federal lands in the ecosystem during 2002 to 2014. Hunter-focused educational efforts have been implemented in an attempt to reduce hunter-bear encounters and defensive shootings. This educational material warns of the inherent risks of hunting in grizzly habitat and advocates carrying bear-spray, appropriate camping techniques, and rapid game retrieval.

Wilderness Management—In contrast to an emphasis on resource extraction, the multiple-use approach to management practices on national forests also includes preservation of wildlands and the associated natural processes. This is formally recognized within designated wilderness areas. There are 11 U.S. Forest Service areas in the Greater Yellowstone Ecosystem with wilderness designation included. This involves about 36% of national forest land in the Greater Yellowstone Ecosystem, or 3,948,813 acres.

The Wilderness Act of 1964 created the legal definition of wilderness areas. Wilderness designation is a protective constraint Congress applies to selected portions of existing federal lands. Motorized and mechanized conveyance is excluded from wilderness, resulting in a pristine environment favorable to wildlife, including the grizzly bear. The Wilderness Act offers a careful and yet poetic definition of wilderness: "A wilderness, in contrast with those areas where man and his own works dominate the landscape, is hereby recognized as an area where the earth and its community of life are untrammeled by man, where man himself is a visitor who does not remain."

The constraints placed on human use of wilderness areas results in a landscape where grizzly bears are less likely to encounter humans and, consequently, human-bear conflicts are comparatively few. The management focus is on educating the public on how to travel and camp to avoid contacts with grizzly bears, especially during big-game hunting seasons. Ensuring that food rewards are not available to bears where humans camp is central to this educational emphasis. To facilitate attractant storage, food-hanging poles may be provided.

Management of Human-Grizzly Bear Conflicts—The U.S. Forest Service has responsibility for determining the extent of wildlife use on national forests, but wildlife regulations direct managers to cooperate with the states in both the planning and action stages of management, and stipulate that the harvesting of wildlife must conform with state laws. Thus, comprehensive forest plans are prepared to ensure the conservation of biological diversity and sustainable populations of native wildlife and their habitats. However, the respective states have traditionally exercised primary management authority over wildlife on national forest lands. Therefore, the U.S. Forest Service sustains habitat for grizzly bears and provides bear-resistant garbage receptacles, food storage boxes, and educational efforts on national forest lands, while the respective states have the primary role in managing bears and human-bear conflicts.

## Management on State and Private Lands

Preventing bears from obtaining human-related foods and garbage is the foundation of bear management programs on state and private lands in the Greater Yellowstone Ecosystem. The states of Idaho, Montana, and Wyoming have implemented bear-wise community efforts throughout the ecosystem that promote the use of bear-resistant garbage receptacles, food storage boxes, electric fencing, and other tactics in combination with public outreach to minimize human-bear conflicts. However, the task of bear-proofing entire communities and isolated rural homes, farms, and ranches is extremely difficult given many private land owners are unable or reluctant to incur the financial costs and lifestyle changes required to store bear attractants in a bear-resistant manner. This challenge is further exacerbated by the expansion of grizzly bears into long vacant habitats that are now dominated by people, livestock, and agriculture. The state wildlife management agencies are required to resolve conflicts occurring on private lands in a timely manner. Generally speaking, management activities favor the land owner or resident when grizzly bear activity is incompatible with human activities on private lands. As described in Chapter 8, most conflicts occurring on private lands involve damage to buildings, vehicles, gardens, fruit trees, and apiaries by bears attempting to obtain human foods, garbage, fruit, vegetables, and livestock and pet feed.

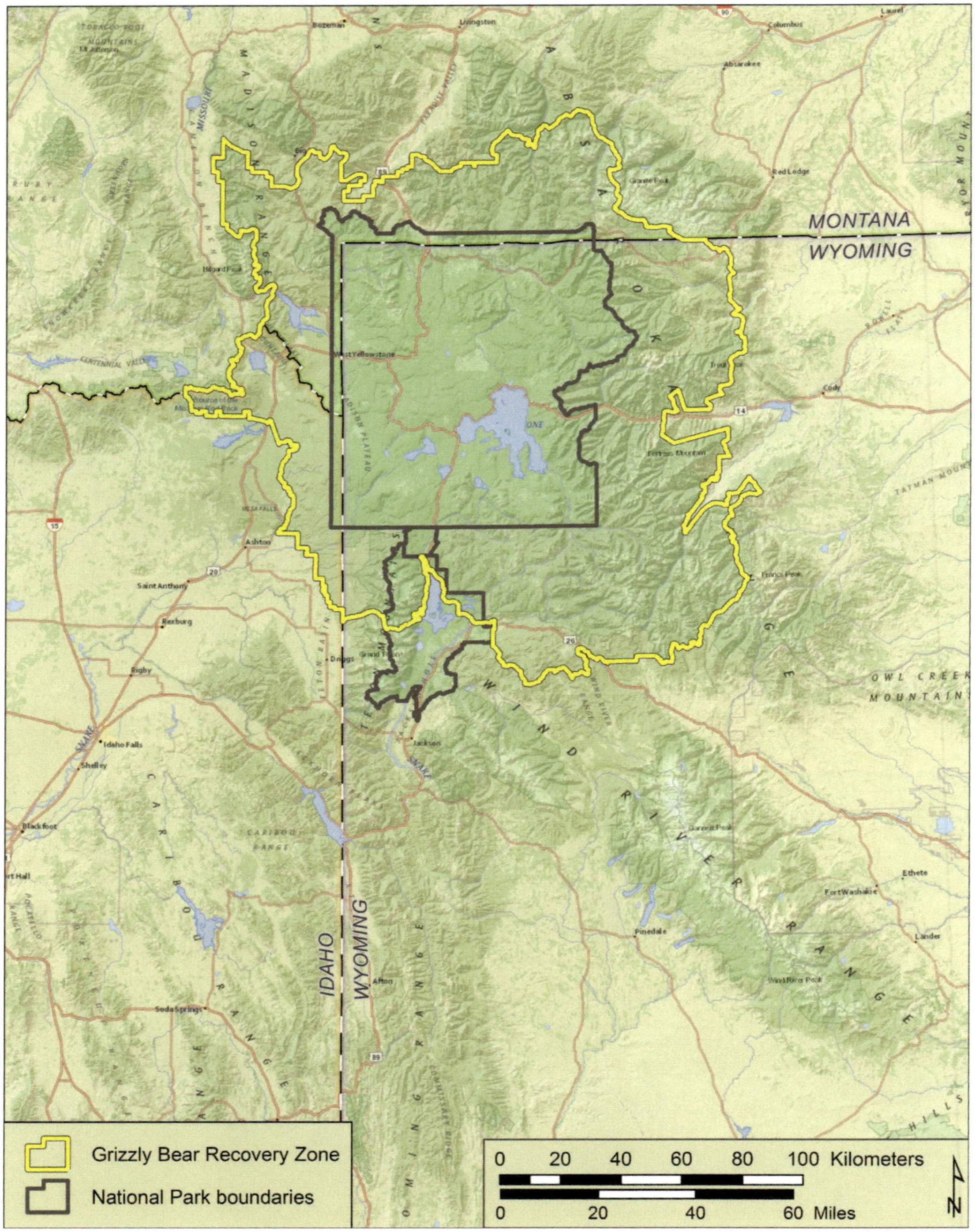

*Figure 10.1. The Recovery Zone/Primary Conservation Area for grizzly bears in the Greater Yellowstone Ecosystem. Base map source: National Geographic World Map, ESRI, Redlands, California.*

## Grizzly Bear Conservation Strategy

The grizzly bear was protected as a threatened species under the Endangered Species Act in 1975 because of unsustainable levels of human-caused mortality, loss of habitat, and significant habitat alteration. Since then, public and tribal agencies, non-governmental organizations, and private landowners have worked together to recover grizzly bears and conserve their habitats. Previous chapters described these efforts and the biological data indicating population recovery. Consequently, the U.S. Fish and Wildlife Service has proposed to remove Yellowstone grizzly bears from protection under the Endangered Species Act (Craighead et al. 1974, Haroldson and Frey 2007, U.S. Fish and Wildlife Service 2007a, Haroldson and Frey 2010, Bjornlie et al. 2015, Haroldson and Frey 2015, U.S. Fish and Wildlife Service 2016).

However, the potential removal of grizzly bears from threatened species status does not mean monitoring and protection of bears and their habitat will no longer be a priority. The Yellowstone grizzly bear population will likely always need to be closely monitored and carefully managed, including efforts to control human-caused mortality. In 2007, the federal and state managers responsible for managing grizzly bears and their habitat completed a *Conservation Strategy for the Grizzly Bear in the Greater Yellowstone Area*, which was updated during 2016. This strategy will guide grizzly bear management by federal and state agencies if grizzly bears are removed from protection under the Endangered Species Act. Oversight will be coordinated by the Yellowstone Grizzly Coordinating Committee, which will have representatives from participating federal and state agencies, Native American tribes, and affected counties. The strategy describes coordinated efforts to manage the grizzly bear population and its habitat to ensure its continued conservation. The strategy specifies standards for abundance, distribution, and habitat necessary to maintain a recovered grizzly population into the future. (U.S. Fish and Wildlife Service 2007b, U.S. Fish and Wildlife Service 2016)

In addition, the *Conservation Strategy* documents the regulatory mechanisms and legal authorities, policies, management, and monitoring programs in place to maintain the recovered Yellowstone grizzly bear population. The foundation of the strategy is the protection of habitat inside a 9,210-square-mile (23,854-square kilometer) Primary Conservation Area (equivalent to the Grizzly Bear Recovery Zone) where development, livestock grazing, and roads are limited (Figure 10.1). This area is primarily managed by the U.S. Forest Service (59%) and the National Park Service (39%). The Primary Conservation Area is intended to help sustain the grizzly bear population into the future, while facilitating the dispersal of bears elsewhere. The states of Wyoming, Montana, and Idaho have plans for management on lands outside the Primary Conservation Area that allow grizzly bears to inhabit biologically suitable and socially acceptable areas. (U.S. Fish and Wildlife Service 2007b, U.S. Fish and Wildlife Service 2016)

Conserving a recovered grizzly bear population in the Greater Yellowstone Ecosystem requires having an adequate number of widely distributed bears and maintaining a balance between reproduction and mortality. Under the *Conservation Strategy*, state and federal wildlife management agencies will maintain a population of around 674 grizzly bears (based on the average of estimates derived during 2002 to 2014 using a conservative model known as Chao2), with females and young widely distributed throughout the Primary Conservation Area and total mortality rates below sustainable limits. Also, the State of Montana has agreed to manage discretionary mortality in areas potentially linking the Greater Yellowstone and Northern Continental Divide ecosystems to retain the opportunity for natural movements of bears and genetic interchange between ecosystems. In addition, federal land management agencies agreed to maintain secure habitat within the Primary Conservation Area with no net increase in development, livestock grazing, or roads. Secure habitat is defined as areas larger than 10 acres (4 hectares) and more than 547 yards (500 meters) from a motorized access route or recurring helicopter flight line during the non-denning period. (Dood et al. 2006, Cherry et al. 2007, U.S. Fish and Wildlife Service 2007b, Schwartz et al. 2008, Kamath et al. 2015, U.S. Fish and Wildlife Service 2016)

*Management of human-bear conflicts often starts with resolving the human causes of conflict. To prevent bears from accessing human foods and other attractants, food-storage boxes are provided at most frontcountry campsites in Yellowstone National Park.*

The management of grizzly bears causing conflicts in the Greater Yellowstone Ecosystem will vary depending on whether they are within or outside the Primary Conservation Area. Inside, management will follow guidelines outlined in the *Conservation Strategy*. Elsewhere, appropriate state and federal agency management plans will govern how conflict bears are handled. Within the Primary Conservation Area, guidelines are designed to prevent human-bear conflicts instead of just reacting to conflicts after they occur. Wildlife management agencies will continue to emphasize the prevention of human-bear conflicts through visitor education; proper storage of human foods, garbage, and other bear attractants; use of bear-resistant dumpsters, garbage cans, food storage boxes, and food-hanging poles; and strict enforcement of food and garbage storage regulations in frontcountry and backcountry areas. Management of human-bear conflicts will emphasize resolving human causes of the conflict, but additional actions may be taken when bears pose a significant threat to human safety, the human causes of conflict cannot be resolved, or bears persist in causing conflict after human causes have been corrected.

The long-term survival of bears in the Greater Yellowstone Ecosystem depends on the people who live, work, visit, and recreate in the area having an understanding of bear behavior and bear management practices. Also, addressing the causes and sources of human-bear conflicts is critical because public attitudes will play a large role in determining the success of grizzly bear conservation efforts. Under the *Conservation Strategy*, an interagency Information and Education Working Group will develop a public outreach program to cultivate an appreciation of grizzly bears as a wildlife resource and teach people how to coexist with them. (U.S. Fish and Wildlife Service 2007b, U.S. Fish and Wildlife Service 2016)

## Conclusions

Unsustainable levels of human-caused grizzly bear mortality were the primary cause of the decrease in numbers and distribution that led to the species being listed under the Endangered Species Act in 1975.

Most human-caused grizzly bear mortalities are the direct result of human-bear conflicts. During the 4 decades that grizzly bears have been protected as a threatened species, federal, state, and tribal land and wildlife managers have implemented ecosystem-wide measures to reduce human-bear conflicts, including the management of motorized access, garbage management and food storage requirements, and reduced livestock grazing on public lands in some areas. These measures have helped reduce grizzly bear mortality to sustainable levels, thereby allowing the recovery of the population. The *2016 Conservation Strategy for the Grizzly Bear in the Greater Yellowstone Ecosystem* was written, in part, to standardize as much as possible the management of grizzly bears occupying lands under many different federal and state jurisdictions. The standards contained in the *Conservation Strategy* ensure these measures to protect habitat and reduce human-bear conflicts and human-caused bear mortality will continue after grizzly bears are removed from threatened species status.

Photograph by Cory Richards

*Crossing boundaries near Tom Miner Basin, Montana, outside of Yellowstone National Park. The future of grizzly bears in the Greater Yellowstone Ecosystem will depend on people working together across a spectrum of social values.*

# Chapter 11

## THE FUTURE—CONSIDERATIONS FOR GRIZZLY BEAR CONSERVATION

*P. J. White, Kerry A. Gunther, Frank T. van Manen, Mark A. Haroldson, and Daniel J. Thompson*

### Introduction

THE RECOVERY OF grizzly bears in the Greater Yellowstone Ecosystem is a remarkable achievement. National parks and surrounding national forest lands provided the foundation for this restoration, with about 6 million acres (2.4 million hectares) of mostly remote wilderness providing habitat for grizzly bears and serving as a proving ground for the development of effective methods to reduce human-bear conflicts. Likewise, state wildlife management agencies, non-governmental organizations, and private landowners demonstrated strong commitments and a proud tradition of preserving sustainable populations of wildlife and their habitats, including grizzly bears. Several key points arose from these efforts, many of which are pertinent to the continued conservation of grizzly bears in the Greater Yellowstone Ecosystem and elsewhere. (Lonner et al. 2009, Bjornlie et al. 2014a, van Manen et al. 2016b)

**Key Points**

Wild Bears Need Vast, Remote Places—Grizzly bears are wild animals that need sizeable expanses of habitat to procure the various resources needed for their survival and reproduction, without getting into conflicts with humans. Sustaining a healthy, recovered population in the Greater Yellowstone Ecosystem requires having many hundreds of bears widely distributed across suitable habitat within the region. The *2016 Conservation Strategy for the Grizzly Bear in the Greater Yellowstone Ecosystem*, which was developed by the Yellowstone Ecosystem Subcommittee of the Interagency Grizzly Bear Committee, designates a 9,210 square mile (23,850 square kilometer) Primary Conservation Area (formerly the Grizzly Bear Recovery Zone) that includes all of Yellowstone National Park, about one-third of Grand Teton National Park, and large tracts of surrounding national forest lands. The purpose of this area is to reduce human-caused mortalities to grizzly bears by maintaining secure habitat and preventing additional access-related disturbances caused by development, roads, and livestock grazing. Currently, human-caused mortality is very low in the national parks, with an average of about 1 human-caused grizzly bear death per year since 1990, but higher in surrounding national forest lands within the Primary Conservation Area. Portions of the Greater Yellowstone Ecosystem in private ownership outside the Primary Conservation Area are experiencing human population growth and rapid changes in land use. In many areas, land development is exceeding human population growth due to low-density, rural, residential development, which may affect range use by grizzly bears and increase the risk of conflicts with people. Long-term viability of Yellowstone grizzly bears would be enhanced by continuing to preserve secure habitat and maintaining relatively low levels of human-caused mortality within the Primary Conservation Area, while preserving habitat elsewhere in the ecosystem that enables bears to occupy suitable historically used areas and, potentially, connect with other populations. (Gude et al. 2006, Schwartz et al. 2006d, U.S. Fish and Wildlife Service 2007b, Schwartz et al. 2012, U.S. Fish and Wildlife Service 2016)

Preventing Bear Access to Human Foods is Crucial—A healthy bear population must not have access to sources of human foods or garbage because, as a famous slogan during the 1980s maintained, "a fed bear is a dead bear." In other words, bears that become dependent on human foods pose a danger to people and must be removed from the population for the sake of human safety. A great deal of work is conducted by managers throughout the Greater Yellowstone Ecosystem to prevent the food conditioning of bears. Also, managing the behavior of people to prevent bears from obtaining human foods has been successful at reducing injuries to people and property damage. Thus, managers will continue work to prevent conflicts by using and advocating for the bear-resistant storage of human foods and garbage. This includes the use of bear-resistant receptacles (dumpsters, garbage cans, and food storage boxes), food-hanging poles, and the enforcement of food and garbage storage regulations in both frontcountry and backcountry areas. Education and public ownership of the overall concept of attractant storage and bear awareness is vital toward long-term conservation of grizzly bears because securing food and garbage is a personal choice and responsibility for everyone living in, or visiting, bear country. (Gunther 2015a)

In Some Areas, a Certain Level of Habituation to People is Inevitable—Some grizzly bears in the Greater Yellowstone Ecosystem, particularly in national parks, are habituated to people due to frequent, nonthreatening encounters along roadways and trails. Such habituation can be benign and is inevitable in some areas given the high and increasing numbers of human residence and visitors to the region. Many of these areas are productive habitats and habituation allows bears to make full use of available food resources. Bears that are habituated to the presence of people may appear unresponsive or unaffected as they forage in close proximity to roads or other places near people.

Photograph by Michael Nichols with Ronan Donovan and the National Park Service

A grizzly bear, caught with a camera trap, forages for fruit from an apple tree in the front yard of a historic house near the boundary of Yellowstone National Park. This image underscores the importance of living thoughtfully in these places where wild and urban intersect.

However, this does not mean these bears are tame and safe to approach. All grizzly bears in the ecosystem are wild and sometimes dangerous. People should stay more than 100 yards (91 meters) away and keep that distance if bears move closer. While habituated bears provide viewing opportunities for the public and are a source of revenue for parks and local communities, the impacts of raising habituated offspring that may disperse to other areas and pose a potential increased risk of human-bear conflicts should continue to be evaluated. (Aumiller and Matt 1994, Herrero et al. 2005, Smith et al. 2005, Gunther et al. 2015c)

Intensive Management of Some Grizzly Bears is Necessary at Times—Management of the human-bear interface to lessen or resolve conflicts occurs across the Greater Yellowstone Ecosystem. Bears are generally excluded from frontcountry developments, which are managed for people to the exclusion of wildlife when conflicts occur. Road corridors are managed for human transportation and wildlife viewing in some places such as national parks. Management along transportation corridors in national parks initially emphasizes resolving the human causes of any conflicts. In these settings, managers have demonstrated that managing the human component of bear jams is more successful than attempting to alter bear behavior. However, management actions such as hazing may be taken with bears if the human causes of conflict cannot be resolved or bears persist in causing conflicts and pose a significant threat to people. Wilderness and backcountry areas in national parks are managed primarily for bears and other wildlife. Elsewhere, these areas are managed for multiple uses with a focus on providing optimum habitat for wildlife. Visitation in backcountry areas is often limited by the number of backpackers, campsites, or outfitters. Also, seasonal recreational use closures are implemented in some high-use bear areas. While every situation regarding human-bear conflicts is distinct, food-conditioned bears and bears that pose an impending threat to people are not tolerated.

Sustained Recovery is Contingent on Public Support and Human Tolerance—People are the driving force behind actions taken to recover and sustain the population of grizzly bears in the Greater Yellowstone

Ecosystem, but they also continue to be the primary cause of death for bears in the region (see Chapters 3 and 8). Thus, the long-term viability of grizzly bears depends on people having an understanding of bears, their behavior, and best management practices to reduce the risk and severity of human-bear conflicts. A coordinated information and education campaign can, and does, facilitate an appreciation of the value of grizzly bears as a wildlife resource and teaches people how to live with them. Because public attitudes play a crucial role in determining the success of wildlife conservation efforts, it is essential for managers to lessen conflicts between bears and people, and address the causes and sources of conflicts to maintain support for grizzly bear conservation. At times, it will also be necessary to restrict some human activities in certain areas, such as occurs within Bear Management Areas encompassing about 21% of Yellowstone National Park. (National Park Service 1982, Haroldson and Frey 2016)

Monitoring, Research, and Frequent Assessments are Crucial for Effective Conservation—Grizzly bears are vulnerable to excessive human-caused mortality, which requires greater management attention than may be considered for many other wildlife species. Experience in the Greater Yellowstone Ecosystem indicates a careful, science-based management approach can effectively maintain a recovered, self-sustaining population of grizzly bears. Such an approach requires annual monitoring of the population and habitat, along with research to address questions relevant to managers. The Interagency Grizzly Bear Study Team has monitored and conducted research on the Yellowstone grizzly bear population for many decades and continuation of this cooperative interagency program will be crucial to ensure the long-term health of the population. Monitoring programs will focus on assessing whether the population and habitat standards described in the *Conservation Strategy* are being achieved and maintained. (Scott et al. 2005, U.S. Fish and Wildlife Service 2016)

## Issues and Considerations

Although the recovery of grizzly bears in the Greater Yellowstone Ecosystem is a great success story, there is still substantial debate regarding issues related to their conservation. People from around the world are extremely interested in these bears, but opinions vary on their management, role on the landscape, and status. When dealing with wide-ranging opinions, it is critical to understand the underlying issues, including stakeholder values, and consider rigorous science to make informed decisions for the continued conservation of grizzly bears. The following sections describe some of the contentious issues regarding Yellowstone grizzly bears.

Increasing Abundance and Distribution—As mentioned previously, the sustainability of grizzly bears in the Greater Yellowstone Ecosystem depends on them having access to large expanses of suitable habitat with a relatively low risk of death from conflicts with people. The Primary Conservation Area encompasses federal lands that provide secure habitat with restrictions on development, roads, and livestock grazing so bears can subsist with less human disturbance and fewer deaths caused by people. As grizzly bear numbers in this core area reached high densities, bears expanded elsewhere throughout the ecosystem and their numbers continued to increase. In turn, agencies responsible for grizzly bear conservation responded by increasing educational efforts and providing proactive management responses to alleviate and rectify potential conflict situations. Nonetheless, in areas with higher human habitation there will always be challenges to maintaining a sustainable population of grizzly bears, while ensuring human safety and tolerance are evaluated and addressed. (Bjornlie et al. 2014a, van Manen et al. 2016a)

Human-induced Mortality—Management efforts to minimize human-bear conflicts greatly reduced injuries to people and property damage in the Greater Yellowstone Ecosystem from high historic levels associated primarily with food-conditioned bears. However, human-bear conflicts have begun to increase again as grizzly bears continue to expand into habitats with more human presence on landscapes that have not been occupied by grizzly bears for many decades. There is generally less human tolerance for grizzly bears in these areas and bears are more likely to be removed from the population due to human safety issues, livestock depredations, and property damage. Conflicts may be reduced through greater awareness and tolerance, proper management of garbage, and proactive measures to protect human lifestyles and property. However, certain areas are not conducive for occupancy by grizzly bears due to landscape changes over more than a century and, as a result, occupancy is not promoted in all areas where grizzly bears historically occurred. (Schwartz et al. 2006d, Gunther and Wyman 2008, Meagher 2008, Bjornlie et al. 2015, Lasseter 2015)

Sport Hunting—The states of Wyoming, Montana, and Idaho may decide to implement regulated, sustainable harvests of grizzly bears in the Greater Yellowstone Ecosystem if they are removed from protection under the Endangered Species Act. While any form of hunting would be regulated by state agencies to maintain a recovered population, hunting is probably the most controversial issue confronting the future of grizzly bear conservation and management in the Greater Yellowstone Ecosystem. Hunting could possibly increase support for the conservation of grizzly bears in some areas at the periphery of the ecosystem, but many stakeholders are concerned harvests would contribute to reduced population growth and fewer bears. There is also concern about the potential harvest of well-known, recognizable grizzly bears that primarily live in national parks, but at times venture beyond. The harvest of these habituated bears would be highly contentious. (Miller et al. 2003, Schwartz et al. 2003a, Schwartz et al. 2003b, Creel et al. 2015, National Park Service 2016a, U.S. Fish and Wildlife Service 2016)

The three states have committed to meeting annually with the other land management agencies and Native American tribes to discuss harvest strategies should delisting occur. Conservative harvests of grizzly bears would have minimal impacts on the overall population demographics of grizzly bears in the Greater Yellowstone Ecosystem. However, the potential use of hunting would be a significant change in population management from the recovery period. Thus, monitoring

*When dealing with wide-ranging opinions, it is critical to understand the underlying issues, including stakeholder values, and consider rigorous science to make informed decisions for the continued conservation of grizzly bears.*

and research should evaluate the overall and regional influence of harvest on grizzly bear population demographics (such as dispersal, recruitment, and survival), habitat use, and other factors, as well as from a human dimensions standpoint. Regulated hunts, rigorous monitoring, and timely adaptive management adjustments would result in sustainable harvests and the maintenance of a viable population of grizzly bears. (Creel et al. 2015, U.S. Fish and Wildlife Service 2016)

Climate Warming and Food Resources—Many previous studies have reported, and recent studies by the Interagency Grizzly Bear Study Team have confirmed, that grizzly bears consume a wide diversity of plant and animal species, which provides flexibility to respond to changing food resources. As a result, grizzly bears in the Greater Yellowstone Ecosystem so far have compensated for recent decreases in cutthroat trout and whitebark pine seeds by shifting to other nutritious foods without a loss in body mass or condition. However, there is still uncertainty regarding the future extent of climate changes, the magnitude of their effects on grizzly bears, and the resilience of bears to adapt to these changes. Minimum spring and summer temperatures in the Greater Yellowstone Ecosystem increased by 1.1 degrees Fahrenheit (0.6 degrees Celsius) during the past century, with more warming at higher elevations. As a result, the ecosystem is slightly drier, with spring snow pack about 20% lower than the 800-year average and reduced stream runoff and warmer stream temperatures during spring and summer. If temperatures warm another 1 to 3 degrees over the next century, as predicted, wildlife would experience higher temperatures, more frequent and severe droughts and fires, and associated changes in vegetation communities. Such warming could also adversely affect several food resources for grizzly bears that have already decreased in some areas during recent decades. Consequently, monitoring and research should continue to provide early detection of any adverse changes and trends. Conversely, some positive benefits could result from certain climatological changes if soft mast producing vegetation such as berries or other plant foods increase in some areas. Also, managers at Yellowstone National Park are continuing to implement the Native Fish Conservation Plan to recover cutthroat trout in Yellowstone Lake, its tributaries, and other rivers and streams, in part, to restore a food source for grizzly bears and other wildlife. Above all, maintaining large tracts of secure habitats will be critical for bears to adapt to future environmental conditions. (Mattson et al. 1992, Miller et al. 1997, Haroldson et al. 2006, Schwartz et al. 2006d, Warwell et al. 2007, McWethy et al. 2010, National Park Service 2010, Schwartz et al. 2010b, Westerling et al. 2011, Center for Biological Diversity 2014, Costello et al. 2014, Gunther et al. 2014, Chang and Hansen 2015, Ebinger et al. 2016, van Manen et al. 2016a)

Genetic Isolation—There was some evidence of a slight decrease in genetic diversity in Yellowstone grizzly bears after 1900, which led to concerns about the genetic integrity and viability of the population. However, recent genetic analyses suggest the historic loss of genetic diversity was not as severe as previously thought. Also, there has been little inbreeding and stable genetic diversity since 1985. The increase in population size undoubtedly was a contributing factor and should reduce chance losses of genetic diversity. Thus, the population does not appear to be vulnerable to a significant loss of genetic diversity under current environmental conditions. The Yellowstone grizzly bear population would still benefit from periodic gene flow from other populations given its isolation over many generations, low genetic diversity compared to many other interior grizzly bear populations, and inevitable future changes in environmental conditions. It would be favorable for gene flow to occur with the North Continental Divide population to the north, which is currently separated by about 68 miles (110 kilometers; see Chapter 7). Several bears immigrating to the Yellowstone population each generation that survive and breed would augment genetic diversity. If genetic diversity decreases without evidence of immigration, periodic translocations of grizzly bears by managers could occur to mimic the ecological processes of dispersal and gene flow. (Miller and Waits 2003, Allendorf and Luikart 2007, Becker et al. 2013, Kamath et al. 2016, U.S. Fish and Wildlife Service 2016)

Increasing Visitation—Since the 1960s, food storage requirements and the education and management of people have contributed to minimizing conflicts with bears in the Greater Yellowstone Ecosystem. However, visitation has steadily increased over the past several decades to nearly 4.3 million visits during 2016 in Yellowstone National Park alone.

Managers within national parks need to evaluate and lessen the unintended effects of increased visitation, including displacement and habituation, on grizzly bears and other wildlife. National parks and forests provide the majority of secure habitats for grizzly bears in the Greater Yellowstone Ecosystem. As a result, the challenge for managers is to enable bears to use backcountry and roadside habitats on these public lands, while ensuring the safety of bears and visitors. Managers should continue efforts to minimize conflicts through visitor education and safety messaging, sanitation and storage of human foods, use of bear-resistant dumpsters and garbage cans, use of food storage boxes and food-hanging poles, strict enforcement of food storage regulations, management of bear jams and enforcement of no feeding and approach-distance regulations, and removal of food-conditioned bears and others posing a significant threat to human safety. The "a fed bear is a dead bear" and "stay safe and keep bears wild" messaging campaigns have been successful at bluntly conveying the consequences of human misbehavior or negligence on bears and, in turn, have likely contributed to far fewer conflicts and bear removals. (Gunther 2008, Gunther and Wyman 2008, Haroldson et al. 2008b, Coleman et al. 2013a, Coleman et al. 2013b, Haroldson and Gunther 2013, Richardson et al. 2014, Gunther 2015a, Gunther et al. 2015b)

Safety precautions are important as well because most bear attacks occur in response to surprise encounters with people, often in protection of food or cubs. As a result, the National Park Service recommends all hikers, regardless of their experience or the distance being traveled, carry bear spray that is readily accessible, travel in groups, make noise on the trail, and be alert for bears. Unfortunately, fewer than 30% of visitors entering the backcountry in Yellowstone National Park carry bear spray. Thus, the park has embarked on a new campaign called "a bear doesn't care," which encourages people to carry bear spray whether they are an angler, backpacker, hiker, geyser gazer, photographer, or wildlife watcher. As Superintendent Dan Wenk stated "a bear doesn't care how far you are hiking, if you are just fishing, or even if you work here. No matter who you are or what you are doing, you should always carry bear spray and know how to use it."

Photography and Bear Viewing Ethics—Many photographers learn about specific bears and their daily movements along roadside habitats to increase their efficiency to garner and perhaps sell photographs. Although many of these photographers believe they have developed a special bond with their favorite roadside bear, in many instances their actions may negatively influence the behavior and energetics of these bears and their offspring. For example, persistent stalking of bears by photographers could lead to increased levels of habituation. Indeed, recent research indicates the length of time bears spend in roadside habitats is increasing, while the distance at which habituated bears tolerate roadside photographers is decreasing. The result is bear jams of longer duration with closer interaction distances between bears and photographers. In some circumstances, habituation may make bears more vulnerable to becoming conditioned to human foods, which ultimately can lead to the bears' death. Habituation can also increase the odds of human-bear encounters eventually leading to conflicts and human-caused bear mortality. Large numbers of photographers, patiently waiting at roadside meadows for bears to appear, also compound traffic congestion problems. Many drivers stop when they see large groups of people with spotting scopes and long-lensed cameras, creating large traffic jams even when no bears are present. While the handling of bear jams is often manageable in national parks, roadside bear situations on state highways may result in a higher risk of injury or death to bears, motorists, photographers, and wildlife viewers. As bears expand their distribution, managers must continue to develop interagency strategies to deal with these types of situations. (Haroldson and Gunther 2013, Richardson et al. 2015)

*A typical scene in spring and summer; photographers queue up in droves for the chance to take pictures of bears in Yellowstone National Park. Approximately 2,500 to 3,000 personnel hours are spent managing bear jams every year.*

The actions of photographers may not only alter the behavior and survivorship of individual bears, but also influence the behavior of many other bystanders who may be relatively naïve of bear behavior and mimic the photographer's viewing etiquette, whether good or bad. In national parks, the popularity of bear viewing and photography, combined with significantly increasing visitation and an increasing level of habituation of bears to people and people to bears, will likely be among the greatest challenges bear managers face in the future. In addition, most park visitors now come from urban areas and/or foreign countries where they have little exposure to wild nature or bears and, therefore, little knowledge of bear behavior, safety, or viewing etiquette. New, innovative methods for teaching visitors how to view bears safely, while not disturbing, harassing, or contributing to their mortality, are imperative for the conservation of bears and the well-being of photographers and other visitors. (Gunther et al. 2015c)

Public Engagement—Many people who share an interest in grizzly bears want more opportunity for meaningful input and discussion with decision-makers prior to the implementation of management strategies. To address these concerns and provide more transparency, managers should continue to incorporate presentations and discussion into meetings regarding Yellowstone grizzly bears that allow information and ideas to be transferred and deliberated among managers, scientists, and the public. Also, public confidence in decisions could be enhanced by soliciting independent reviews of analyses and proposed plans, as well as consultation with Native American tribes and meetings with local community leaders to gain their input. These actions can be accomplished under the umbrella of the Yellowstone Ecosystem Subcommittee of the Interagency Grizzly Bear Committee. (Bidwell 2010, National Research Council 2013, Berger and Cain 2014)

## Conclusions

Occupied grizzly bear habitat in the Greater Yellowstone Ecosystem is managed by many different federal, state, and tribal agencies, with many bears frequently crossing jurisdictional boundaries. As a result, interagency cooperation is essential for successful long-term conservation, especially with expanding human occupation of the area and factors that could affect the availability of bear foods in the future, such as changing climate, invasive species, and wildlife diseases. Knowledge gained from management, monitoring, and research over the past 50 years provides a strong foundation for making decisions about the future management of grizzly bears. However, their continued conservation will largely depend on human behaviors, values, and decisions. The grizzly bear is an intelligent and opportunistic animal capable of adapting to environmental changes. It is usually human factors and values that determine where bears will or will not survive. As a result, human tolerance, preservation of habitat, and a willingness to accept grizzly bears in suitable habitats will continue to be crucial for their conservation. Regional planning, increased public engagement, innovative and prompt responses to lessen human-bear conflicts, and adequate funding and staff for management will be essential. Collaborative efforts by agencies, non-government organizations, and private landowners brought Yellowstone grizzly bears back from the brink of extirpation. The continued dedication and commitment of these agencies, groups, and people, combined with the adaptability of grizzly bears, should ensure a viable population well into the future. (Gunther 2008, Gunther et al. 2014)

Photograph by Jake Davis

*An alert grizzly bear investigates its surroundings. Bears can see in color, can hear in the ultrasonic range, and possess an incredible sense of smell.*

# Yellowstone Grizzly Bear Facts

*Kerry A. Gunther, Mark A. Haroldson, and Frank T. van Manen*

This fact sheet summarizes interesting aspects of the nomenclature, physiology, ecology, and behavior of grizzly bears in the Greater Yellowstone Ecosystem.

**Taxonomy**
Kingdom: Animalia
Phylum: Chordata
Class: Mammalia
Order: Carnivora
Family: Ursidae
Subfamily: Ursinae
Genus: *Ursus* (Latin word for bear)
Species: *arctos* (Greek word for bear)

**Common Names:** Grizzly bear; Brown bear; Silvertip

**Estimated Number Currently Living in the Greater Yellowstone Ecosystem (2016 estimate):** 690 (range = 615 to 764) (Interagency Grizzly Bear Study Team, unpublished data ; estimate does not include bears outside the Demographic Monitoring Area)

**Area Occupied in Greater Yellowstone Ecosystem (2000-2014):** 22,515 square miles or 14,409,600 acres (58,314 square kilometers) (method based on Bjornlie et al. 2014a)

**Average Lifetime Home Range in the Greater Yellowstone Ecosystem:** Females 108 square miles (281 square kilometers); Males 337 square miles (874 square kilometers) (Schwartz et al. 2003b)

**Average Annual Home Range in the Greater Yellowstone Ecosystem:** Subadult males 197 square miles (509 square kilometers); Adult males 154 square miles (399 square kilometers); Adult females 66 square miles (170 square kilometers); Females with cubs 62 square miles (161 square kilometers); Subadult females 59 square miles (153 square kilometers)

**Group of Bears:** Called a "sleuth" (Brown 2009)

**Life Span:** 20 to 30 years. The oldest known Yellowstone bears are a 31-year-old male and a 30-year-old female.

**Pelage (fur):** From black to brown to light blonde

**Molt:** Brown/grizzly bears replace their hair annually. In general, adult males molt first, followed by young males and other lone individuals. Females with dependent young molt last. The molt is generally complete by late July or August. (Schwartz et al. 2003b)

**Eyes:** Blue at birth; Brown as adults; Greenish yellow in headlights in the dark (Brown 2009)

**Vision:** Possibly equal to human vision, with color and excellent night vision (Brown 2009)

**Sense of Smell:** Excellent; unlike most humans where sight is the primary sense, olfaction (smell) is the primary sense in grizzly bears. Bears have a 9-inch (22.5-centimeter) nose and millions of nerve endings that send olfactory information to their brains. A bloodhound dog's sense of smell is about 300 times greater than a human's, but a bear's sense of smell is 7 times better than a bloodhound's. (Stevenson 2007)

**Hearing:** Bears have good hearing and can hear in the ultrasonic range of 16 to 20 megahertz, perhaps higher (Brown 2009)

**Average Body Height at Shoulders When Standing on All Four Legs:** Adult males 38 inches (95 centimeters); Adult females 34 inches (86 centimeters). Measurements were estimated from the top of the shoulder to the foot pad while bears were lying on their sides.

**Average Standing Height:** 6 feet, 8 inches (205 centimeters). Measurements were estimated from hind paw to top of head when standing on two hind legs. (Brown 2009)

**Average Body Length:** Adult males 65 inches (166 centimeters); Adult females 58 inches (147 centimeters). Measurements were estimated from the tip of the nose to the end of the tail while bears were lying on their sides.

**Tail Length:** 3 to 4.5 inches (7.5 to 11.3 centimeters) (Brown 2009)

**Average Body Mass (Weight):** Adult males 413 pounds (187 kilograms); Adult females 269 pounds (122 kilograms)

**Heaviest Known Body Mass in the Greater Yellowstone Ecosystem:** Adult male 715 pounds (324 kilograms); Adult female 436 pounds (198 kilograms)

**Speed:** 35 to 40 miles per hour (56 to 64 kilometers per hour) (Brown 2009)

**Strength:** 2.5 to 5 times greater than humans (Ellig 2006)

**Bite Pressure:** Carnassial: 1,895 Newtons (2,748 psi); Canine: 1,410 Newtons (2,045 psi) (Christianse and Wroe 2007)

**Claw Length:** Average 2 inches (5.1 centimeters); Longest 5.6 inches (14.2 centimeters). Claw length and shape allow efficient digging of foods from the ground, but claws are less efficient for tree climbing than black bear claws.

**Body Temperature:** 98.6 to 100.4 degrees Fahrenheit (37 to 38 degrees Celsius) during the active season and 86.0 to 96.8 degrees Fahrenheit (30 to 36 degrees Celsius) during hibernation

**Respiration:** 6 to 10 breaths per minute, but slows to less than 1 breath per minute during hibernation

**Heart Rate:** 40 to 50 beats per minute, but slows to 8 to 19 beats per minute during hibernation

**Genetics:** 74 diploid chromosomes

**Number of Bones:** Male 225; Female 224 (not counting the metapodial sesamoid bones and hyoid bones)

**Number of Teeth:** 42

**Adult Sex Ratio:** 50 males to 50 females

**Dental Formulae:** Incisors 3/3; Canines 1/1; Premolars 4/4; Molars 2/3; Upper (each side) = 3 incisors, 1 canine, 4 premolars, and 2 molars; Lower (each side) = 3 incisors, 1 canine, 4 premolars, and 3 molars

**Age Composition:** 20% cubs; 11% yearlings; 16% subadults (2 to 4 years old); 53% adults (Interagency Grizzly Bear Study Team 2012)

**Mating System:** Polygamous/Promiscuous. Females mate with multiple males and may have a litter with offspring sired by different males. Males can sire litters with multiple females. (Schwartz et al. 2003b)

**Period of Courtship:** Generally mid-May through mid-July, though later on occasion

**Delayed Implantation:** Implantation of embryo is delayed until late November or early December. (Schwartz et al. 2003b)

**Gestation:** 235 days

**Birth:** Birth occurs late January or early February inside the winter den.

**Typical Den Types:** Dug/excavated 91%; Natural cavity 6%; Snow 3% (Judd et al. 1986)

**Den Entry:** Pregnant females in first week of November; Other females in second week of November; Males in second week of November (Haroldson et al. 2002)

**Average Denning Duration:** Females with cubs 171 days; Other females 151 days; Males 131 days (Haroldson et al. 2002)

**Den Emergence:** Females with newborn cubs fourth week of April; Other females third week of April; Males fourth week of March (Haroldson et al. 2002)

**Hibernation:** Bears are true hibernators that reduce their metabolism to about 25% of active metabolism and heart rate by 20% to 45% during denning. However, the decrease in body temperature (36 to 46 degrees Fahrenheit; 2 to 8 degrees Celsius) is moderate and bears typically remain reactive and do not undergo the cyclical arousals common in small mammals that hibernate. This specialized response of bears involves no consumption of foods or water, and relies primarily on the metabolism of stored fat for sustenance.

**Weight Loss During Hibernation:** 15% to 30% of body weight

**Age at First Reproduction:** 5.8 years (Schwartz et al. 2006a)

**Litter Size:** Range 1 to 4 cubs per litter; Average 2.0 cubs per litter (Schwartz et al. 2006a)

**Inter-birth Interval:** Average 2.8 years (Schwartz et al. 2006a)

**Reproductive Rate:** 0.3 female cubs per female per year (Schwartz et al. 2006a)

**Annual Survival Rate:** Cubs 55%; Yearlings 54%; Subadults 95%; Adult females 95%; Adult males 95% (Interagency Grizzly Bear Study Team 2012)

**Causes of Death in the Greater Yellowstone Ecosystem:** Human causes 85%; Natural causes 15% (Schwartz et al. 2006a)

**Period of Maternal Care:** Average 30 months (range 18 to 42 months)

**Nursing Characteristics:** Females have 3 pairs of functional nipples (Brown 2009)

**Milk Content:** 30% fat, 15% protein; 2.3 kilocalories per gram of energy (Brown 2009, Schwartz et al. 2003b)

**Eyes of Cubs:** Open at approximately 21 days (Brown 2009)

**Weaning:** After 24 weeks, cubs are no longer dependent on their mother's milk, but young bears may continue to nurse occasionally until they separate from their mother as 2- or 3-year-olds. (Brown 2009)

**Offspring Dispersal:** Young females establish home ranges overlapping or adjacent to their mother's range, while young males establish home ranges in more distant areas. This reduces the chances of inbreeding and provides added security to young females that are critical to population viability.

**Social Behavior:** Generally solitary except during courtship, when accompanied by young, or at concentrated food sources such as ungulate carcasses, trout spawning streams, and moth aggregation sites.

**Feeding Habits:** Grizzly bears are omnivorous, which means they consume both plants and animals. They also have a generalist diet, eating a wide variety of foods.

**Types of Foods Eaten:** Hoofed animals, small mammals, insects, seeds, fruits, foliage, flower heads, stems, roots, and tubers. In the Greater Yellowstone Ecosystem, grizzly bear diets include more than 260 plant and animal species. (Gunther et al. 2014)

**Tree Climbing Ability:** All grizzly bears can climb trees, though cubs, yearlings, and other smaller bears are more proficient.

**Female Reproductive Senescence:** Reproductive senescence occurs before physical senescence; maximum per capita litter production occurs at 8.7 years and reproductive performance remains high between 8 and 25 years of age. Thereafter, productivity decreases rapidly. (Schwartz et al. 2003b)

Photograph by Ronan Donovan

*A grizzly bear swims across the Yellowstone River with iconic thermal features in the background. Although the recovery of the Yellowstone grizzly bear population is a remarkable conservation success story, continued recovery will be overwhelmingly influenced by human behavior, values, and decisions.*

# History of Yellowstone Grizzly Bear Conservation and Management

*Daniel B. Tyers, Kevin L. Frey, and Kerry A. Gunther*

THIS CHRONOLOGY SUMMARIZES key historical events affecting the Greater Yellowstone Ecosystem and the conservation and management of Yellowstone grizzly bears.

**1806:** The Lewis and Clark expedition traveled through the northern portion of the Greater Yellowstone Ecosystem and observed 2 gray or white bears, probably grizzly bears, between present-day Big Timber and Livingston, Montana. (Schullery and Whittlesey 1992, Schullery 2002)

**1837:** Osborne Russell's trapping party killed a grizzly bear near Yellowstone Lake in present-day Yellowstone National Park. (Schullery and Whittlesey 1992)

**1848:** Gold was discovered in California, which induced a mass migration of settlers into the western United States. (Gill 2010)

**1872:** Yellowstone National Park was established by Congress and endorsed by President Grant.

**1879:** The transcontinental railway system was completed, which enabled the cost-effective and efficient transport of domestic livestock to markets in the eastern United States and Europe. In turn, numbers of cattle and sheep produced in western states rapidly increased. (Gill 2010)

**1884:** There were about 35 to 40 million cattle in the western United States. Livestock associations and federal, state, and territorial governments implemented bounty programs for predators to reduce depredation on cattle, pigs, poultry, and sheep. Grizzly bears were poisoned, shot, and trapped to near extinction in most of the western United States. (Gill 2010)

**1886:** Hunting of grizzly bears and black bears inside Yellowstone National Park became illegal and a company of Army cavalry was sent to the park to prevent poaching. (Schullery 1992)

**1888:** One of the first reported grizzly bear attacks on a human in the Greater Yellowstone Ecosystem occurred when a man was chased and pulled from a tree by a female grizzly with 2 cubs in the Cinnabar Basin of Montana, a short distance outside of Yellowstone National Park. (Whittlesey 2014)

**1890:** Grizzly bears were congregating at garbage piles behind hotels in Yellowstone National Park. (Schullery 1992)

**1891:** The Superintendent of Yellowstone National Park reported food-conditioned bears were causing problems at camps and hotels and indicated removing these bears was necessary to alleviate problems. (Schullery 1992)

**1891:** Congress passed the Forest Reserve Act, which allowed the President to set aside or "reserve" portions of the public domain for the protection of natural resources. The law set aside the public lands withdrawn under its provision from further settlement and appropriation, but there were no specific management directions or monies to provide for the protection of the forest reserves until enactment of the Organic Administration Act in 1897. The Forest Reserve Act was the first step toward protecting the public domain's remaining stands of timber in the west. This legislation had profound impacts on the conservation of land in the Greater Yellowstone Ecosystem. The national forests surrounding Yellowstone National Park are the direct result of this legislation.

**1891:** President Benjamin Harrison set aside the Yellowstone Park Timber Land Reserve, which was located along the eastern and southern boundary of Yellowstone National Park and encompassed 1,239,040 acres (5,014 square kilometers). The Reserve was first suggested by General Philip Sheridan in 1882 after he observed Yellowstone National Park did not include important portions of the Greater Yellowstone Ecosystem worthy of conservation. The first Reserve was created, in part, to secure a protective buffer around the park, which was followed by a series of similar efforts to protect other lands with intrinsic natural value. Although the preservation of the Yellowstone grizzly bear population and necessary habitat for its survival were not stated goals of these actions, it was an associated effect.

**1891:** The Fountain Hotel was constructed in Yellowstone National Park by the Northern Pacific Railroad. A garbage dump was located within walking distance of the hotel to provide visitors with entertainment through bear viewing at the dump. These bear "shows" were so popular that they were later instituted near hotels at Lake, Old Faithful, and Canyon. (Wondrak Biel 2006)

**1892:** The first known human death from a grizzly bear mauling in the Greater Yellowstone Ecosystem occurred when Phillipe Henry Vetter, a 37-year old buffalo hunter, was killed by a grizzly bear along the Greybull River in Wyoming.

**1897:** President William McKinley signed into law the U.S. Forest Service Organic Administration Act, which provided the primary statutory basis for managing Forest Reserves. The Act opened the reserves for public use, granted the Secretary of the Interior the authority in making regulations, and allowed the general Land Office to hire employees to perform necessary administrative tasks. The Act specified the intent of the reserves was timber production, watershed protection, and forest protection. The U.S. Geological Survey was given responsibility for mapping the reserves. This law is an important legislative event in U.S. Forest Service history because it established forest reserves and the means to protect and manage them; thereby establishing the basic elements of federal forestry.

**1897:** President Cleveland, by executive order, created the Teton Forest Reserve from 829,440 acres (3,356 square kilometers) of public domain land. The Reserve included areas south of the original Yellowstone Park Timber Land Reserve.

**1902:** Regulations prohibiting the hand feeding of bears in Yellowstone National Park were established, but largely ignored by visitors and rarely enforced by park rangers. Also, bears were still allowed to feed on garbage at dumps and bear feeding stations. (Schullery 1992)

**1902:** President Theodore Roosevelt added 5 million acres (20,235 square kilometers) to the Forest Reserve system in northwest Wyoming and southwest Montana. Also, he renamed the Yellowstone

Park Timber Land Reserve as the Yellowstone Forest Reserve, which was divided into 4 divisions adjacent to Yellowstone National Park: Absaroka to the north, Shoshone to the east, Teton to the south, and Wind River to the southeast. The Yellowstone Forest Reserve at that time included 6,580,920 acres (26,632 square kilometers).

**1905:** Through the influence of President Roosevelt, the Transfer Act moved the administration of the Forest Reserves of the United States from the Department of the Interior, General Land Office, to the Department of Agriculture, Bureau of Forestry. Gifford Pinchot, head of the Division of Forestry, was a strong advocate for this action. This transfer included over 63 million acres (250,000 square kilometers) of Forest Reserves and over 500 employees, including the reserves in the Greater Yellowstone Ecosystem. This act was significant because it caused the National Forest Reserves to shift roles from a recreational focus to an economic approach, as determined by science-based management. Ultimately, the Division of Forestry was renamed the U.S. Forest Service. Pinchot framed the creed for managing these public lands: "for the greatest good of the greatest number in the long run."

**1907:** The name Forest Reserve was changed to National Forest. The Yellowstone Park Timber Land Reserve became the Yellowstone National Forest.

**1908:** President Roosevelt abolished the Yellowstone National Forest with its separate divisions and created the Teton, Wyoming (now Bridger), Absaroka (now Gallatin), Beartooth (now Custer), Shoshone, Bonneville (now Caribou), and Targhee national forests. He also established the Beaverhead and Deerlodge national forests, pulling together land west of Yellowstone National Park which earlier presidents had withdrawn as the Hell Gate, Bitter Root, and Big Hole forest reserves between 1897 and 1906. In the decades that followed, this aggregation of reserved lands went through multiple additions, consolidations, and name changes. At present, they are administered by the U.S.

Forest Service. In their current configuration, the national forest lands around Yellowstone National Park are the Custer Gallatin, Shoshone, Bridger-Teton, Caribou-Targhee, and Beaverhead-Deerlodge national forests. The assemblage of public lands as national forests and national parks in the Greater Yellowstone Ecosystem provided the land base necessary for the conservation of the Yellowstone grizzly bear.

**1913:** A report on conditions in Yellowstone National Park conducted by Robert Dole of the U.S. Geological Survey recommended "all garbage should be burned or buried, and all incinerators and dump operations should be fenced with barbed wire to keep out the bears." (Schullery 1992)

**1916:** Congress passed the National Park Service Act to create the National Park Service, which assumed management of Yellowstone National Park from the Army cavalry.

**1916:** The first confirmed human fatality caused by a grizzly bear in Yellowstone National Park occurred when a wagon teamster named Frank Welch was dragged from a roadside camp and killed by a grizzly bear. (Schullery 1992)

**1921:** The State of Montana prohibited the use of dogs when hunting grizzly bears and black bears.

**1931:** A bear feeding area was built at Otter Creek in the Canyon area of Yellowstone National Park with parking for 600 cars, log-bench seating for 250 people, and standing room for another 1,250 people. It attracted 50 to 70 grizzly bears each evening. (Wondrak Biel 2006)

**1931:** One in every 2,800 visitors to Yellowstone National Park reported a bear-related injury, and 1 in every 1,000 visitors reported bear-related property damage.

**1934:** Public viewing of bears at dumps in Yellowstone National Park was restricted to the Old Faithful and Canyon dumps. (Schullery 1992)

**1935:** Public viewing of bears at the Old Faithful dump in Yellowstone National Park was closed. (Schullery 1992)

**1939:** Yellowstone National Park considered building a fence around the Fishing Bridge development and campground to protect visitors and their property from bears. (Wondrak Biel 2006)

**1941:** The Wyoming National Forest was renamed the Bridger National Forest.

**1942:** The Canyon Public Bear Feeding Ground at Otter Creek was closed due to changing National Park Service philosophy regarding wildlife management and substantially reduced visitation during World War II. (Schullery 1992, Wondrak Biel 2006)

**1942:** A woman was killed at the Old Faithful campground by a large brown-colored bear (species unknown). Congress criticized the National Park Service for not alleviating problems with food-conditioned bears in national parks. (Schullery 1992)

**1944:** Olaus Murie concluded bears in Yellowstone National Park did not need garbage to survive because only 10% of their diet was composed of garbage. He experimented with electric cattle prods to teach bears to avoid campgrounds, but concluded "the bear learns to recognize the particular person or car that administers the shock or other punishment, and simply avoids that person or car in the future, but does not fear other persons or cars." (Murie 1944)

**1946:** The State of Idaho prohibited the hunting of grizzly bears.

**1948:** The State of Montana prohibited the use of baits for hunting grizzly and black bears.

**1950:** By this decade, the Greater Yellowstone Ecosystem was one of the last places inhabited by grizzly bears south of Canada.

**1959-1971:** Research, which included the marking of individual grizzly bears, was conducted in Yellowstone National Park by Drs. John and Frank Craighead. During 1968 to 1971, human-derived garbage was the most important dietary source for grizzly bears. In 1971, the National Park Service research permit for this study was not renewed. (Craighead et al. 1995)

**1960:** New bear management guidelines were implemented in Yellowstone National Park to reduce the availability of human foods and garbage. Education efforts to reduce human-bear conflicts were increased and the park began converting all garbage cans and dumpsters to a bear-resistant design. Regulations prohibiting the hand feeding of bears were strictly enforced.

**1963:** A special advisory board on wildlife management in national parks (Leopold Report) recommended allowing natural processes to function with minimal human influence so animal and plant communities would remain as "primitive" as possible. (Leopold et al. 1963)

**1967:** Two women were killed by grizzly bears in separate incidents in Glacier National Park during August 12-13. These deaths were a catalyst for changing how bears were managed in national parks.

**1967:** Montana required separate licenses for grizzly bears and black bears. Prior to 1967, hunters could take one bear per season of either species. (Beckworth 1971)

**1968:** The West Thumb and Tower Falls dumps in Yellowstone National Park were closed.

**1969:** A Natural Sciences Advisory Committee of the National Park Service completed a report entitled "A bear management policy and program for Yellowstone National Park." (Leopold et al. 1969)

**1969:** The Rabbit Creek dump near Old Faithful in Yellowstone National Park was closed and capped.

**1970:** Additional bear management guidelines were implemented in Yellowstone National Park to prevent bears from obtaining human foods or garbage and reduce human-bear conflicts and human-caused bear mortalities. Regulations required all human foods and garbage to be stored in a bear-resistant manner in frontcountry and backcountry areas. Remaining garbage dumps in the park were closed and remaining non-bear proof garbage cans and dumpsters were converted to bear-resistant designs.

**1970:** The Trout Creek dump in Yellowstone National Park was closed.

**1971:** Yellowstone National Park finished installing bear-resistant garbage cans in developed areas.

**1971:** The West Yellowstone municipal dump outside of West Yellowstone, Montana, was closed. The dump was moved 2 miles north to a fenced facility.

**1972:** Yellowstone National Park restricted backcountry camping to designated sites and installed food-hanging poles or bear-resistant food storage boxes at all sites to reduce the number of human-bear conflicts occurring in the backcountry.

**1973:** The period of high management removals following the dump closures in Yellowstone National Park ended. No bears were killed in management actions in the park.

**1973:** The Interagency Grizzly Bear Study Team was formed by the Department of the Interior to conduct grizzly bear monitoring and research in the Greater Yellowstone Ecosystem through an agreement signed by the National Park Service, U.S. Fish and Wildlife Service, U.S. Forest Service, and the state wildlife agencies of Idaho, Montana, and Wyoming.

**1974:** Two separate population estimates for grizzly bears in the Greater Yellowstone Ecosystem were 136 and 237 to 540, respectively. (Craighead et al. 1974, Knight et al. 1975)

**1975:** The U.S. Fish and Wildlife Service protected the grizzly bear as threatened under the Endangered Species Act of 1973, as amended, in the conterminous 48 states via 40 *Federal Register* 31734-31736 and subsequent regulations. A moratorium was placed on grizzly bear hunting in the Greater Yellowstone Ecosystem.

**1975:** Wyoming and Montana closed their respective portions of the Greater Yellowstone Ecosystem to grizzly bear hunting. Idaho had previously protected grizzly bears in 1946. Hunting continued in the Northern Continental Divide Ecosystem in northwestern Montana under a quota system.

**1977-1987:** A study of grizzly bear food habits indicated garbage was not a significant diet item for grizzly bears in the Greater Yellowstone Ecosystem. (Mattson et al. 1991a)

**1978:** The open-pit garbage dump in Gardiner, Montana, was closed.

**1979:** The open-pit garbage dump near Cooke City, Montana, was closed and replaced with a fenced compound with dumpsters.

**1979:** The sanitation of Yellowstone National Park was considered mostly complete because human foods and garbage were no longer available to bears and all grizzly bears with prior knowledge or use of these food sources had been removed from the population. (Meagher and Phillips 1983)

**1981:** The grizzly bear population in the Greater Yellowstone Ecosystem was estimated at 197 bears. (Knight et al. 1982)

**1982:** The U.S. Fish and Wildlife Service issued the first National Grizzly Bear Recovery Plan, which was facilitated by Don Brown, Director of Montana Fish, Wildlife & Parks.

**1982:** The Environmental Impact Statement (started in 1974) regarding the management of grizzly bears in Yellowstone National Park was completed. The new revised Bear Management Program incorporated backcountry habitat protections by seasonally restricting human recreational activities in areas of high-quality bear habitat.

**1983:** The Interagency Grizzly Bear Committee was created by the Undersecretaries of the Departments of Agriculture and the Interior and the Governors of Idaho, Montana, and Wyoming to oversee the recovery of grizzly bears in the lower 48 states.

**1983:** The Interagency Grizzly Bear Committee formed the Yellowstone Ecosystem Subcommittee to coordinate grizzly bear recovery efforts in the Greater Yellowstone Ecosystem.

**1983:** The West Yellowstone dump was capped and transitioned to a waste transfer station.

**1984:** State representatives from Montana, Idaho, and Wyoming were included in the Interagency Grizzly Bear Committee.

**1984:** The first bear-resistant food storage boxes, poles, and platforms were installed in selected backcountry campsites (some in federal wilderness) on the Shoshone National Forest.

**1986:** For two consecutive years, research studies indicated an increase in the number of grizzly bears in the Greater Yellowstone Ecosystem; 25 females and 48 new cubs were counted.

**1987:** West Yellowstone, Montana, adopted City Ordinance 122 making it illegal to feed or leave food available to bears; thereby requiring "bear-resistant" storage of food.

**1987:** Montana statute (87-2-702) limited grizzly bear hunters in Montana to 1 bear per lifetime.

**1990:** Each national forest issued "special orders" requiring the storage of attractants associated with humans so they were unavailable to bears. Wildlife and wilderness managers from the U.S. Forest Service Region 1 Leadership Team met to discuss providing the public with attractant storage devices in designated wilderness. The intent was to give the public a reasonable means of storing attractants to comply with food storage orders, but not compromise wilderness values. The consensus was to allow placement of storage containers at popular campsites. Allowances were made for outfitter camps to use collapsible metal boxes or vaults at kitchen tents and "Alaskan-style" platforms for horse feed storage.

**1990:** A special order was issued for portions of the Gallatin, Beaverhead, Custer, Shoshone, Bridger-Teton, and Targhee national forests requiring appropriate storage of food and garbage to minimize human-bear encounters. The special order covered the Grizzly Bear Recovery Area and additional areas.

**1993:** The U.S. Fish and Wildlife Service initiated efforts to develop a Yellowstone Grizzly Bear Conservation Strategy by an interagency technical team under the direction of the Interagency Grizzly Bear Committee.

**1994:** The Shoshone National Forest expanded the food storage order to include Jack Creek, Francs Fork, Timber Creek, and the upper Wood River drainages, as well as the rest of Carter Mountain outside the Grizzly Bear Recovery Area.

**1996:** Counts of female grizzly bears with cubs inside Yellowstone National Park stabilized, suggesting grizzly bear numbers in the park had reached carrying capacity.

**1996:** Due to an increase in bear activity in the Greybull district of the Shoshone National Forest, an effort was initiated to include the rest of the District under the food storage order. The effort was terminated due to objections from the public and other agencies. This area was later added by redrawing the boundary, rather than issuing a new order.

**1998:** The area covered by the food storage order was expanded on the Custer Forest, involving the Beartooth Ranger District and Pryor Mountains.

**2000:** One county commissioner from Idaho, Montana, and Wyoming were included on the Yellowstone Ecosystem Subcommittee of the Interagency Grizzly Bear Committee.

**2000:** A notice of the availability of the Yellowstone Conservation Strategy was published for public review and comment (65 *Federal Register* 11340).

**2000:** Portions of the Madison District in the Beaverhead-Deerlodge National Forest were included under the provisions of the food storage order.

**2001:** The Montana Legislature adopted a statute making it illegal to purposely or knowingly leave attractants for bears and other wildlife.

**2001:** Additional portions of the Caribou-Targhee National Forest were included under the provisions of the food storage order.

**2001:** An effort was initiated to extend the food storage order to all portions of the Shoshone and Bridger-Teton national forests not already covered. The proposal was abandoned due to public opposition.

**2002:** The Interagency Grizzly Bear Committee approved a process to append the Yellowstone Grizzly Bear Conservation Strategy with approved state management plans for Montana, Idaho, and Wyoming that allowed grizzly bear expansion into "biologically suitable and socially acceptable habitat."

**2002:** The Interagency Grizzly Bear Committee approved the Yellowstone Grizzly Bear Conservation Strategy.

**2003:** The fenced compound with enclosed dumpsters in Cooke City, Montana, was replaced with a metal-sided building that contained roll-out trash compactors for garbage storage and removal.

**2003:** Representatives from the Shoshone-Bannock and Northern Arapaho tribes were included on the Yellowstone Ecosystem Subcommittee.

**2003-2004:** The Conservation Strategy for the Grizzly Bear in the Yellowstone Area was completed.

**2004:** Two bands of domestic sheep, with permits allowing up to 2,200 sheep in each band, were removed from the Absaroka-Beartooth Wilderness.

**2005:** The U.S. Fish and Wildlife Service announced a proposed rule designating the Greater Yellowstone Ecosystem population of grizzly bears as a distinct population segment and removing it from protection under the Endangered Species Act (70 *Federal Register* 69854).

**2005:** The U.S. Fish and Wildlife Service announced the availability for public review of the draft document produced by the Interagency Grizzly Bear Study Team entitled, "Reassessing methods to estimate population size and sustainable mortality limits for the Yellowstone grizzly bear" (70 *Federal Register* 70632). The final revised methodology was later appended to the Grizzly Bear Recovery Plan and the final Conservation Strategy for the grizzly bear in the Greater Yellowstone Ecosystem.

**2007:** The final Conservation Strategy for the grizzly bear in the Greater Yellowstone Ecosystem was released.

**2007:** The U.S. Fish and Wildlife Service announced the availability of a document describing the habitat-based and demographic recovery criteria to be amended into the 1993 Grizzly Bear Recovery Plan, as well as the *Final Conservation Strategy for the Grizzly Bear in the Greater Yellowstone Area* (72 *Federal Register* 11376).

**2007:** The U.S. Fish and Wildlife Service announced the availability of a final rule and notice of petition finding for the Yellowstone grizzly bear distinct population segment, which was deemed recovered and removed from protection pursuant to the Endangered Species Act (72 *Federal Register* 14865).

**2007:** The food storage order was extended to include all of the Gallatin National Forest under its provisions.

**2009:** The United States District Court for Montana in Missoula issued an order vacating the removal of the Yellowstone distinct population segment of grizzly bears from protection pursuant to the Endangered Species Act.

**2009:** A Memorandum of Understanding was signed between the U.S. Geological Survey and the Eastern Shoshone and Northern Arapaho Tribes to establish cooperation and coordination in the exchange of technical information and services and allow the tribes to appoint a member to the Interagency Grizzly Bear Study Team.

**2010:** The U.S. Fish and Wildlife Service restored the Yellowstone grizzly bear as a threatened species pursuant to the Endangered Species Act (75 *Federal Register* 14496).

**2010:** The U.S. Fish and Wildlife Service and Department of Justice appealed the 2009 ruling by the United States District Court to the Ninth Circuit Court of Appeals.

**2011:** The Ninth Circuit Court of Appeals concluded the 2007 *Conservation Strategy* for the grizzly bear in the Greater Yellowstone Ecosystem provided adequate regulatory mechanisms to conserve bears. However, the appellate court also concluded the U.S. Fish and Wildlife Service failed to articulate a rational connection between the data in the record and its determination that whitebark pine declines were not a threat to the Yellowstone grizzly bear population. Thus, Yellowstone grizzly bears remained protected pursuant to the Endangered Species Act.

**2013:** Fifty-eight adult female grizzly bears accompanied by cubs and 126 total cubs were counted in the Greater Yellowstone Ecosystem. This was the highest number females with cubs and the highest number of cubs counted since the Interagency Grizzly Bear Study Team was created in 1973.

**2013:** The Interagency Grizzly Bear Study Team issued a report addressing grizzly bear responses to whitebark pine decline. They concluded that changes in food resources did not have profound negative effects on grizzly bears at the individual or population level. Grizzly bears obtained sufficient alternative foods through diet shifts and have maintained body mass and percent body fat over time. Additionally, demographic analyses indicated that increased bear density, rather than a decline in food resources, may be associated with a documented slowing of population growth since the early 2000s, possibly indicating the population is nearing carrying capacity in portions of the ecosystem.

**2014:** The food storage order was extended to include all of the Beaverhead-Deerlodge National Forest under its provisions.

**2016:** On March 3, the U.S. Fish and Wildlife Service proposed to remove the grizzly bear in the Greater Yellowstone Ecosystem from the Federal List of Endangered and Threatened Wildlife (81 *Federal Register* 13173).

**2016:** In December, the Yellowstone Ecosystem Subcommittee released the *2016 Conservation Strategy for the Grizzly Bear in the Greater Yellowstone Ecosystem*, accompanied by a signed Memorandum of Understanding for its implementation.

Photograph by Michael Nichols with Ronan Donovan and the National Park Service

*A natural seep, often called a "bear bathtub," where grizzly and black bears frequent.*

# Acknowledgments

Very special thanks to Grant Hilderbrand, U.S. Geological Survey, Alaska Science Center, Anchorage, Alaska; Rachel Mazur, National Park Service, Yosemite National Park; Sterling Miller, Dunrovin Ranch and Research, LLC (retired from Alaska Game and Fish and the National Wildlife Federation) for sharing their time and expertise reviewing a draft version of this book and providing insightful suggestions for improvement.

We thank Yellowstone Forever for financial support to produce this book. We also thank Jake Davis, Ronan Donovan, Neal Herbert, Michael Nichols, Jim Peaco, Diane Renkin, Cory Richards, Drew Rush, the Craighead Institute, The National Geographic Society, and the National Park Service for sharing the images used in this book. Thanks to Karin Bergum for providing a technical review of the book, as well as Lisa Landenburger and Thi Pruitt for assisting with maps. Book design by Jennifer Jerrett.

The views and opinions in this book are those of the authors and should not be construed to represent any views, determinations, or policies of federal or state agencies. Any use of trade, firm, or product names is for descriptive purposes only and does not imply endorsement by the U.S. Government.

Photograph by Jake Davis

A female grizzly bear with her 3 cubs. Grizzly bears typically have litters of 1 to 3 cubs, with occasional litters of 4.

# Glossary of Terms

**Adaptive capabilities:** Behaviors and traits that enable bears and other animals to adjust to changing environmental conditions.

**Adaptive management:** A decision-making process with repeated cycles of (1) describing the problem and desired results, (2) modeling the system, (3) predicting the effects of management actions, (4) implementing management actions, (5) monitoring to evaluate their effectiveness, and (6) making adjustments based on learning to enhance progress.

**Adult:** A bear reproductively mature and capable of breeding; age of 5 years or older in Yellowstone grizzly bears. Approximately 10% of 3-year-old females breed and produce cubs at 4 years of age and are considered adults.

**Aggressive behavior:** A bear threatening other animals or people.

**Allele:** An alternate form of a gene at a specific site, or locus, on a chromosome. A diploid organism has 2 alleles at each locus, one inherited from each parent.

**Allelic richness:** The total number of alleles at each gene locus in a population.

**Aversive conditioning:** The use of deterrents such as clapping, cracker shells, paint balls, and rubber bullets to make bears uncomfortable and encourage them to stop an undesirable behavior and/or leave the area.

**Backcountry:** Areas 250 yards (230 meters) or more from roads or developments.

**Bear jam:** Traffic congestion caused when visitors stop their vehicles and disembark to view bears feeding or conducting other activities near roadways.

**Bear Management Area:** Management closures of certain areas to people during certain times of year to maintain undisturbed foraging opportunities for bears, decrease habituation of bears, and increase safety for people.

**Biomass:** The amount of living or recently living material in an area, such as animals, plants, or meat, measured by weight.

**Birth:** The process of bearing offspring, which is also known as parturition.

**Blastocyst:** Cluster of cells from which the embryo and placenta eventually develop.

**Body condition:** The state of fat and protein stores in an animal that reflects nutritional intake and deposition or metabolism based on their physiological requirements and environmental conditions.

**Bottleneck:** A reduction in population size to a small number of animals containing less genetic variation than the original, larger population; also known as the founder effect.

**Carnivore/Carnivorous:** Meat eater.

**Carrion:** Tissues of dead animals.

**Carrying capacity:** The number of animals that can live in an area based on the amount of available food, space, and other resources.

**Cecum:** A pouch at the beginning of the large intestine where water and salts are absorbed from undigested foods and bacteria begin to break down plant materials.

**Clade:** A group of biological taxa, such as species, that includes all descendants from a common ancestor.

**Competition:** A direct or indirect interaction with another animal that influences the ability of the animal to survive and reproduce.

**Conflict (or management) bear:** A bear repeatedly involved in conflicts with humans over food or property.

**Conservation:** The preservation and stewardship of natural resources and the ecological processes that sustain them.

**Copulation:** The act of mating between a female and male.

**Crepuscular:** Twilight at dawn and before dusk.

**Cub:** Same as cub-of-the-year. While some biologists may use this term to describe any bear still living with its mother, in this book we use the term yearling to refer to a bear between 1 and 2 years of age.

**Cub-of-the-year:** A bear between birth and 1 year of age.

**Delayed implantation:** A delay in embryonic development. After sexual reproduction, the embryo develops only to the blastocyst stage and does not immediately implant in the uterus, extending the normal gestation period. In grizzly bears, implantation of the blastocyst occurs around late November.

**Demographics/Demography:** Statistics related to births, deaths, emigration, and immigration.

**Density:** The number of animals in a defined area.

**Density-dependence:** A response that occurs when there are a high number of animals within a given area.

**Deterrents:** *See* Aversive conditioning.

**Digestion:** Breaking down food into substances that can be absorbed by the body.

**Digestive system:** A group of organs that convert food into energy and nutrients.

**Dispersal:** Movement to another area without returning shortly thereafter.

**DNA:** Deoxyribonucleic acid containing genetic instructions for the development and functioning of animals.

**Dominance hierarchy:** Relationships in animal groups based on a tiered ranking, often as a function of body size, and established and maintained through behavioral interactions.

**Ecological plasticity:** The ability of an organism to adapt its ecological relationships in response to changes in the environment.

**Ecosystem:** A community of living organisms interacting with each other and the nonliving components and processes in the environment that sustain them.

**Effective population size ($N_e$):** A genetic measure of the number of individuals in a population that contribute offspring to the next generation.

**Emigration:** Movements of animals out of a population or area.

**Energetics:** The movement and transformation of energy.

**Estrus:** A recurring period of sexual receptivity and fertility in female mammals. Grizzly bears are considered monestrous because females typically have 1 period of estrus per year.

**Euro-Americans:** Americans with ancestry in Europe.

**Fecundity:** The number of female cubs produced per reproductive-age female per year.

**Fitness:** How successful an animal with particular traits is at surviving, reproducing, and transmitting their genetic characteristics to succeeding generations compared to animals with different traits.

**Fixation index ($F_{ST}$):** A measure of population differentiation due to genetic structure at various population levels such as a subpopulation (S) compared with total population (T).

**Food-conditioned:** A bear associates people with obtaining food and, possibly, becomes dependent on human food sources.

**Food web:** The foraging relationships among organisms in a community.

**Forage:** Food.

**Frontcountry:** Areas less than 250 yards (230 meters) from roads or developments.

**Gene:** The basic unit of heredity (inheritance) consisting of DNA with instructions to make proteins.

**Gene flow:** The transfer of genes (alleles) from one population to another.

**Generation time:** The approximate time it takes individuals to replace themselves in a population or, in other words, the time between successive generations (about 10 to 14 years in Yellowstone grizzly bears).

**Genetic distance:** A measure of the genetic divergence between species or populations within a species. Populations with many similar alleles have small genetic distances, which indicate they are closely related and have a recent common ancestor.

**Genetic diversity:** Variation of heritable characteristics in a population that allows some animals to adapt to a changing environment.

**Genetic drift:** Stochastic fluctuations in the frequency of a genetic variant in a population due to the random sampling of individual offspring from the parental gene pool. As a population becomes smaller, the rate of genetic drift increases.

**Genetic integrity:** The preservation of existing genetic diversity and substructure.

**Genetics:** The study of heredity.

**Geothermal:** Heat from the earth that flows to the surface and produces hydrothermal features such as geysers, hot springs, fumaroles, and mud pots in some areas, while warming more extensive portions of the landscape and reducing or eliminating snow pack.

**Greater Yellowstone Ecosystem:** The general area surrounding the Yellowstone Plateau (including Yellowstone and Grand Teton national parks) where the states of Idaho, Montana, and Wyoming share a boundary.

**Green-up (of vegetation):** Commencement and continuation of new growth by live green plants.

**Habitat:** The environment in which an animal lives that includes cover, food, space, water, and other resources necessary for an animal to survive and reproduce.

**Habituation:** A bear does not visibly respond to people following recurrent interactions without adverse consequences.

**Hazing (of bears):** People using deterrents to stop bears from conducting undesirable behaviors and/or move them away from locations where they are not wanted.

**Herbivore:** Plant eater.

**Heredity:** Inheritance or the genetic transfer of traits to offspring.

**Heterozygosity:** An index of genetic diversity that sums the proportion of genes with different alleles (alternative forms of a gene) across a representative sample of a population.

**Hibernation:** Bears in their winter dens enter a physiological state in which they decrease their body temperature and metabolic rate, metabolize body fat and protein for sustenance, and do not eat, drink, defecate, or urinate. Females give birth and nurse cubs in the den during hibernation.

**Home range:** Area in which an animal lives; can be estimated daily, seasonally, annually, or for a lifetime.

**Human-bear conflict:** An adverse interaction between humans and bears such as death, feeding, injury, physical contact, predatory behavior, property damage, or removal.

**Human-bear interaction:** Humans and bears are in the same vicinity and aware of each other.

**Human foods:** Food materials eaten by humans and garbage or waste.

**Hunting:** Harvest; pursuing an animal to kill it for food (subsistence), sport, and/or spiritual or cultural reasons.

**Hyperphagia:** Period of increased food consumption to store fat and protein for hibernation.

**Immigration:** Movements of animals into a population or area.

**Inbreeding:** Reproduction between closely related individuals that often produces offspring with deleterious traits.

**Inbreeding depression:** A reduction in the fitness of a population due to the breeding of related individuals.

**Independent-age bears:** Yellowstone grizzly bears that are more than 2 years of age.

**Inter-birth interval:** The time period between successive birthing events; typically 3 years for Yellowstone grizzly bears, but can be shorter if a female loses an entire litter of cubs.

**Invertebrates:** Animals that do not have a spinal column, including insects, snails, and worms.

**Known-fate monitoring:** Monitoring of wildlife populations based on the frequent assessment of survival and reproduction using data from telemetry transmitters affixed to a sample of study animals.

**Management (wildlife):** The conservation of populations of wild animals and the ecological processes that sustain them, while considering other biological, economic, political, and social factors.

**Management closure:** Human access to an area is restricted to prevent conflicts with bears.

**Metabolic rate:** The amount of energy expended by an animal during a certain time period.

**Metabolism/Metabolize:** The chemical processes that convert food into energy and other products necessary to sustain life.

**Microsatellite markers:** Short segments of DNA that have a repeated sequence of nucleotides, which are nucleic acids that form the basic structural unit of DNA, and tend to occur in non-coding DNA. In diploid organisms such as bears, each individual animal will have 2 copies of any particular microsatellite segment, one from the mother and one from the father. Over time, as animals in a population breed, they will recombine their microsatellites during sexual reproduction and the population will maintain a variety of microsatellites that is distinct from other populations with which there is no interbreeding.

**Mitochondrial DNA:** The DNA (mtDNA or mDNA) located in mitochondria, cellular organelles within eukaryotic cells that convert chemical energy from food into a form cells can use (adenosine triphosphate; ATP). Mitochondrial DNA is passed down almost unchanged from a mother to her offspring.

**Mortality:** Death or death rate.

**Natal:** Birth.

**Native people:** Indigenous people that have certain inherent rights based on their prehistoric occupation of an area.

**Niche:** The place or role of an animal in its community, including how it uses resources and interacts with other animals.

**Nutrition:** The process of ingesting and using food substances.

**Nutritional ecology:** The study of how nutrition influences growth, reproduction, and survival, as well as the different strategies animals use, such as seasonally, to meet their nutritional needs.

**Omnivores:** Animals that feed on a variety of animals and plants.

**Organism:** A life form such as an animal, bacteria, or plant composed of interdependent parts that maintain vital processes.

**Placental:** Female mammals that maintain 1 or more fetuses in their uterus (womb) during gestation (pregnancy) and provide nourishment to developing fetuses through an umbilical cord.

**Population:** A collection of individuals of the same species that live in the same area and interbreed.

**Population dynamics:** Changes in the size and composition (age, sex) of a population, and the factors and processes influencing those changes.

**Population estimation:** The total number of animals in a population is approximated by sampling a portion of the population and then using these data to draw conclusions about the entire population. An estimate differs from a census, or a complete count of all animals in the population, which are almost impossible to accurately obtain with wild animals over vast landscapes.

**Population trajectory:** The change in population size or growth rate over time (may be positive or negative).

**Predation:** An interaction in which one organism (the predator) attacks and feeds on another (the prey).

**Predatory:** A bear attempting or successfully attacking other animals or people for food.

**Pregnancy:** A female animal carrying 1 or more fetuses in her body from fertilization to birth.

**Radio collar:** *See* Radio telemetry.

**Radio telemetry (wildlife):** The transmission of information such as direction and location from a transmitter attached to an animal to a receiver where the information can be processed or downloaded.

**Range expansion:** The outward dispersal of animals beyond current limits of the distribution of a population.

**Recovery:** *See* Restoration.

**Recruitment:** The number of young that survive to enter a population in a given year.

**Relocation:** The capture and transport of a bear to another area.

**Removal (of bears):** The culling or harvest of animals from a population.

**Reproduction:** Procreation or the process of creating new offspring.

**Resource (natural):** A naturally occurring material that could be used by humans or wildlife.

**Restoration:** The return of something that was removed or nearly extirpated.

**Rumen:** The first compartment of the 4-chambered stomach of ungulates with microorganisms such as bacteria and protozoa to break down plant material into volatile fatty acids and other compounds.

**Scavengers:** Animals that feed on dead or injured animals.

**Senescence:** Becoming old and dying; a decrease in reproduction or survival with age.

**Species:** A group of populations that contain individuals that resemble each other and can interbreed.

**Stable isotope analysis:** A technique in which ratios of certain elements (such as carbon-12 or nitrogen-14) to their stable isotope form (such as carbon-13 or nitrogen-15) in bones, hair, or blood serum of animals reflect their diet in a predictable manner, generally exhibiting a stepwise enrichment at each trophic level. In bear studies, stable isotope analyses are used to determine the dietary proportion of meat and plant matter over different time periods.

**Stakeholders:** People and organizations that use, influence, and have an interest (or stake) in a given resource.

**Subadult:** A young bear no longer dependent on its mother and is living independently, but not yet full-grown or mature; from 2 to 4 years for Yellowstone grizzly bears.

**Survival:** Continuing to live.

**Tolerance:** Acceptance of some animal or thing.

**Translocation:** *See* Relocation.

**Trophic cascade:** A progression of direct and indirect effects of predators or herbivores on successively lower trophic levels.

**Trophic levels:** Species with similar feeding habits such as producers, herbivores, carnivores, top predators, or decomposers.

**Ungulates:** Hoofed mammals such as bighorn sheep, bison, cattle, deer, elk, moose, and pronghorn.

**Vegetation:** Plants.

**Vertebrates:** Animals with spinal columns, including amphibians, birds, fish, mammals, and reptiles.

**Weaning:** A mother stops nursing (milk) her offspring so it will begin eating other foods.

**Wild (bears):** Untamed, free-roaming bears that live in an environment not dominated by humans and whose behaviors, movements, survival, and reproductive success are predominantly affected by their own capabilities, traits, and daily decisions.

**Wildlife:** Wild animals, birds, and other living things.

**Yearling:** A bear between 1 and 2 years of age.

**Yellowstone grizzly bears:** Bears that live in the Greater Yellowstone Ecosystem.

**Yellowstone National Park:** The world's first national park established in 1872 and located on 2.2 million acres in the states of Idaho, Montana, and Wyoming.

NPS Photo/Neal Herbert

*A grizzly bear comes into view through the trees, Yellowstone National Park.*

# Scientific Names

**Fish**
    Cutthroat trout, *Oncorhynchus clarkii*
    Lake trout, *Salvelinus namaycush*

**Fungi**
    Black truffle, *Tuber melanosporum*
    False truffle, *Rhizopogon* spp.

**Insects**
    Ants, *Componotus* spp. and *Formica* spp.
    Army cutworm moth, *Euxoa auxiliaris*
    Mountain pine beetle, *Dendroctonus ponderosae*

**Mammals**
    American black bear, *Ursus americanus*
    Asiatic black bear, *Ursus thibetanus*
    Beaver, *Castor canadensis*
    Bison (buffalo), *Bison bison*

Brown bear, *Ursus arctos*
Deer, *Odocoileus hemionus* and *O. virginianus*
Elk, *Cervus canadensis*
Grizzly bear, *Ursus arctos*
Moose, *Alces alces*
Packrat, *Neotoma* spp.
Pocket gopher, *Thomomys talpoides*
Porcupine, *Erethizon dorsatus*
Pronghorn, *Antilocapra americana*
Mountain lion (cougar, puma), *Puma concolor*
Red squirrel, *Tamiasciurus hudsonicus*
Voles, *Microtus* spp. and *Clethrionomys gapperi*
Wolf, *Canis lupus*

## Parasites
Blister rust, *Cronartium ribicola*
Whirling disease, *Myxobolus cerebralis*

## Plants
Biscuitroot, *Lomatium* spp.
Bistort, *Bistorta bistortoides*
Black hawthorne, *Crataegus douglasii*
Buffaloberry, *Shepherdia canadensis*
Chokecherry, *Prunus virginiana*
Clover, *Trifolium* spp.
Cowparsnip, *Heracleum sphondylium*
Dandelion, *Taraxacum* spp.
Fireweed, *Chamerion angustifolium*
Glacier lily, *Erythronium grandiflorum*
Grouse whortleberry, *Vaccinium scoparium*
Horsetail, *Equisetum* spp.

Huckleberry, *Vaccinium membranaceum*
Lodgepole pine, *Pinus contorta*
Oniongrass, *Melica spectabilis*
Pondweed, *Potamogeton* spp.
Serviceberry, *Amelanchier alnifolia*
Soapberry, *Shepherdia canadensis*
Spring beauty, *Claytonia lanceolata*
Strawberries, *Fragaria virginiana* and *F. vesca*
Sweet cicely, *Osmorhiza berteroi* and *O. occidentalis*
Thistle, *Cirsium* spp.
Vacciniums, *Vaccinium scoparium* and *V. membranaceum*
Whitebark pine, *Pinus albicaulis*
Yampa, *Perideridia gairdneri*

Photograph by Ronan Donovan

*A grizzly bear travels along the bank of the Yellowstone River in Yellowstone National Park.*

# References

Allendorf, F., and G. Luikart. 2007. Conservation and the genetics of populations. Blackwell Publishing, Malden, Massachusetts.

Anderson, C. R., M. A. Ternent, and D. S. Moody. 2002. Grizzly bear-cattle interactions on two grazing allotments in northwest Wyoming. Ursus 13:247-256.

Anderson, N. J. 1994. Grizzly bear food production on clearcuts within the western and northwestern Yellowstone ecosytem. Thesis, Montana State University, Bozeman, Montana.

Archambault, D. II. 2014. Letter dated December 8, 2014 from the Standing Rock Sioux tribe opposing the federal government's intention to delist the grizzly bear from the Endangered Species Act. Fort Yates, North Dakota.

Ashrafzadeh, M. R., M. Kaboli, and M. R. Naghavi. 2016. Mitochondrial DNA analysis of Iranian brown bears (*Ursus arctos*) reveals new phylogeographic lineage. Mammalian Biology 81:1-9.

Auger, J. S., E. Meyer, and H. L. Black. 2002. Are American black bears (*Ursus americanus*) legitimate seed dispersers for fleshy-fruited shrubs? American Midland Naturalist 147:352-367.

Aumiller, L. D., and C. A. Matt. 1994. Management of McNeil River State Game Sanctuary for viewing of brown bears. International Conference on Bear Research and Management 9:51-61.

Austin, C. G., and B. Kohring. 2013. Branding of an ecosystem-wide bear safety message. College of Business, Montana State University, Bozeman, Montana.

Bagget, J. A. 1984. Hibernation. Science World 40:8-11.

Ballard, W. B., L. N. Carbyn, and D. W. Smith. 2003. Wolf interactions with non-prey. Pages 259-271 in L. D. Mech and L. Boitani, editors. Wolves: Ecology, behavior, and conservation. University of Chicago Press, Chicago, Illinois.

Barber-Meyer, S. M. 2015. Trophic cascades from wolves to grizzly bears or changing abundance of bears and alternate foods? Journal of Animal Ecology 84:647-651.

Barber-Meyer, S. M., L. D. Mech, and P. J. White. 2008. Elk calf survival and mortality following wolf restoration to Yellowstone National Park. Wildlife Monographs 169:1-30.

Barboza, P. S., S. D. Farley, and C. T. Robbins. 1997. Whole-body urea cycling and protein turnover during hyperphagia and dormancy in growing bears (*Ursus americanus* and *U. arctos*). Canadian Journal of Zoology 75:2129-2136.

Barnes, V. G., and O. E. Bray. 1967. Final report: Population characteristics and activities of black bears in Yellowstone National Park. National Park Service, Colorado Cooperative Wildlife Research Unit, Colorado State University, Fort Collins, Colorado.

Bascompte, J., C. J. Melián, and E. Sala. 2005. Interaction strength combinations and the overfishing of a marine food web. Proceedings National Academy Sciences 102:5443-5447.

Becker, C. D., Life Net Nature, B. Bergstrom, J. T. Bruskotter, F. J. Camenzind, *et al*. 2013. Comments on draft revised supplement to the grizzly bear recovery plan; specifically, revisions to the demographic recovery criteria for the Greater Yellowstone Ecosystem. Letter dated June 20 to the Grizzly Bear Recovery Coordinator, U.S. Fish and Wildlife Service, Missoula, Montana.

Beckworth, R. 1971. Grizzly bear. Pages 121-125 in T. W. Mussehl and F. W. Howeller, editors. Game management in Montana. Montana Fish and Game Department, Helena, Montana.

Belant, J. L., K. Kielland, E. H. Follmann, and L. G. Adams. 2006. Interspecific resource partitioning in sympatric ursids. Ecological Applications 16:2333-2343.

Ben-David, M., K. Titus, and L. R. Beier. 2004. Consumption of salmon by Alaskan brown bears: A trade-off between nutritional requirements and the risk of infanticide. Behavioral Ecology 138:465-474.

Berger, J., and S. L. Cain. 2014. Moving beyond science to protect a mammalian migration corridor. Conservation Biology 28:1142-1150.

Bergstrom, R., and L. M. B. Harrington. 2013. Balancing communities, economies, and the environment in the Greater Yellowstone Ecosystem. Journal of Rural and Community Development 8:228-241.

Bidwell, D. 2010. Bison, boundaries, and brucellosis: Risk perception and political ecology at Yellowstone. Society and Natural Resources 23:14-30.

Bienen, L., and G. Tabor. 2006. Applying an ecosystem approach to brucellosis control: Can an old conflict between wildlife and agriculture be successfully managed? Frontiers in Ecology and the Environment 4:319-327.

Bjornlie, D. D., and M. A. Haroldson. 2015a. Grizzly bear use of insect aggregation sites documented from aerial telemetry observations. Pages 41-45 in F. T. van Manen, M. A. Haroldson, and S. C. Soileau, editors. Yellowstone grizzly bear investigations: Annual report of the Interagency Grizzly Bear Study Team, 2014. U.S. Geological Survey, Bozeman, Montana.

Bjornlie, D. D., and M. A. Haroldson. 2015b. Grizzly bears and army cutworm moths. Yellowstone Science 23:49-51.

Bjornlie, D. D., M. A. Haroldson, D. J. Thompson, C. C. Schwartz, K. A. Gunther, *et al*. 2015. Expansion of occupied grizzly bear range. Yellowstone Science 23:54-57.

Bjornlie, D. D., D. J. Thompson, M. A. Haroldson, C. C. Schwartz, K. A. Gunther, *et al*. 2014a. Methods to estimate distribution and range extent of grizzly bears in the Greater Yellowstone Ecosystem. Wildlife Society Bulletin 38:182-187.

Bjornlie, D. D., F. T. van Manen, M. R. Ebinger, M. A. Haroldson, D. J. Thompson, *et al.* 2014b. Whitebark pine, population density, and home-range size of grizzly bears in the Greater Yellowstone Ecosystem. PLOS ONE 9:e88160.

Blanchard, B. M. 1983. Grizzly bear: Habitat relationships in the Yellowstone area. International Conference on Bear Research and Management 5:118-123.

Blanchard, B. M. 1987. Size and growth patterns of the Yellowstone grizzly bear. International Conference on Bear Research and Management 7:99-107.

Blanchard, B. M., and R. R. Knight. 1991. Movements of Yellowstone grizzly bears. Biological Conservation 58:41-67.

Brown, G. 2009. The bear almanac: A comprehensive guide to the bears of the world. Lyons Press, Guilford, Connecticut.

Burt, W. H. 1943. Territoriality and home range concepts as applied to mammals. Journal of Mammalogy 24:346-352.

Caughley, G. 1977. Analysis of vertebrate populations. John Wiley and Sons, New York, New York.

Center for Biological Diversity. 2014. Petition for a recovery plan for the grizzly bear (*Ursus arctos horribilis*) across its native range in the conterminous United States. Tucson, Arizona.

Chang, T., and A. J. Hansen. 2015. Historic and projected climate change in the Greater Yellowstone Ecosystem. Yellowstone Science 23:14-19.

Chapron, G., P. Kaczensky, J. D. C. Linnell, M. von Arx, D. Huber, *et al.* 2014. Recovery of large carnivores in Europe's modern human-dominated landscapes. Science 346:1517-1519.

Cherry, S., G. C. White, K. A. Keating, M. A. Haroldson, and C. C. Schwartz. 2007. Evaluating estimators of the numbers of females with cubs-of-the-year in the Yellowstone grizzly bear population. Journal of Agricultural Biological and Environmental Statistics 12:195-215.

Christianse, P., and S. Wroe. 2007. Bite forces and evolutionary adaptations to feeding ecology in carnivores. Ecology 88(2): 347-358.

Cohen, J. E., S. L. Pimm, P. Yodzis, and J. Saldaña. 1993. Body sizes of animal predators and animal prey in food webs. Journal of Animal Ecology 62:67-78.

Cole, G. F. 1971a. Preservation and management of grizzly bears in Yellowstone National Park. BioScience 21:858-864.

Cole, G. F. 1971b. Progress in restoring a natural grizzly bear population in Yellowstone National Park. Transactions of the National Park Centennial Symposium, Annual Meeting of the American Association for the Advancement of Science, December 28-29, 1971, Philadelphia, Pennsylvania. Research in the Parks, National Park Service Symposium Series No. 1 released in 1976.

Cole, G. F. 1976. Management involving grizzly and black bears in Yellowstone National Park, 1970-1975. Department of the Interior, National Park Service, Yellowstone National Park, Mammoth, Wyoming.

Cole, L. C. 1954. The population consequences of life history phenomena. Quarterly Review of Biology 29:103-137.

Coleman, T. H., C. C. Schwartz, K. A. Gunther, and S. Creel. 2013a. Grizzly bear and human interaction in Yellowstone National Park: An evaluation of bear management areas. Journal of Wildlife Management 77:1311-1320.

Coleman, T. H., C. C. Schwartz, K. A. Gunther, and S. Creel. 2013b. Influence of overnight recreation on grizzly bear movement and behavior in Yellowstone National Park. Ursus 24:101-110.

Costello, C. M., S. L. Cain, S. Pils, L. Frattaroli, M. A. Haroldson, *et al.* 2016a. Diet and macronutrient optimization in wild ursids: A comparison of grizzly bears with sympatric and allopatric black bears. PLoS ONE 11:e0153702.

Costello, C. M., R. D. Mace, and L. Roberts. 2016b. Grizzly bear demographics in the Northern Continental Divide Ecosystem, Montana: Research results (2004-2014) and suggested techniques for management and mortality. Montana Department of Fish, Wildlife and Parks, Helena, Montana.

Costello, C. M., F. T. van Manen, M. A. Haroldson, M. R. Ebinger, S. L. Cain, *et al.* 2014. Influence of whitebark pine decline on fall habitat use and movements of grizzly bears in the Greater Yellowstone Ecosystem. Ecology and Evolution 4:2004-2018.

Cowan, I. M., D. G. Chapman, R. S. Hoffmann, D. R. McCullough, G. A. Swanson, *et al.* 1974. Report of the committee on the Yellowstone grizzlies. National Academy of Sciences, Washington, D.C.

Craighead, F. C. Jr. 1982. Track of the grizzly. Sierra Club Books, San Francisco, California.

Craighead, F. C. Jr., and J. J. Craighead. 1972. Grizzly bear prehibernation and denning activities as determined by radiotracking. Wildlife Monographs 32:1-35.

Craighead, F. L., D. Paetkau, H. V. Reynolds, C. Strobeck, and E. R. Vyse. 1998. Use of microsatellite DNA analyses to infer breeding behavior and demographic processes in an arctic grizzly bear population. Ursus 10:323-327.

Craighead, J. J., and F. C. Craighead. 1967. Management of bears in Yellowstone National Park. Montana Cooperative Wildlife Research Unit, University of Montana, Missoula.

Craighead, J. J., K. R. Greer, R. R. Knight, and H. I. Pac. 1988. Grizzly bear mortalities in the Yellowstone ecosystem, 1959-1987. Montana Department of Fish, Wildlife and Parks, Bozeman, Montana.

Craighead, J. J., and J. A. Mitchell. 1982. Grizzly bear. Pages 515-556 in J. A. Chapman and G. A. Feldhamer, editors. Wild mammals of North America: Biology, management, and economics. John Hopkins University Press, Baltimore, Maryland.

Craighead, J. J., J. S. Sumner, and J. H. Mitchell. 1995. The grizzly bears of Yellowstone: Their ecology in the Yellowstone ecosystem, 1959-1992. Island Press, Covelo, California.

Craighead, J. J., J. R. Varney, and F. C. Craighead, Jr. 1974. A population analysis of the Yellowstone grizzly bears. Montana Forest and Conservation Station Bulletin 40, University of Montana, Missoula, Montana.

Creel, S., M. Becker, D. Christianson, E. Dröge, N. Hammerschlag, *et al.* 2015. Questionable policy for large carnivore hunting. U.S. wolf-hunting policies do not align with ecological theory or data. Science 350:1473-1475.

Cullinane Thomas, C., and L. Koontz. 2016. 2015 national park visitor spending effects. Economic contributions to local communities, states, and the nation. Natural Resource Report NPS/NRSS/EQD/NRR—2016/1200. National Park Service, Natural Resource Stewardship and Science, Fort Collins, Colorado.

Dahle, B., O.- G. Stoen, and J. E. Swenson. 2006b. Factors influencing home-range size in subadult brown bears. Journal of Mammalogy 87:859-865.

Dahle, B., and J. E. Swenson. 2003a. Factors influencing length of maternal care in brown bears (*Ursus arctos*) and its effect on offspring. Behavioral Ecology and Sociobiology 54:352-358.

Dahle, B. and J. E. Swenson. 2003b. Home ranges in adult Scandinavian brown bears (*Ursus arctos*): Effect of mass, sex, reproductive category, population density, and habitat type. Journal of Zoology 260:329-335.

Dahle, B., A. Zedrosser, and J. E. Swenson. 2006a. Correlates of body size and mass in yearling brown bears (*Ursus arctos*). Journal of Zoology 269:273-283.

Darwin, C. 1859. On the origin of species by means of natural selection. Down, Bromley, and Kent, London, UK.

Davison, J., S. Y. W. Ho, S. C. Bray, M. Korsten, E. Tammeleht, *et al.* 2011. Late-Quaternary biogeographic scenarios for the brown bear (*Ursus arctos*), a wild mammal model species. Quaternary Science Reviews 30:418-430.

De Barba, M., L. P. Waits, E. O. Garton, P. Genovesi, E. Randi, *et al.* 2010. The power of genetic monitoring for studying demography, ecology and genetics of a reintroduced brown bear population. Molecular Ecology 19:3938-3951.

DeBolt, B., Z. Turnbull, L. Ellsbury, M. Boyce, K. Bayles, *et al.* 2015. Grizzly bear-human conflicts in Wyoming. Pages 64-68 in F. T. van Manen, M. A. Haroldson, and S.C. Soileau, editors. Yellowstone grizzly bear investigations: Annual report of the Interagency Grizzly Bear Study Team, 2014. U.S. Geological Survey, Bozeman, Montana.

Dittrich, L., and H. Kronberger. 1963. Biological-anatomical research concerning the biology of reproduction of brown bear (*Ursus arctos* L.) and other bears in captivity. Zeitschrift für Säugetierkunde 28:129.

Dood, A. R., S. J. Atkinson, and V. J. Boccadori. 2006. Grizzly bear management plan for western Montana: Final programmatic environmental impact statement 2006. Montana Department of Fish, Wildlife and Parks, Helena, Montana.

Eberhardt, L. L. 1977. Optimal policies for conservation of large mammals, with special reference to marine ecosystems. Environmental Conservation 4:205-212.

Eberhardt, L. L. 2002. A paradigm for population analysis of long-lived vertebrates. Ecology 83:2841-2854.

Eberhardt, L. L., B. M. Blanchard, and R. R. Knight. 1994. Population trend of the Yellowstone grizzly bear as estimated from reproductive and survival rates. Canadian Journal of Zoology 72:360-363.

Ebinger, M. R., M A. Haroldson, F. T. van Manen, C. M. Costello, D. D. Bjornlie, *et al.* 2016. Detecting grizzly bear use of ungulate carcasses using global positioning system telemetry and activity data. Oecologia 181:695-708.

Edwards, M. A., A. E. Derocher, and J. A. Nagy. 2013. Home range size variation in female arctic grizzly bears relative to reproductive status and resource availability. PLoS ONE 8:e68130.

Ellig, T. 2006. MSU researcher tests grizzly bear strength for National Geographic. Montana State University News Service, Montana State University, Bozeman, Montana.

Enders, M. S., and S. B. Vander Wall. 2012. Black bears *Ursus americanus* are effective seed dispersers, with a little help from their friends. Oikos 121:589-596.

Erlenbach, J. A., K. D. Rode, D. Raubenheimer, and C. T. Robbins. 2014. Macronutrient optimization and energy maximization determine diets of brown bears. Journal of Mammalogy 95:160-168.

Evans, A. L., N. J. Singh, A. Friebe, J. M. Arnemo, T. G. Laske, *et al*. 2016. Drivers of hibernation in the brown bear. Frontiers in Zoology 13:7 doi: 10.1186/s12983-016-0140-6.

Farley, S. D., and C. T. Robbins. 1995. Lactation, hibernation, and mass dynamics of American black bears and grizzly bears. Canadian Journal of Zoology 73:2216-2222.

Felicetti, L. A., C. C. Schwartz, R. O. Rye, M. A. Haroldson, K. A. Gunther, *et al*. 2003. Use of sulfur and nitrogen stable isotopes to determine the importance of whitebark pine nuts to Yellowstone grizzly bears. Canadian Journal of Zoology 81:763-770.

Fisher, L. 2014. Letter dated September 12, 2014 from the Northern Cheyenne tribe Administration in support of the GOAL tribal coalition. Lame Deer, Montana.

Fortin, J. K. 2012. Niche separation of grizzly bears (*Ursus arctos*) and American black bears (*Ursus americanus*) in Yellowstone National Park. Dissertation, Washington State University, Pullman, Washington.

Fortin, J. K., C. C. Schwartz, K. A. Gunther, J. E. Teisberg, M. A. Haroldson, *et al*. 2013. Dietary adjustability of grizzly bears and American black bears in Yellowstone National Park. Journal of Wildlife Management 77:270-281.

Franklin, I. R. 1980. Evolutionary change in small populations. Pages 135-140 in M. E. Soulé, and B. A. Wilcox, editors. Conservation biology: An evolutionary-ecological perspective. Sinauer Associates, Sunderland, Massachusetts.

Franklin, I. R., and R. Frankham. 1998. How large must populations be to retain evolutionary potential? Animal Conservation 1:69-70.

French, S. P., M. G. French, and R. R. Knight. 1994. Grizzly bear use of army cutworm moths in the Yellowstone ecosystem. International Conference on Bear Research and Management 9:389-399.

Frey, K. L. 2015. Grizzly bear-human conflicts in Montana. Pages 59-63 in F. T. van Manen, M. A. Haroldson, and S.C. Soileau, editor. Yellowstone grizzly bear investigations: Annual report of the Interagency Grizzly Bear Study Team, 2014. U.S. Geological Survey, Bozeman, Montana.

Garrott, R. A., D. R. Stahler, and P. J. White. 2013. Competition and symbiosis: The indirect effects of predation. Pages 94-108 in P. J. White, R. A. Garrott, and G. E. Plumb, editors. Yellowstone's wildlife in transition. Harvard University Press, Cambridge, Massachusetts.

Gende, S. M., and T. P. Quinn. 2004. The relative importance of prey density and social dominance in determining energy intake by bears feeding on Pacific salmon. Canadian Journal of Zoology 82:75-85.

Gill, R. B. 2010. To save a mountain lion: Evolving philosophy of nature and cougars. Pages 5-16 in M. Hornocker and S. Negri, editors. Cougar ecology and conservation. University of Chicago Press, Chicago, Illinois.

GOAL [Guardians of Our Ancestors Legacy]. 2014. Tribal coalition to protect the grizzly bear. http://www.goaltribal.org/

Gonzalez, O., A. Zedrosser, F. Pelletier, J. E. Swenson, and M. Festa-Bianchet. 2012. Litter reductions reveal a trade-off between offspring size and number in brown bears. Behavioral Ecology and Sociobiology 66:1025-1032.

Green, G. I., D. J. Mattson, and J. M. Peek. 1997. Spring feeding on ungulate carcasses by grizzly bears in Yellowstone National Park. Journal of Wildlife Management 61:1040-1055.

Griffin, K. A., M. Hebblewhite, H. S. Robinson, P. Zager, S. M. Barber-Meyer, *et al*. 2011. Neonatal mortality of elk driven by climate, predator phenology and predator community composition. Journal of Animal Ecology 80:1246-1257.

Gude, P. H., A. J. Hansen, R. Rasker, and B. Maxwell. 2006. Rates and drivers of rural residential development in the Greater Yellowstone. Landscape and Urban Planning 77:131-151.

Gunther, K. A. 1990. Visitor impact on grizzly bear activity in Pelican Valley, Yellowstone National Park. International Conference on Bear Research and Management 8:73-78.

Gunther, K. A. 1994. Bear management in Yellowstone National Park, 1960-93. International Conference on Bear Research and Management 9:549-560.

Gunther, K. A. 2003. Yellowstone National Park bear management area program, YELL 705 information paper BMO-5. Yellowstone National Park, Mammoth, Wyoming.

Gunther, K. A. 2008. Delisted but not forgotten: Management, monitoring, and conservation of grizzly bears in Yellowstone National Park after delisting. Yellowstone Science 16:30-34.

Gunther, K. A. 2015a. A fed bear is a dead bear: How this catchy phrase and management philosophy led to positive changes for bears and visitors in Yellowstone National Park. Presentation at 20th International Conference on Bear Research and Management, Session 11, Invited Panel on Bear Feeding, July 17-23. Ottawa, Ontario, Canada.

Gunther, K. A. 2015b. Risk, frequency, and trends in grizzly bear attacks in Yellowstone National Park. Yellowstone Science 23:62-64.

Gunther, K. A. 2015c. Yellowstone National Park recreational use. Pages 49-50 in F. T. van Manen, M. A. Haroldson, and S. C. Soileau, editors. Yellowstone grizzly bear investigations: Annual report of the Interagency Grizzly Bear Study Team, 2014. U.S. Geological Survey, Bozeman, Montana.

Gunther, K. A., staff reviewer. 2016. Bears. Pages 173-184 in J. Waller, V. Warner, T. Blackford, and L. Young, editors. Yellowstone resources and issues handbook, 2016. National Park Service, Yellowstone National Park, Mammoth, Wyoming.

Gunther, K. A., M. J. Biel, N. Anderson, and L. Waits. 2002. Probable grizzly bear predation on an American black bear in Yellowstone National Park. Ursus 28:372-374.

Gunther, K. A., M. A. Haroldson, K. Frey, S. L. Cain, J. Copeland, *et al.* 2004a. Grizzly bear-human conflicts in the Greater Yellowstone Ecosystem, 1992-2000. Ursus 15:10-22.

Gunther, K. A., M. A. Haroldson, M. Nichols, and R. Donovan. 2015a. The bear bath tub. Yellowstone Science 23:66-67.

Gunther, K. A., and H. E. Hoekstra. 1998. Bear inflicted human injuries in Yellowstone National Park, 1970-1994. Ursus 10:378-384.

Gunther, K. A., and E. G. Reinertson. 2016. Visitor compliance with bear spray and hiking group size bear safety recommendations in Yellowstone National Park. Pages 93-97 in F. T. van Manen, M. A. Haroldson, and S. C. Soileau, editors. Yellowstone grizzly bear investigations: Annual report of the Interagency Grizzly Bear Study Team, 2015. U.S. Geological Survey, Bozeman, Montana.

Gunther, K. A., E. Reinertson, T. M. Koel, P. E. Bigelow, and B. Ertel. 2016. Spawning cutthroat trout availability and use by grizzly bears in Yellowstone National Park. Pages 44-50 in F. T. van Manen, M. A. Haroldson, and B. E. Karabensh, editors. Yellowstone grizzly bear investigations: Annual report of the Interagency Grizzly Bear Study Team, 2015. U.S. Geological Survey, Bozeman, Montana.

Gunther, K. A., E. G. Reinertson, T. C. Wyman, D. Bergum, N. R. Bowersock, *et al.* 2015b. Visitor compliance with bear spray and hiking group size in Yellowstone National Park. Yellowstone Science 23:41-43.

Gunther, K. A., and R. A. Renkin. 1990. Grizzly bear predation on elk calves and other fauna of Yellowstone National Park. International Conference on Bear Research and Management 8:329-334.

Gunther, K. A., R. R. Shoemaker, K. L. Frey, M. A. Haroldson, S. L. Cain, *et al.* 2014. Dietary breadth of grizzly bears in the Greater Yellowstone Ecosystem. Ursus 25:60-72.

Gunther, K. A., and D. W. Smith. 2004. Interactions between wolves and female grizzly bears with cubs in Yellowstone National Park. Ursus 15:232-238.

Gunther, K. A., K. Tonnessen, P. Dratch, and C. Servheen. 2004b. Management of habituated grizzly bears in North America: Report from a workshop. Transactions of the 69th North American Wildlife and Natural Resources Conference. Washington, D.C.

Gunther, K., F. T. van Manen, M. A. Haroldson, C. Servheen, and S. Haas, editors. 2015c. Grizzly bear recovery in the Greater Yellowstone Ecosystem. Yellowstone Science 23:1-100.

Gunther, K. A., K. R. Wilmot, S. L. Cain, T. C. Wyman, E. G. Reinertson, *et al.* 2015d. Habituated grizzly bears: A natural response to increasing visitation in Yellowstone & Grand Teton National Parks. Yellowstone Science 23:33-39.

Gunther, K. A., and T. C. Wyman. 2008. Human habituated bears. The next challenge in bear management in Yellowstone National Park. Yellowstone Science 16:35-41.

Gunther, K. A., and T. C. Wyman. 2016. Human-grizzly bear interactions in Yellowstone National Park. Pages 87-92 in F. T. van Manen, M. A. Haroldson, and S. C. Soileau, editors. Yellowstone grizzly bear investigations: Annual report of the Interagency Grizzly Bear Study Team, 2015. U.S. Geological Survey, Bozeman, Montana.

Hadley, E. A., M. H. Kohn, J. A. Leonard, and R. K. Wayne. 1998. A genetic record of population isolation in pocket gophers during

Holocene climatic change. Proceedings of the National Academy of Sciences 95:6893-6896.

Haggerty, J. H., and W. R. Travis. 2006. Out of administrative control: Absentee owners, resident elk and the shifting nature of wildlife management in southwestern Montana. Geoforum 37:816-830.

Haines, A. L. 1977. The Yellowstone story—A history of our first national park: Volume 1. Yellowstone Library and Museum Association, Yellowstone National Park, and Colorado Associated University Press, Boulder, Colorado.

Hamer, D., and S. Herrero. 1990. Courtship and use of mating areas by grizzly bears in the Front Ranges of Banff National Park, Alberta. Canadian Journal of Zoology 68:2695-2697.

Hansen, A. J. 2009. Species and habitats most at risk in greater Yellowstone. Yellowstone Science 17:27-36.

Hansen, A. J., R. Rasker, B. Maxwell, J. J. Rotella, J. D. Johnson, *et al*. 2002. Ecological causes and consequences of demographic change in the new west. BioScience 52:151-162.

Haroldson, M. 1999. Mortalities. Pages 25-28 in C. C. Schwartz and M. A. Haroldson, editors. Yellowstone grizzly bear investigations: Annual report of the Interagency Grizzly Bear Study Team, 1998. U.S. Geological Survey, Bozeman, Montana.

Haroldson, M. A., and K. L. Frey. 2005. Grizzly bear mortalities. Pages 24-29 in C. C. Schwartz, M. A. Haroldson, and K. West, editors. Yellowstone grizzly bear investigations: Annual report of the Interagency Grizzly Bear Study Team, 2004. U.S. Geological Survey, Bozeman, Montana.

Haroldson, M. A., and K. L. Frey. 2007. Grizzly bear mortalities. Pages 16-18 in C. C. Schwartz, M. A. Haroldson, and K. West, editors. Yellowstone grizzly bear investigations: Annual report of the Interagency Grizzly Bear Study Team, 2006. U.S. Geological Survey, Bozeman, Montana.

Haroldson, M. A., and K. L. Frey. 2008. Estimating sustainability of annual grizzly bear mortalities. Pages 24-27 in C. C. Schwartz, M. A. Haroldson, and K. West, editors. Yellowstone grizzly bear investigations: Annual report of the Interagency Grizzly Bear Study Team, 2007. U.S. Geological Survey, Bozeman, Montana.

Haroldson, M. A., and K. L. Frey. 2010. Grizzly bear mortalities. Pages 20-23 in C. C. Schwartz, M. A. Haroldson, and K. West, editors. Yellowstone grizzly bear investigations: Annual report of the Interagency Grizzly Bear Study Team, 2009. U.S. Geological Survey, Bozeman, Montana.

Haroldson, M. A., and K. L. Frey. 2015. Estimating sustainability of annual grizzly bear mortalities. Pages 26-30 in F. T. van Manen, M. A. Haroldson, and S. C. Soileau, editors. Yellowstone grizzly bear investigations: Annual report of the Interagency Grizzly Bear Study Team, 2014. U.S. Geological Survey, Bozeman, Montana.

Haroldson, M. A., and K. L. Frey. 2016. Documented grizzly bear mortalities in the GYE and estimated percent mortality for the Demographic Monitoring Area. Pages 29-37 in F. T. van Manen, M. A. Haroldson, and B. E. Karabensh, editors. Yellowstone grizzly bear investigations: Annual report of the Interagency Grizzly Bear Study Team, 2015. U.S. Geological Survey, Bozeman, Montana.

Haroldson, M. A., and K. A. Gunther. 2013. Roadside bear viewing opportunities in Yellowstone National Park: Characteristics, trends, and influence of whitebark pine. Ursus 24:27-41.

Haroldson, M. A., K. A. Gunther, S. L. Cain, K. R. Wilmot, and T.C. Wyman. 2015a. Grizzly cub adoptions confirmed in Yellowstone and Grand Teton National Parks. Yellowstone Science 23:58-61.

Haroldson, M. A., K. A. Gunther, D. P. Reinhart, S. R. Podruzny, C. Cegelski, *et al*. 2005. Changing numbers of spawning cutthroat trout in tributary streams of Yellowstone Lake and estimates of grizzly bears visiting streams from DNA. Ursus 16:167-180.

Haroldson, M. A., K. A. Gunther, and T. C. Wyman. 2008a. Possible grizzly cub adoption in Yellowstone National Park. Yellowstone Science 16:42-44.

Haroldson, M. A., C. C. Schwartz, S. Cherry, and D. S. Moody. 2004. Possible effects of elk harvest on fall distribution of grizzly bears in the Greater Yellowstone Ecosystem. Journal of Wildlife Management 68:129-137.

Haroldson, M. A., C. C. Schwartz, and K. A. Gunther. 2008b. Grizzly bears in the Greater Yellowstone Ecosystem: From garbage, controversy, and decline to recovery. Yellowstone Science 16:13-24.

Haroldson, M. A., C. C. Schwartz, K. C. Kendall, K. A. Gunther, D. S. Moody, et al. 2010. Genetic analysis of individual origins supports isolation of grizzly bears in the Greater Yellowstone Ecosystem. Ursus 21:1-13.

Haroldson, M. A., C. C. Schwartz, and G. C. White. 2006. Survival of independent grizzly bears in the Greater Yellowstone Ecosystem, 1983-2001. Pages 33-42 in C. C. Schwartz, M. A. Haroldson, G. C. White, R. B. Harris, S. Cherry, et al., editors. Temporal, spatial, and environmental influences on the demographics of grizzly bears in the Greater Yellowstone Ecosystem. Wildlife Monographs 161:1-68.

Haroldson, M. A., M. A. Ternent, K. A. Gunther, and C. C. Schwartz. 2002. Grizzly bear denning chronology and movements in the Greater Yellowstone Ecosystem. Ursus 13:29-37.

Haroldson, M. A., F. T. van Manen, and D. D. Bjornlie. 2015b. Estimating number of females with cubs. Pages 11-20 in F. T. van Manen, M. A. Haroldson, and S. C. Soileau, editors. Yellowstone grizzly bear investigations: Annual report of the Interagency Grizzly Bear Study Team, 2014. U.S. Geological Survey, Bozeman, Montana.

Haroldson, M. A., F. T. van Manen, and D. D. Bjornlie. 2016. Estimating number of females with cubs. Pages 13-23 in F. T. van Manen, M. A. Haroldson, and B. E Karabensh, editors. Yellowstone grizzly bear investigations: Annual report of the Interagency Grizzly Bear Study Team, 2015. U.S. Geological Survey, Bozeman, Montana.

Harris, R. B., C. C. Schwartz, M. A. Haroldson, and G. C. White. 2006. Trajectory of the Yellowstone grizzly bear population under alternative survival rates. Pages 44-55 in C. C. Schwartz, M. A. Haroldson, G. C. White, R. B. Harris, S. Cherry, *et al.*, editors. Temporal, spatial and environmental influences on the demographics of grizzly bears in the Greater Yellowstone Ecosystem. Wildlife Monographs 161:1-68.

Harris, R. B., G. C. White, C. C. Schwartz, and M. A. Haroldson. 2007. Population growth of Yellowstone grizzlies: Uncertainty, correlation, and future monitoring. Ursus 18:167-177.

Harting, A. L. 1985. Relationships between activity patterns and foraging strategies of Yellowstone grizzly bears. Thesis, Montana State University, Bozeman, Montana.

Hebblewhite, M., and D. W. Smith. 2010. Wolf community ecology: Ecosystem effects of recovering wolves in Banff and Yellowstone National Parks. Pages 69-120 in M. Musiano, P. Paquet, and L. Boitani, editors. The world of wolves. University of Calgary Press, Calgary, Alberta, Canada.

Herrero, S. 1978. A comparison of some features of the evolution, ecology and behavior of black and grizzly/brown bears. Carnivore 1:7-17.

Herrero, S. 2002. Bear attacks: Their causes and avoidance. Lyons & Burford, New York, New York.

Herrero, S., and A. Higgins. 1998. Field use of capsicum spray as a bear deterrent. Ursus 10:533-537.

Herrero, S., T. Smith, T. D. Debruyn, K. A. Gunther, and C. A. Matt. 2005. From the field: Brown bear habituation to people—safety, risks, and benefits. Wildlife Society Bulletin 33:362-373.

Hilderbrand, G. V., S. G. Jenkins, C. C. Schwartz, T. A. Hanley, and C. T. Robbins. 1999a. Effect of seasonal differences in dietary meat intake on changes in body mass and composition in wild and captive brown bears. Canadian Journal of Zoology 77:1623-1630.

Hilderbrand, G. V., C. C. Schwartz, C. T. Robbins, and T. A. Hanley. 2000. Effect of hibernation and reproductive success on body mass and condition of coastal brown bears. Journal of Wildlife Management 64:178-183.

Hilderbrand, G. V., C. C. Schwartz, C. T. Robbins, M. E. Jacoby, T. A. Hanley, *et al.* 1999b. The importance of meat, particularly salmon, to body size, population productivity, and conservation of North American brown bears. Canadian Journal of Zoology 77:132-138.

Holtgrieve, G. W., D. E. Schindler, and P. K. Jewett. 2009. Large predators and biogeochemical hotspots: Brown bear (*Ursus arctos*) predation on salmon alters nitrogen cycling in riparian soils. Ecological Research 24:1125-1135.

Hopkins, J. B. III, S. Herrero, R. T. Shideler, K. A. Gunther, C. C. Schwartz, *et al.* 2010. A proposed lexicon of terms and concepts for human-bear management in North America. Ursus 21:154-168.

Horejsi, B. L. 1985. Uncontrolled land use threatens an international grizzly bear population. Conservation Biology 3:220-226.

Hornocker, M. 1962. Population characteristics and social and reproductive behavior of grizzly bears in Yellowstone National Park. Thesis, Montana State University, Missoula, Montana.

Interagency Grizzly Bear Committee. 1986. Interagency grizzly bear guidelines. U.S. Forest Service, Washington, D.C.

Interagency Grizzly Bear Study Team. 2012. Updating and evaluating approaches to estimate population size and sustainable mortality limits for grizzly bears in the Greater Yellowstone Ecosystem. U.S. Geological Survey, Northern Rocky Mountain Science Center, Bozeman, Montana.

Interagency Grizzly Bear Study Team. 2013. Response of Yellowstone grizzly bears to changes in food resources: A synthesis. Report to the Interagency Grizzly Bear Committee and Yellowstone Ecosystem Subcommittee. U.S. Geological Survey, Northern Rocky Mountain Science Center, Bozeman, Montana.

Jacoby, M. E., G. V. Hilderbrand, C. Servheen, C. C. Schwartz, S. M. Arthur, *et al.* 1999. Trophic relations of brown and black bears in several western North American ecosystems. Journal of Wildlife Management 63:921-929.

Jobes, P. C. 1991. The greater Yellowstone social system. Conservation Biology 5:387-394.

Johnson, C. J., M. S. Boyce, R. L. Case, H. D. Cluff, R. J. Gau, *et al*. 2005. Cumulative effects of human developments on Arctic wildlife. Wildlife Monographs 160:1-36.

Johnson, K. M., and S. I. Stewart. 2005. Recreation, amenity migration and urban proximity. Pages 177-196 in G. P. Green, S. C. Deller, and D. W. Marcouiller, editors. Amenities and rural development theory, methods and public policy. Edward Elgar Publishing Limited, Cheltenham, UK.

Jonkel, C. 1980. Black, brown (grizzly), and polar bears. Pages 227-248 in J. L. Schmidt and D. L. Gilbert, editors. Big game of North America, ecology and management. Stackpole Books, Harrisburg, Pennsylvania.

Jope, K. L. 1985. Implications of grizzly bear habituation to hikers. Wildlife Society Bulletin 13:32-37.

Judd, S. L., R. R. Knight, and B. M. Blanchard. 1986. Denning of grizzly bears in the Yellowstone National Park area. International Conference on Bear Research and Management 6:111-117.

Kamath, P. L., M. A. Haroldson, G. Luikart, D. Paetkau, C. Whitman, *et al*. 2015. Multiple estimates of effective population size for monitoring a long-lived vertebrate: An application to Yellowstone grizzly bears. Molecular Ecology 24:5507-5521.

Kasworm, W. F., and T. L. Manley. 1990. Road and trail influences on grizzly bears and black bears in northwest Montana. International Conference on Bear Research and Management 8:79-84.

Keating, K. A., C. C. Schwartz, M. A. Haroldson, and D. Moody. 2002. Estimating numbers of females with cubs-of-the-year in the Yellowstone grizzly bear population. Ursus 13:161-174.

Keiter, R. B., and M. S. Boyce. 1991. The Greater Yellowstone Ecosystem: Redefining America's wilderness heritage. Yale University Press, New Haven, Connecticut.

Kellert, S. R., M. Black, C. Reid Rush, and A. J. Bath. 1996. Human culture and large carnivore conservation in North America. Conservation Biology 10:977-990.

Kendall, K. C. 1983. Use of pine nuts by grizzly and black bears in the Yellowstone area. International Conference on Bear Research and Management 5:166-173.

Knight, R. L., and D. N. Cole. 1995. Factors that influence wildlife responses to recreationists. Pages 71-79 in R. L. Knight and K. J. Gutzwiler, editors. Wildlife and recreationists, coexistence through management and research. Island Press, Covelo, California.

Knight, R. R., J. Basile, K. Greer, S. Judd, L. Oldenburg, *et al.* 1975. Yellowstone grizzly bear investigations. Report of the Interagency Grizzly Bear Study Team, 1974. U.S. Department of the Interior, National Park Service, Bozeman, Montana.

Knight, R. R., B. M. Blanchard, and K. C. Kendall. 1982. Yellowstone grizzly bear investigations. Report of the Interagency Grizzly Bear Study Team, 1981. U.S. Department of the Interior, National Park Service, Bozeman, Montana.

Knight, R. R., and L. L. Eberhardt. 1985. Population dynamics of the Yellowstone grizzly bear. Ecology 66:323-334.

Knight, R. R., and S. L. Judd. 1983. Grizzly bears that kill livestock. International Association for Bear Research and Management Conference 5:186-190.

Koel, T. M., J. L. Arnold, P. E. Bigelow, B. D. Ertel, and D. L. Mahony. 2003. Yellowstone Fisheries and Aquatic Sciences: Annual report, 2002. National Park Service, Yellowstone Center for Resources, Yellowstone National Park, Wyoming.

Koel, T. M., P. E. Bigelow, P. D. Doepke, B. D. Ertel, and D. L Mahony. 2005. Nonnative lake trout result in Yellowstone cutthroat trout decline and impacts to bears and anglers. Fisheries 30:10-19.

Korsten, M., S. Y. W. Ho, J. Davison, B. Pähn, E. Vulla, *et al.* 2009. Sudden expansion of a single brown bear maternal lineage across northern continental Eurasia after the last ice age: A general demographic model for mammals? Molecular Ecology 18:1963-1979.

Kovach, A. I., and R. A. Powell. 2003. Effects of body size on male mating tactics and paternity in black bears, *Ursus americanus*. Canadian Journal of Zoology 81:1257-1268.

Kovach, S. D., G. H. Collins, M. T. Hinkes, and J. W. Denton. 2006. Reproduction and survival of brown bears in southwest Alaska, USA. Ursus 17:16-29.

Kratina, P., R. M. LeCraw, T. Ingram, and B. R. Anholt. 2012. Stability and persistence of food webs with omnivory: Is there a general pattern? Ecosphere 3:50.

Lanner, R. M., and B. K. Gilbert. 1994. Nutritive value of whitebark pine seeds, and the question of their variable dormancy. Pages 206-211 in W. C. Schmidt and F. K. Holtmeier, editors. Proceedings of the international workshop on subalpine stone pines and their environment: The state of our knowledge. General Technical Report INT-GTR-309. U.S. Department of Agriculture, U.S. Forest Service, Intermountain Research Station, Ogden Utah.

Lasseter, D. 2015. 2014 Wyoming bear wise community project update. Pages 108-118 in F. T. van Manen, M. A. Haroldson, and S. C. Soileau, editors. Yellowstone grizzly bear investigations: Annual report of the Interagency Grizzly Bear Study Team, 2014. U.S. Geological Survey, Bozeman, Montana.

Leopold, A. S., S. Cain, C. M. Cottam, I. N. Gabrielson, and T. L. Kimball. 1963. Wildlife management in the national parks: The Leopold report. Advisory Board on Wildlife Management appointed by Secretary of the Interior Udall. U.S. Department of the Interior, Washington, D.C.

Leopold, A. S., S. Cain, C. Olmsted, and S. Olson. 1969. A bear management policy and program for Yellowstone National Park. Report to the Director by the Natural Sciences Advisory Committee of the National Park Service. U.S. Department of the Interior, National Park Service, Yellowstone National Park, Wyoming.

Lindzey, F. G., and E. C. Meslow. 1976. Winter dormancy in black bears in southwestern Washington. Journal of Wildlife Management 40:408-415.

Linnell, J. D. C., J. E. Swenson, R. Anderson, and B. Barnes. 2000. How vulnerable are denning bears to disturbance? Wildlife Society Bulletin 28:400-413.

Lonner, T. N., T. Manning, and J. Campanella. 2009. Back from the brink: Montana's wildlife legacy. Produced by T. Lonner, Media Works Studio, Bozeman, Montana.

MacNulty, D. R., N. Varley, and D. W. Smith. 2001. Grizzly bear, *Ursus arctos*, usurps bison calf, *Bison bison*, captured by wolves, *Canis lupus*, in Yellowstone National Park, Wyoming. Canadian Field Naturalist 115:495-498.

Mahalovich, M. F., M. J. Kimsey, J. K. Fortin-Noreus, and C. T. Robbins. 2016. Isotopic heterogeneity in whitebark pine (*Pinus albicaulis* Engelm.) nuts across geographic, edaphic and climatic gradients in the Northern Rockies (USA). Forest Ecology and Management 359:174-189.

Matsuhashi, T., R. Masuda, T. Mano, K. Murata, and A. Aiurzaniin. 2001. Phylogenetic relationships among worldwide populations of the brown bear *Ursus arctos*. Zoological Science 18:1137-1143.

Matsuhashi, T., R. Masuda, T. Mano, M. C. Yoshida. 1999. Microevolution of the mitochondrial DNA control region in the Japanese brown bear (*Ursus arctos*) population. Molecular Biology and Evolution 16:676-684.

Mattson, D. J. 1990. Human impacts on bear habitat use. International Conference on Bear Research and Management 8:33-56.

Mattson, D. 1997a. Use of ungulates by Yellowstone grizzly bears *Ursus arctos*. Biological Conservation 81:161-177.

Mattson, D. J. 1997b. Use of lodgepole pine cover types by Yellowstone grizzly bears. Journal of Wildlife Management 61:480-496.

Mattson, D. J. 2004. Exploitation of pocket gophers and their food caches by grizzly bears. Journal of Mammalogy 85:731-742.

Mattson, D. J., B. M. Blanchard, and R. R. Knight. 1991a. Food habits of Yellowstone grizzly bears, 1977-87. Canadian Journal of Zoology 69:1619-1629.

Mattson, D. J., B. M. Blanchard, and R. R. Knight. 1992. Yellowstone grizzly bear mortality, human habituation, and whitebark pine seed crops. Journal of Wildlife Management 56:432-442.

Mattson, D. J., C. M. Gillin, S. A. Benson, and R. R. Knight. 1991b. Bear feeding activity at alpine insect aggregation sites in the Yellowstone ecosystem. Canadian Journal of Zoology 69:2430-2435.

Mattson, D. J., S. Herrero, and T. Merrill. 2005. Are black bears a factor in the restoration of North American grizzly bear populations? Ursus 16:11-30.

Mattson, D. J., and R. R. Knight. 1991. Effects of road access on human-caused mortality of Yellowstone grizzly bears. U.S. Department of the Interior, National Park Service, Interagency Grizzly Bear Study Team Report 1991B.

Mattson, D. J., R. R. Knight, and B. M. Blanchard. 1987. The effects of developments and primary roads on grizzly bear habitat use in Yellowstone National Park, Wyoming. International Conference on Bear Research and Manaagement 7:259-273.

Mattson, D. J., and T. Merrill. 2002. Extirpations of grizzly bears in the contiguous United States, 1850-2000. Conservation Biology 16:1123-1136.

Mattson, D. J., and D. P. Reinhart. 1995. Influences of cutthroat trout (*Oncorhynchus clarki*) on behaviour and reproduction of Yellowstone grizzly bears (*Ursus arctos*), 1975-1989. Canadian Journal of Zoology 73:2072-2079.

Mattson, D. J., and D. P. Reinhart. 1997. Excavation of red squirrel middens by grizzly bears in the whitebark pine zone. Journal of Applied Ecology 34:926-940.

Mattson, D. J., R. G. Wright, K. C. Kendall, and C. J. Martinka. 1995. Grizzly bears. Pages 103-105 in E. T. Laroe, S. S. Farris, C. E. Puckett, P. D. Doran, and M. J. Mac, editors. Our living resources: A report to the nation on the distribution, abundance, and health of U.S. plants, animals, and ecosystems. U.S. National Biological Service, Washington, D.C.

McCullough, D. R. 1982. Behavior, bears, and humans. Wildlife Society Bulletin 10:27-33.

McLellan, B. N. 1994. Density-dependent population regulation of brown bears. Pages 15-24 in M. Taylor, editor. Density-dependent population regulation of brown, black, and polar bears. International Conference on Bear Research and Management, Monograph Series 3.

McLellan, B. N. 2011. Implications of a high-energy and low protein diet on the body composition, fitness and competitive abilities of black (*Ursus americanus*) and grizzly bears (*Ursus arctos*). Canadian Journal of Zoology 89:546-558.

McLellan, B. N, and F. W. Hovey. 1995. The diet of grizzly bears in the Flathead River drainage of southeastern British Columbia. Canadian Journal of Zoology 73:704-712.

McLellan, B. N. and F. W. Hovey. 2001. Natal dispersal of grizzly bears. Canadian Journal of Zoology 79:838-844.

McLoughlin, P. D., S. H. Ferguson, and F. Messier. 2000. Intraspecific variation in home range overlap with habitat quality: A comparison among brown bear populations. Evolutionary Ecology 14:39-60.

McWethy, D. B., S. T. Gray, P. E. Higuera, J. S. Littell, G. T. Pederson, *et al.* 2010. Climate and terrestrial ecosystem change in the U.S. Rocky Mountains and upper Columbia basin: Historic and future perspectives for natural resource management. Natural Resource Report NPS/GRYN/NRR-2010/260. National Park Service, Fort Collins, Colorado.

Meagher, M. 2008. Bears in transition, 1959-1970s. Yellowstone Science 16:5-12.

Meagher, M., and J. R. Phillips. 1983. Restoration of natural populations of grizzly and black bears in Yellowstone National Park. International Conference on Bear Research and Management 5:152-158.

Mealey, S. P. 1975. The natural food habits of free-ranging grizzly bears in Yellowstone National Park, 1973-1974. Thesis, Montana State University, Bozeman, Montana.

Mealey, S. P. 1980. The natural food habits of grizzly bears in Yellowstone National Park, 1973-74. International Conference on Bear Research and Management 4:281-292.

Metz, M. C., D. W. Smith, J. A. Vucetich, D. R. Stahler, and R. O. Peterson. 2012. Seasonal patterns of predation for gray wolves in the multi-prey system of Yellowstone National Park. Journal of Animal Ecology 81:553-563.

Middleton, A. D., T. A. Morrison, J. K. Fortin, C. T. Robbins, K. M. Proffitt, *et al*. 2013. Grizzly bear predation links the loss of native trout to the demography of migratory elk in Yellowstone. Proceedings of the Royal Society B 280:20130870.

Miller, C. R., and L. P. Waits. 2003. The history of effective population size and genetic diversity in the Yellowstone grizzly (*Ursus arctos*): Implications for conservation. Proceedings of the National Academy of Sciences 100:4334-4339.

Miller, C. R., L. P. Waits, and P. Joyce. 2006. Phylogeography and mitochondrial diversity of extirpated brown bear (*Ursus arctos*) populations in the contiguous United States and Mexico. Molecular Ecology 15:4477-4485.

Miller, S. D. 1990. Impact of increased bear hunting on survivorship of young bears. Wildlife Society Bulletin 18:462-467.

Miller, S. D., R. A. Sellers, and J. A. Keay. 2003. Effects of hunting on brown bear cub survival and litter size in Alaska. Ursus 14:130-152.

Miller, S. D., G. C. White, R. A. Sellers, H. V. Reynolds, J. W. Schoen, *et al*. 1997. Brown and black bear density estimation in Alaska using radiotelemetry and replicated mark-resight techniques. Wildlife Monographs 133:1-55.

Montana & Wyoming Tribal Leaders Council. 2014. Open letter approved by official resolution number 11Dec2014-04 signed by Chairman I. Posey on December 11. Billings, Montana.

Morris, J. M., and M. K. McBeth. 2003. The new west in the context of extractive commodity theory: The case of bison-brucellosis in Yellowstone National Park. Social Science Journal 40:233-247.

Morrison, M. L., and L. S. Hall. 2002. Standard terminology: Toward a common language to advance ecological understanding and application. Pages 43-52. in P. J. Heglund, M. L. Morrison, J. B. Haufler, M. G. Raphael, W. A. Wall, *et al.*, editors. Predicting species occurrences: Issues of accuracy and scale. Island Press, Washington, D.C.

Mowat, G., and D. C. Heard. 2006. Major components of grizzly bear diet across North America. Canadian Journal of Zoology 84:473-89.

Murie, O. 1944. Progress report on the Yellowstone bear study. National Park Service, Yellowstone National Park, Wyoming.

Murphy, K. M., G. S. Felzien, M. G. Hornocker, and T. K. Ruth. 1998. Encounter competition between bears and cougars: Some ecological implications. Ursus 10:55-60.

Nabokov, P., and L. Loendorf. 2004. Restoring a presence: American Indians and Yellowstone National Park. University of Oklahoma Press, Norman, Oklahoma.

Nagy, J. A., and M. A. Haroldson. 1990. Comparison of some home ranges and population parameters among four grizzly bear populations in Canada. International Conference on Bear Research and Management 8:227-235.

Naoe, S., I. Tayasu, Y. Sakai, T. Masaki, K. Kobayashi, *et al.* 2016. Mountain-climbing bears protect cherry species from global warming through vertical seed dispersal. Current Biology 26:R307-R318.

National Park Service. 1960. National Park Service bear management program and guidelines. U.S. Department of the Interior, Washington D.C.

National Park Service. 1982. Final environmental impact statement, grizzly bear management program. Yellowstone National Park, Mammoth, Wyoming.

National Park Service. 1995. Draft backcountry management plan. Yellowstone National Park, Mammoth, Wyoming.

National Park Service. 2010. Native fish conservation plan environmental assessment. Yellowstone National Park, Mammoth, Wyoming.

National Park Service. 2016a. NPS comments on proposed rule: Removing the Greater Yellowstone Ecosystem population of grizzly bears from the federal list of endangered and threatened wildlife and final draft 2016 conservation strategy, docket ID: FWS-R6-ES-2016-0042. Letter dated May 10 from S. Masica, Intermountain Regional Director, to the Director of the U.S. Fish & Wildlife Service. Denver, Colorado.

National Park Service. 2016b. Yellowstone resources and issues handbook, 2016. Waller, J., V. Warner, T. Blackford, and L. Young, editors. Yellowstone National Park, Mammoth, Wyoming.

National Research Council. 2013. Using science to improve the BLM wild horse and burro program: A way forward. National Academy Press, Washington, D.C.

Native American Encyclopedia. 2014. Grizzly bear. http://nativeamericanencyclopedia.com/grizzly-bear/

Nelson, N. M., P. A. Taylor, T. Hopkins, and A. Rieser. 2011. Evaluation of the "be bear aware" message to visitors in Grand Teton National Park. Wyoming Survey and Analysis Center, University of Wyoming, Laramie, Wyoming.

Nelson, O. L., and C. T. Robbins. 2015. Cardiovascular function in large to small hibernators: Bears to ground squirrels. Journal of Comparative Physiology B 185:265-279.

Nevin, O. T., and B. K. Gilbert. 2005a. Perceived risk, displacement and refuging in brown bears: Positive impacts of ecotourism? Biological Conservation 121:611-622.

Nevin, O. T., and B. K. Gilbert. 2005b. Measuring the cost of risk avoidance in brown bears: Further evidence of positive impacts of ecotourism. Biological Conservation 123:453-460.

Oftedal, O. T., and J. L. Gittleman. 1989. Patterns of energy output during reproduction in carnivores. Pages 355-378 in J. L. Gittleman, editor. Carnivore behavior, ecology, and evolution. Chapman and Hall, London, UK.

Old Coyote, D. 2014. Letter dated November 26, 2014 from the Crow Tribe Executive Branch opposing the federal government's intention to delist the grizzly bear from the Endangered Species Act. Crow Agency (Baaxuwuaashe), Montana.

Onoyama, K., and R. Haga. 1982. New record of four fetuses in a litter of Yezo brown bear (*Ursus arctos yesoensis*) Lydekker with mention of prenatal growth and development. Journal of the Mammalogy Society of Japan 9:1-8.

Paetkau, D., L. P. Waits, P. Waser, L. Clarkson, L. Craighead, *et al.* 1998. Variation in genetic diversity across the range of North American brown bears. Conservation Biology 12:418-429.

Pasitschniak-Arts, M. 1993. Mammalian species: *Ursus arctos*. American Society of Mammalogy 439:1-10.

Pearson, M. 2014. Letter dated December 17, 2014 from the Spirit Lake Sioux tribe opposing the federal government's intention to delist the grizzly bear from the Endangered Species Act. Fort Totten, North Dakota.

Peterson, C. 2005. Grizzlies have great sniffers. Hungry Horse News, Columbia Falls, Montana.

Picton, H. D., and T. N. Lonner. 2010. Montana's wildlife legacy "decimation to restoration." Media Works Publishing, Bozeman, Montana.

Pimm, S. L. 1982. Food webs. Chapman & Hall, London, UK.

Pimm, S. L., and J. H. Lawton. 1978. On feeding on more than one trophic level. Nature 275:542-544.

Podruzny, S. R., S. Cherry, C. C. Schwartz, and L. A. Landenburger. 2002. Grizzly bear denning and potential conflict areas in the Greater Yellowstone Ecosystem. Ursus 13:19-28.

Podruzny, S. R., D. P. Reinhart, and D. J. Mattson. 1999. Fire, red squirrels, whitebark pine, and Yellowstone grizzly bears. Ursus 11:131-128.

Pritchard, G. T., and C. T. Robbins. 1990. Digestive and metabolic efficiencies of grizzly and black bears. Canadian Journal of Zoology 68:1645-1651.

Proctor, M. F., D. Paetkau, B. N. McLellan, G. B. Stenhouse, K. C. Kendall, *et al.* 2012. Population fragmentation and inter-ecosystem movements of grizzly bears in western Canada and the northern United States. Wildlife Monographs 180:1-46.

Randi, E., L. Gentile, G. Boscagli, D. Huber, and H. U. Roth. 1994. Mitochondrial DNA sequence divergence among some west European brown bear (*Ursus arctos* L) populations - Lessons for conservation. Heredity 73:480-489.

Reinhart, D. P. 1990. Grizzly bear habitat use on cutthroat trout spawning streams in tributaries of Yellowstone Lake. Thesis, Montana State University, Bozeman, Montana.

Reinhart, D. P., and D. J. Mattson. 1990. Bear use of cutthroat trout spawning streams in Yellowstone National Park. International Conference on Bear Research and Management 8:343-350.

Renfree, M. B., and J. H. Calaby. 1981. Background to delayed implantation and embryonic diapause. Journal of Reproductive Fertility (Supplement) 29:1-9.

Reynolds, H. V. 1976. North Slope grizzly bear studies (Federal Aid in Wildlife Restoration, Final Report Project W-17-6 and W-17-7, Jobs 4.8R, 4.9R, 4.10R, and 4.11R). Alaska Department of Fish and Game, Juneau, Alaska.

Richardson, L., K. A. Gunther, T. Rosen, and C. C. Schwartz. 2015. Visitor perceptions of roadside bear viewing and management in Yellowstone National Park. George Wright Forum 32:299-306.

Richardson, L., T. Rosen, K. Gunther, and C. Schwartz. 2014. The economics of roadside bear viewing. Journal of Environmental Management 140:102-110.

Rigano, K. S., J. L. Gehring, B. D. Evans-Hutzenbiler, C. A. Vella, O. L. Nelson, *et al.* 2017. Life in the fat lane: seasonal regulation of insulin sensitivity, food intake, and adipose biology in brown bears. Journal of Comparative Physiology B 187:649-676.

Ripple, W. J., R. L. Beschta, J. K. Fortin, and C. T. Robbins. 2014. Trophic cascades from wolves to grizzly bears in Yellowstone. Journal of Animal Ecology 83: 223-233.

Ripple, W. J., R. L. Beschta, J. K. Fortin, and C. T. Robbins. 2015. Wolves trigger a trophic cascade to berries as alternative food for grizzly bears. Journal of Animal Ecology 84:652-654.

Robbins, C. T. 1993. Wildlife feeding and nutrition. Academic Press, San Deigo, California.

Robbins, C. T., M. Ben-David, J. K. Fortin, and O. L. Nelson. 2012. Maternal condition determines birth date and growth of newborn bear cubs. Journal of Mammalogy 93:540-546.

Robbins, C. T., C. C. Schwartz, and L. A. Felicetti. 2004. Nutritional ecology of ursids: A review of newer methods and management implications. Ursus 15:161-171.

Robison, H. L., C. C. Schwartz, J. D. Petty, and P. F. Brussard. 2006. Assessment of pesticide residues in the army cutworm moths (*Euxoa auxiliaris*) from the Greater Yellowstone Ecosystem and their potential consequences to foraging grizzly bears (*Ursus arctos horribilis*). Chemosphere 64:1704-1712.

Rockwell, D. 1991. Giving voice to the bear. Roberts Rinehart Publishers, Niwot, Colorado.

Rode, K. D., C. T. Robbins, and L. A. Shipley. 2001. Constraints on herbivory by grizzly bears. Oecologia 128:62-71.

Ruth, T. K., D. W. Smith, M. A. Haroldson, P. C. Buotte, C. C. Schwartz, *et al.* 2003. Large-carnivore response to recreational big-game hunting along the Yellowstone National Park and Absaroka-Beartooth Wilderness boundary. Wildlife Society Bulletin 31:1150-1161.

Schleyer, B. O. 1983. Activity patterns of grizzly bears in the Yellowstone ecosystem and their reproductive behavior, predation, and the use of carrion. Thesis, Montana State University, Bozeman, Montana.

Schullery, P. 1992. The bears of Yellowstone. High Plains Publishing Company, Worland, Wyoming.

Schullery, P. 2002. Lewis and Clark among the grizzlies: Legend and legacy in the American west. Globe Pequot, Guilford, Connecticut.

Schullery, P., and L. Whittlesey. 1992. The documentary record of wolves and related wildlife species in the Yellowstone National Park area prior to 1882. Pages 1.4-1.174 in J.D. Varley and W.G. Brewster, editors. Wolves for Yellowstone? A Report to the United States Congress, Volume IV, Research and Analysis. National Park Service, Yellowstone National Park, Wyoming.

Schwartz, C. C., S. L. Cain, S. R. Podruzny, S. Cherry, and L. Frattaroli. 2010a. Contrasting activity patterns of sympatric and allopatric black and grizzly bears. Journal of Wildlife Management 74:1628-1638.

Schwartz, C. C., J. K. Fortin, J. E. Teisberg, M. A. Haroldson, C. Servheen, *et al.* 2014. Body and diet composition of sympatric black and grizzly bears in the Greater Yellowstone Ecosystem. Journal of Wildlife Management 78:68-78.

Schwartz, C. C., P. H. Gude, L. A. Landenburger, M. A. Haroldson, and S. R. Podruzny. 2012. Impacts of rural development on Yellowstone wildlife: Linking grizzly bear *Ursus arctos* demographics with projected residential growth. Wildlife Biology 18:246-257.

Schwartz, C. C., M. A. Haroldson, and S. Cherry. 2006a. Reproductive performance of grizzly bears in the Greater Yellowstone Ecosystem, 1983-2002. Pages 18-23 in C. C. Schwartz, M. A. Haroldson, G. C. White, R. B. Harris, S. Cherry, *et al.*, editors. Temporal, spatial, and environmental influences on the demographics of grizzly bears in the Greater Yellowstone Ecosystem. Wildlife Monographs 161:1-68.

Schwartz, C. C., M. A. Haroldson, S. Cherry, and K. A. Keating. 2008. Evaluation of rules to distinguish unique female grizzly bears with cubs in Yellowstone. Journal of Wildlife Management 72:543-554.

Schwartz, C. C., M. A. Haroldson, K. A. Gunther, and D. Moody. 2002. Distribution of grizzly bears in the Greater Yellowstone Ecosystem, 1990-2000. Ursus 13:203-212.

Schwartz, C. C., M. A. Haroldson, K. A. Gunther, and D. Moody. 2006b. Distribution of grizzly bears in the Greater Yellowstone Ecosystem in 2004. Ursus 17:63-66.

Schwartz, C. C., M. A. Haroldson, K. A. Gunther, and C. T. Robbins. 2013. Omnivory and the terrestrial food web: Yellowstone grizzly bear diets. Pages 109-124 in P. J. White, R. A. Garrott, and G. E. Plumb, editors. Yellowstone's wildlife in transition. Harvard University Press, Cambridge, Massachusetts.

Schwartz, C. C., M. A. Haroldson, and G. C. White. 2006c. Survival of cub and yearling grizzly bears in the Greater Yellowstone Ecosystem, 1983-2001. Pages 25-31 in C. C. Schwartz, M. A. Haroldson, G. C. White, R. B. Harris, S. Cherry, *et al.*, editors. Temporal, spatial, and environmental influences on the demographics of grizzly bears in the Greater Yellowstone Ecosystem. Wildlife Monographs 161:1-68.

Schwartz, C. C., M. A. Haroldson, and G. C. White. 2010b. Hazards affecting grizzly bear survival in the Greater Yellowstone Ecosystem. Journal of Wildlife Management 74:654-667.

Schwartz, C. C., R. B. Harris, and M. A. Haroldson. 2006d. Impacts of spatial and environmental heterogeneity on grizzly bear demographics in the Greater Yellowstone Ecosystem: A source-sink dynamic with management consequences. Pages 57-68 in C. C. Schwartz, M. A. Haroldson, G. C. White, R. B. Harris, S. Cherry, *et al.*, editors. Temporal, spatial, and environmental influences on the demographics of grizzly bears in the Greater Yellowstone Ecosystem. Wildlife Monographs 161:1-68.

Schwartz, C. C., K. A. Keating, H. V. Reynolds III, V. G. Barnes Jr., R. A. Sellers, *et al.* 2003a. Reproductive maturation and senescence in the female brown bear. Ursus 14:109-119.

Schwartz, C. C., S. D. Miller, and M. A. Haroldson. 2003b. Grizzly bear. Pages 556-586 in G. A. Feldhamer, B. C. Thompson, and J. A. Chapman, editors. Wild mammals of North America: Biology, management, and conservation. Johns Hopkins University Press, Baltimore, Maryland.

Scott, J. M., D. D. Goble, J. A Wiens, D. S. Wilcove, M. Bean, *et al.* 2005. Recovery of imperiled species under the Endangered Species Act: The need for a new approach. Frontiers in Ecology and the Environment 3:383-389.

Servheen, C. 1990. The status and conservation of the bears of the world. International Conference on Bear Research and Management, Monograph Series 2. Knoxville, Tennessee.

Servheen, C., and M. Cross. 2010. Climate change impacts on wolverines and grizzly bears in the northern U.S. Rockies: Strategies for conservation. Workshop summary report, October 6-7, 2009. Wildlife Conservation Society and the U.S. Fish and Wildlife Service, Bozeman, Montana.

Servheen, C., and R. R. Shoemaker. 2008. Delisting the Yellowstone grizzly bear. A lesson in cooperation, conservation, and monitoring. Yellowstone Science 16:25-29.

Shepard, P., and B. Sanders. 1985. The sacred paw: The bear in nature, myth and literature. Viking Penguin Books, New York, New York.

Sibly, R. M., and J. H. Brown. 2009. Mammal reproductive strategies driven by offspring mortality-size relationships. American Naturalist 173:E185-E199.

Simberloff, D. 1999. Biodiversity and bears: A conservation paradigm shift. Ursus 11:25-31.

Singer, F. J., and J. E. Norland 1994. Niche relationships within a guild of ungulate species in Yellowstone National Park, Wyoming, following release from artificial controls. Canadian Journal of Zoology 72:1383-1394.

Skrbinšek, T., M. Jelencic, L. Waits, I. Kos, K. Jerina, *et al.* 2012. Monitoring the effective population size of a brown bear (*Ursus arctos*) population using new single-sample approaches. Molecular Ecology 21:862-875.

Small, N. 2014. Declaration dated November 4, 2014 from the Fort Hall Business Council opposing the U.S. Fish and Wildlife Service's intention to move forward with a new rule to delist the Yellowstone grizzly bear from the Endangered Species Act. Shoshone-Bannock tribes, Fort Hall, Idaho.

Smith, T. S., S. Herrero, and T. D. DeBruyn. 2005. Alaskan brown bears, humans, and habituation. Ursus 16:1-10.

Smith, T. S., S. Herrero, T. D. Debruyn, and J. M. Wilder. 2008. Efficacy of bear deterrent spray in Alaska. Journal of Wildlife Management 72:640-645.

St. Clair, D. Jr. 2014. Memorandum dated October 29, 2014 from the Eastern Shoshone Business Council regarding delisting of the grizzly bear from the Endangered Species Act. Eastern Shoshone tribe, Fort Washakie, Wyoming.

Stevenson, G. 2007. Neurosurgeon: Griz are sniffing champs of the wild. Missoulian, July 29, 2007.

Stirling, I., and A. E. Derocher. 1990. Factors affecting the evolution and behavioral ecology of the modern bears. International Conference on Bear Research and Management 8:189-204.

Støen, O.- G., A. Zedrosser, S. Saebo, and J. E. Swenson. 2006a. Inversely density-dependent dispersal in brown bears (*Ursus arctos*). Oecologia 148:356-364.

Støen, O.- G., A. Zedrosser, P. Wegge, and J. E. Swenson. 2006b. Socially induced delayed primiparity in brown bears *Ursus arctos*. Behavioral Ecology and Sociobiology 61:1-8.

Stonorov, D., and A.W. Stokes. 1972. Social behavior of the Alaska brown bear. International Conference on Bear Research and Management 2:232-242.

Swenson, J. E., and M. A. Haroldson. 2008. Observations of mixed-aged litters in brown bears. Ursus 19:73-79.

Swenson, J. E., F. Sandegren, S. Brunberg, and P. Segerström. 2001. Factors associated with loss of brown bear cubs in Sweden. Ursus 12:69-80.

Swenson, J. E., F. Sandegren, A. Söderberg, A. Bjärvall, R. Franzén, *et al.* 1997. Infanticide caused by hunting of male bears. Nature 386:450-451.

Taberlet, P., and J. Bouvet. 1994. Mitochondrial DNA polymorphism, phylogeography, and conservation genetics of the brown bear Ursus arctos in Europe. Proceedings of the Royal Society B-Biological Sciences 255:195-200.

Takahashi, K., T. Shiota, H. Tamatani, M. Koyama, and I. Washitani. 2008. Seasonal variation in fleshy fruit use and seed dispersal by the Japanese black bear (*Ursus thibetanus japonicus*). Ecological Research 23:471-478.

Tardiff, S. E., and J. A. Stanford. 1998. Grizzly bear digging: Effects on subalpine meadow plants in relation to mineral nitrogen availability. Ecology 79:2219-2228.

Taylor, P. A., K. A. Gunther, and B. D. Grandjean. 2014. Viewing an iconic animal in an iconic national park: Bears and people in Yellowstone. George Wright Forum 31:300-310.

Teisberg, J. E., M. A. Haroldson, C. C. Schwartz, K. A. Gunther, J. K. Fortin, *et al.* 2014. Contrasting past and current numbers of bears visiting Yellowstone cutthroat trout streams. Journal of Wildlife Management 78:369-378.

Thompson, R. M., M. Hemberg, B. M. Starzomski, and J. B. Shurin. 2007. Trophic levels and trophic tangles: The prevalence of omnivory in real food webs. Ecology 88:612-617.

Tsubota, T., Y. Takahashi, and H. Kanagawa. 1987. Changes in serum progesterone levels and growth of fetuses in Hokkaido brown bear, *Ursus arctos yesoensis*. International Conference on Bear Research and Management 7:355-358.

U.S. Environmental Protection Agency. 2004. Reference notebook. Abandoned Mine Lands Team, Washington, D.C.

U.S. Fish and Wildlife Service. 1975. Grizzly bear. Federal Register 40:31734-31736.

U.S. Fish and Wildlife Service. 1993. Grizzly bear recovery plan. Missoula, Montana.

U.S. Fish and Wildlife Service. 2007a. Endangered and threatened wildlife and plants; designating the Greater Yellowstone Ecosystem population of grizzly bears as a distinct population segment; removing the Yellowstone distinct population segment of grizzly bears from the federal list of endangered and threatened wildlife; 90-day finding on a petition to list as endangered the Yellowstone distinct population segment of grizzly bears. Federal Register 72:14866-14938.

U.S. Fish and Wildlife Service. 2007b. Final conservation strategy for the grizzly bear in the Greater Yellowstone Area. Interagency Conservation Strategy Team, Missoula, Montana.

U.S. Fish and Wildlife Service. 2016. Endangered and threatened wildlife and plants; Removing the Greater Yellowstone Ecosystem population of grizzly bears from the federal list of endangered and threatened wildlife; Proposed rule. Federal Register 81:13174-13227.

Van Daele, L. J., V. G. Barnes Jr., and J. L. Belant. 2012. Ecological flexibility of brown bears on Kodiak Island, Alaska. Ursus 23:21-29.

van Manen, F. T., M. R. Ebinger, M. A. Haroldson, R. B. Harris, M. D. Higgs, *et al.* 2014. Re-evaluation of Yellowstone grizzly bear population dynamics not supported by empirical data: Response to Doak & Cutler. Conservation Letters 7:323-331.

van Manen, F. T., M. A. Haroldson, D. D. Bjornlie, M. R. Ebinger, D. J. Thompson, *et al.* 2016a. Density dependence, whitebark pine, and vital rates of grizzly bears. Journal of Wildlife Management 80:300-313.

van Manen, F. T., M. A. Haroldson, and B. E. Karabensh, editors. 2016b. Yellowstone grizzly bear investigations: Annual report of the Interagency Grizzly Bear Study Team, 2015. U.S. Geological Survey, Bozeman, Montana.

van Manen, F. T., M. A. Haroldson, and S. C. Soileau, editors. 2015. Yellowstone grizzly bear investigations: Annual report of the Interagency Grizzly Bear Study Team, 2014. U.S. Geological Survey, Bozeman, Montana.

Waits, L., D. Paetkau, C. Strobeck, and R. H. Ward. 1998a. A comparison of genetic diversity in North American brown bears. Ursus 10:307-314.

Waits, L., P. Taberlet, J. E. Swenson, F. Sandegren, and R. Franzen. 2000. Nuclear DNA microsatellite analysis of genetic diversity and gene flow in the Scandinavian brown bear (*Ursus arctos*). Molecular Ecology 9:421-431.

Waits, L. P., S. L. Talbot, R. H. Ward, and G. F. Shields. 1998b. Mitochondrial DNA phylogeography of the North American brown bear and implications for conservation. Conservation Biology 12:408-417.

Wang, J., P. Brekke, E. Huchard, L. A. Knapp, and G. Cowlishaw. 2010. Estimation of parameters of inbreeding and genetic drift in populations with overlapping generations. Evolution 64:1704-1718.

Waples, R. S. 1989. A generalized approach for estimating effective population size from temporal changes in allele frequency. Genetics 121:379-391.

Warwell, M. V., G. E. Rehfeldt, and N. L. Crookston. 2007. Modeling contemporary climate profiles of whitebark pine (*Pinus albicaulis*) and predicting responses to global warming. Pages 139-142 in Proceedings of the conference whitebark pine: A Pacific Coast perspective. USDA Forest Service R6-NR-FHP-2007-01. Forestry Sciences Laboratory, Moscow, Idaho.

Westerling, A. L., M. G. Turner, E. A. H. Smithwick, W. H. Romme, and M. G. Ryan. 2011. Continued warming could transform

Greater Yellowstone fire regimes by mid-21st century. Proceedings of the National Academy of Sciences 108:13165-13170.

White, D. Jr., K. C. Kendall, and H. D. Picton. 1998. Seasonal occurrence, body composition, and migration potential of army cutworm moths in northwest Montana. Canadian Journal of Zoology 76:835-842.

White, P. J., R. L. Wallen, D. E. Hallac, and J. A. Jerrett, editors. 2015. Yellowstone bison—Conserving an American icon in modern society. Yellowstone Association, Yellowstone National Park, Wyoming.

Whittlesey, L. H. 2014. Death in Yellowstone: Accidents and foolhardiness in the first national park. Roberts Rinehart Publishers, Lanham, Maryland.

Whittlesey, L., S. Bone, A. Klein, P. J. White, A. W. Rodman, *et al.* 2015. Using historical accounts (1796-1881) to inform contemporary wildlife management in the Yellowstone area. National Park Service, Yellowstone National Park, Mammoth, Wyoming.

Wickelgren, I. 1988. Bone loss and the three bears: A circulating secret of skeletal stability. Science News 134:424-4.

Wilmers, C. C., and E. Post. 2006. Predicting the influence of wolf-provided carrion on scavenger community dynamics under climate change scenarios. Global Change Biology 12:403-409.

Wilson, S. M., M. J. Madel, D. J. Mattson, J. M. Graham, J. A. Burchfiled, *et al.* 2005. Natural landscape features, human-related attractants, and conflict hotspots: A spatial analysis of human-grizzly bear conflicts. Ursus 16:117-129.

Wondrak Biel, A. 2006. Do not feed the bears: The fitful history of wildlife and tourists in Yellowstone. University Press of Kansas, Lawrence, Kansas.

Yarkovich, J., J. D. Clark, and J. L. Murrow. 2011. Effects of black bear relocation on elk calf recruitment at Great Smoky Mountains National Park. Journal of Wildlife Management 75:145-1154.

Yeakel, J. D., P. R. Guimarães, Jr., H. Bocherens, and P. L. Koch. 2013. The impact of climate change on the structure of Pleistocene food webs across the mammoth steppe. Proceedings of the Royal Society B 280:20130239.

Zager, P., and J. Beecham. 2006. The role of American black bears and brown bears as predators on ungulates in North America. Ursus 17:95-108.

Zedrosser, A., B. Dahle, and J. E. Swenson. 2006. Population density and food conditions determine adult female body size in brown bears. Journal of Mammalogy 87:510-518.

Zedrosser, A., G. Rauer, and L. Kruckenhauser. 2004. Early primiparity in brown bears. Acta Theriologica 49:427-432.

Photograph by Jake Davis

*Grizzly bear in summer, Grand Teton National Park.*

# Index

Absaroka-Beartooth Wilderness: 69, 181, 191, 244.

Abundance. *See* Counts; Population dynamics.

Activities: breeding (mating), 3, 30, 31, 34, 43, 63-65, 67, 68, 100, 101, 173, 197, 199; denning, 3, 59, 60; feeding, 4, 5, 49-55, 76-80; interactions, 5, 6, 80-89; movements, 64-73; raising young, 36, 37; timing, 3.

Adaptive capabilities: 9, 60, 91-101, 118, 197.

Adaptive management: 161, 197.

Adult: 2-6, 8, 18, 20, 22, 30, 35, 37, 42-44, 49, 53, 54, 56, 64, 66-68, 77, 84, 85, 112, 123, 124, 141, 170, 171, 173, 174, 193, 197. *See also* Age.

Age, of grizzly bears: adults, 174, 197; cubs, 3, 199; distribution, 42, 170, 173; sub-adults, 173, 208; yearlings, 30, 199.

Alaska: 1, 13, 31, 43, 55, 67, 83, 85, 87, 99, 188.

Alleles: 93, 96, 197, 202, 203.

Ants: 5, 51, 53, 211.

Army cutworm moths: 4, 5, 52, 57, 58, 82, 84, 85.

Asia: 1, 99.

Attacks, by bears. *See* Human-bear encounters/interactions.

Attributes: 1, 2, 103.

Aversive conditioning: 21, 198, 203. *See also* Hazing.

Backcountry: attacks/injuries, 107, 110-112, 135, 138; bear encounters, ix, 10, 26, 107, 110-113, 119, 135, 138; bear safety guidelines, 21, 22, 113, 132-138, 157, 163, 164, 187; bear spray use, 106, 110, 113-115, 135, 138, 139, 144, 163-164; campsites, 18, 21, 22, 26, 107, 108, 110-112, 133-137, 157, 188; definition, 198; food storage, 73, 134-138, 150, 155, 156, 163, 185, 188; Grand Teton National Park, 110, 133, 135, 136; hiking, 15, 21, 106, 108, 112, 113, 134-138, 157; mode of travel, 134; overnight stays, 110, 111,

133-137; permits, 134-136, 157; trails, 21, 22, 26, 107, 108, 110-113, 134-138; Yellowstone National Park, 18, 21, 22, 110, 111, 134-138, 185.

Bear-human conflict. *See* Human-bear conflict.

Bear-human interaction. *See* Human-bear interaction.

Bear jams: bears involved in, 20, 123; definition, x, 119, 198; factors influencing, 20-21, 26, 118-119, 122-126, 164; historical, x, 20, 119, 123; management of, 21, 26, 119-127, 166; numbers of, 20-21, 120-125; people management at, 120-123, 125, 157, 164, 166; personnel hours to manage, xi, 122, 125; safety, 120-125, 164-166. *See also* Habituation; Roadside bears.

Bear Management Areas: 136-137, 158.

Bear-resistant infrastructure (dumpsters, fencing, food storage boxes/containers, garbage cans): 15, 18, 105, 106, 115, 117, 129, 134-138, 142, 145, 150, 155, 163, 182-185, 187, 188, 190.

Bear safety guidelines: 115, 135, 136.

Bear spray: compliance, 106, 113, 138, 163; effectiveness, 138; messaging, 113, 163-164; recommendations, 106, 113, 115, 135, 144, 163-164; use of, 110, 113, 114, 139. *See also* Education; Human-bear encounters/interactions.

Behavior. *See* Breeding; Competition; Digging; Ecological role; Foods; Hibernation; Movements; Parturition; Predation; Scavenging; Seed dispersal.

Berries: 8, 48, 50, 53, 54, 56, 57, 77, 81, 161. *See also* Foods.

Birth: age of first, 32, 33; factors influencing, 32, 33, 35; fat reserves and, 36; inter-birth interval, 33, 34, 174, 204; litter size, 33, 34, 48; location, 173, 203; population dynamics and, 29, 200; rates, 5, 31-33, 35, 174, 201; sex ratio and, 42; timing, 30, 32, 173. *See also* Demography; Hibernation; Pregnancy; Weight.

Bison: mortality from, 39; predation on, 76, 77, 80; scavenging on, 5, 49-50, 52, 53, 76, 78, 84; rut, 53.

Black bears: American, xv, 8, 10, 14, 20, 21, 39, 60, 61, 77, 80, 81, 84-86, 106, 111, 118-121, 123, 124, 172, 178, 182, 184, 211; Asiatic, 86, 211.

Body condition. *See* Nutritional condition.

Bottleneck. *See* Gene/Genetics.

Breeding: age, 197; copulations, 30, 199; frequency, 31, 34, 43; litters, 30; longevity, 30; movements, 63-65, 67, 68; number of breeders, 100, 101; season, 3, 30, 31, 32; sires, 3, 30, 43, 48, 173.

Brown bears: 1, 31-34, 36, 64, 65, 67, 68, 87, 93, 94, 96, 99, 170, 211.

Bureau of Land Management: 2, 20, 105, 131.

Campgrounds/Campsites: avoidance of (by bears), 136, 137; backcountry, 18, 21, 22, 107, 108, 119, 133-137, 150, 155, 185; food storage boxes/containers, 18, 134, 135, 138, 149, 150, 155, 163, 185, 188; food-hanging poles, 18, 134, 135, 144,

150, 155, 156, 163, 185,188; frontcountry, 18, 110, 111, 123, 149, 150, 155, 157, 185; Grand Teton National Park, 135, 136; historic, xv, xvi, 9, 10, 13-19, 182, 183, 185, 188; human-bear conflicts, 26, 104-106, 108, 110-112, 135, 178, locations of, 18, 134, 135; numbers of, 134, 135, 157; outfitters, 134, 157, 188; overnight stays, 134, 135; patrols of, 115, 119, 123, 134, 163; permits, 134-136; safety messages, 123, 135-138, 143, 144, 163; Yellowstone National Park, 18, 21, 22, 134, 135, 156; zones, 21, 22, 134-136.

Canada: 1, 14, 67, 99, 184.

Canyon, Yellowstone National Park: 179-180, 182, 183.

Carcasses/Carrion: biomass obtained/lost, 80, 84, 86; black bears, 8, 80; defense/dominance, 4, 8, 82, 84; displacement from, 4, 8, 82, 84; effects on kill rates of other predators, 80; energetic rewards, 54, 55, 78, 82, 84, 86; feeding rates, 49, 84, 86; hunter-killed ungulates, 41, 143; importance of, 54, 55, 78, 82, 84, 86; influence of climate warming, 80; locating, 8, 78, 80; mountain lions, 8, 80, 89; multiple bears at, 4, 53, 78, 82; olfactory cues, 8, 78, 80; scavenging of, 51,53, 76, 78, 80; usurping of, 8, 80, 89; wolves, 5, 8, 49, 89.

Carnivore/Carnivory: xii, 47, 49, 75, 78, 80, 81, 89, 127, 169, 198, 209.

Carrying capacity: definition, 199; evidence bears near, 44, 189; infanticide and, 43.

Cattle. *See* Livestock and cattle.

Census. *See* Counts.

Chronology, of grizzly bear conservation and management: 177-193.

Clade: 99, 199.

Claws: 1, 172.

Cleveland, Grover: 180.

Climate, warming: ability of bears to adapt, 61, 80, 160, 161, 162, 167; effects of, xvi, 26, 61, 80, 161, 162; temperatures, 161, 162; trout, 26, 161, 162; uncertainties, 161, 162; whitebark pine, 26, 61, 161.

Closures. *See* Bear management area.

Cold pools, 82, 194. *See also* Water.

Color: fur/pelage, 1; eyes, 170; truffles, 53; vision, 2, 171.

Competition: black bears, 61, 81, 84; carcasses, 81; effects on reproduction and survival, 43; exploitation, 84, 199; home ranges and, 64; interference, 7, 84, 199; mates, 9, 30, 35, 43; mountain lions, 81; nutritional costs, 84; siblings, 36; wolves, 81.

Congress: 14, 144, 178, 179, 182, 183.

Connectivity, of habitat: xvi, 72, 94-96, 148, 162.

Conservation, of bears: history, xii, 13-27, 37, 42, 177-193; issues/threats regarding, 7, 11, 26, 112, 126, 151, 159-167; lessons, 38, 44, 106, 115, 122, 151, 153-158, 166, 167; strategies, 20, 37, 128, 136, 144, 145, 147-151, 154, 158, 159, 166, 167; support for, xii, 25, 106, 112, 122, 126, 128, 155, 159, 160, 166, 167.

Conservation strategy: dealing with conflicts, 150, 151; description of, 147-151;

development of, 189-192; education, 150; habitat, 147, 148, 151, 154, 158; hunting, 160-161; Interagency Grizzly Bear Study Team, xi, 6, 19, 22, 27, 38, 39, 158, 161, 186, 192, 193, 205; population, 147, 148, 158; primary conservation area, 148, 150, 154 surveys, 148, 158. *See also* Endangered Species Act; Management.

Cooke City, Montana: 142, 187, 190.

Copulation. *See* Breeding.

Cougar. *See* Mountain lion.

Counts, estimates of abundance/numbers/population size: xv, xvi, 6, 7, 13, 14, 16, 33, 42, 58, 92, 100, 148, 170, 186-188, 189, 191, 206.

Courts. *See* Litigation.

Craighead, Frank and John: 16-18, 60, 184.

Cubs: adoptions, 33, 82; age, 173, 199; birth, 3, 31, 32, 36, 173, 174; climbing, 175; denning, 3, 32, 36; eyes, 170, 175; growth, 36, 37, 48; infanticide, 4, 43; litter size, 18, 30, 31, 33, 35, 48, 174; mass, 2, 30, 48; maternal care, 3, 36, 37, 48, 64, 82, 123, 163, 174; milk intake, 48, 174; population dynamics, 42, 43, 45; protection, 3, 4, 8, 36, 64, 82, 123, 163; sex ratio, 42, 173; sires, 3, 30, 43, 48, 173; size, 30; survival, 18, 39, 42, 43, 45, 174; wean, 4, 32, 175. *See also* Age distribution, of grizzly bears.

Cultural importance: 24, 25.

Cutthroat trout. *See* Trout.

Delayed implantation. *See* Pregnancy.

Demographic Monitoring Area (DMA): 6-7, 170.

Demography: age structure, 3, 30, 42, 170, 173, 174, 197, 199, 208; birth/reproductive rates, 5, 29, 30-36, 42, 48, 173, 174, 200, 201, 203, 204; carrying capacity, 6, 43, 44, 189, 199; counts, xv, xvi, 6, 7, 13, 14, 16, 33, 42, 58, 92, 100, 148, 170, 186-188, 189, 191, 206; dispersal (emigration), 29, 67-69, 94-96, 99, 148, 161, 175, 200, 201, 207; effects of hunting on, 160, 161; lifespan/longevity, 21, 30, 38; mortality, 7, 37-39, 41-43, 45, 159-160, 205; recruitment, 5, 6, 19, 161, 207; reproduction, 5, 7, 16, 19, 22, 29-35, 42-45, 58, 63, 94, 99, 148, 154, 174, 175, 199, 201, 207, 208; population size, xi, 5-7, 13, 14, 19, 20, 92, 99-101, 162, 186, 187, 206; population growth rates, 5-7, 9, 19, 20, 22, 29, 42-45, 96, 106, 162, 206, 207; population models, 6, 16, 88, 148, 197; removals, 5, 7, 18, 39, 42, 92, 106, 120, 121, 141; senescence, 32, 34, 35, 175, 208; survival, 5-7, 16, 18, 19, 22, 35-45, 63, 87, 118, 122, 123, 132, 154, 160, 161, 166, 167, 174, 199, 201, 204, 206-209. *See also* Birth; Population.

Denali National Park: 55.

Dens: bedding, 3; birth/lactation in, 3, 36, 48, 173; description, 3, 173; emergence, 3, 32, 36, 39, 69, 173; entry/duration, 32, 37, 61, 69, 104, 173; hibernation in, 60, 104, 174; movements and, 3, 64; predation during, 77.

Denning. *See* Hibernation.

Density: effects on competition, 84; effects on demography and population dynamics 31, 32, 35, 42, 43, 132; effects on foraging efficiency, 84; effects of habituation, 126; effects on movements and home-range size, 64, 67; roads and residential development, 154. *See also* Demography; Nutrition; Nutritional condition; Population dynamics.

Dentition. *See* Teeth.

Dependent young. *See* Cubs; Yearlings.

Deterrents, for bears. *See* Aversive conditioning.

Development, residential: 7, 13, 14, 16, 18, 19, 26, 37, 95, 104, 107, 108, 110, 118, 126, 127, 129, 132, 133, 142, 148, 154,157, 159. *See also* Roads.

Diet/Diet flexibility/plasticity. *See* Foods; Food habits.

Digestion. *See* Nutrition.

Digestive system/tract: 4, 47-48, 86, 200. *See also* Nutrition.

Digging: 1, 59, 60, 77, 86-87, 172.

Dispersal: age of, 68, 175; gene flow, 94-96; harvests and, 161; home range and, 67; inbreeding and, 69, 175; population dynamics and, 29, 200, 201; range expansion and, 69, 94-96, 148, 200, 207; seeds, 86, 89; sex and, 68-69, 99, 175.

Distinct population segment. *See* Endangered Species Act.

Distribution: area, Table of Contents, 2, 6, 40, 41, 71, 159; clades, 99; constraints in modern society, 25, 45, 147-150, 159, 164; historical, 13, 14, 22, 71, 91,92; worldwide (brown bears), 99. *See also* Dispersal; Home ranges; Movements; Range expansion.

DNA (deoxyribonucleic acid): 92, 200, 201; microsatellite, 93, 205; mitochondrial, 96, 99, 205.

Dominance hierarchy: 30, 48, 82, 123, 200. *See also* Carcasses/Carrion.

Drought: 76, 161.

Dumps. *See* Garbage.

Ecological plasticity: 75, 89, 118, 200.

Ecological role: 7, 8, 75-89; competition, 7, 43, 9, 30, 35, 36, 43, 61, 64, 81, 84, 199; effects on community structure, 85-87; omnivory, 47, 49, 85-89, 175, 206; predation, 5, 7, 8, 42, 49, 50-52, 64, 76-78, 80, 81, 84, 87-89; ; redistribution of nutrients, 7, 87-89; scavenging, 8, 78-80, 89; seed dispersal, 86, 89; soil tilling, 86, 87; trophic cascades, 85-89, 208, 209.

Economics: attributed to Yellowstone National Park, 127-128; jobs, 122, 128; mining, 25, 143; of bear viewing, 122, 126-128; of tourism, 11, 25, 128; timber, 25, 140, 181; values and, 25, 45, 205.

Ecosystem. *See* Greater Yellowstone Ecosystem.

Education, of people: bear safety messaging/recommendations, 113, 115, 129, 138, 163, 164; bear spray, 110, 113, 115, 138, 163, 164; camping, 134-136, 138; communities, 106, 145, 153; food storage, 18, 106, 113, 115, 123, 134, 145, 150,

151, 155, 163; hiking, 113, 136, 163, 164; hunters, 110, 143, 144; media, 107, 113, 138; personal responsibility, 7, 115, 155; slogans, 155, 163, 164.

Effective population size: 92, 99-101, 200. *See also* Gene/Genetics.

Elk: bear predation on, 5, 7, 49, 51, 76-78, 87-89; calves, 5, 7, 49, 56, 64, 76-78, 80, 81, 87-89; carcasses/scavenging, 5, 49, 53, 78, 89; competition for, 81, 84; meat contribution to diet/digestibility, 47, 54-55, 76, 84; hunter killed, 53, 78, 80, 110; hunters killing bears, 41, 110, 143; scientific name, 211; trends in numbers, 49, 54-55, 77, 78, 87-89.

Emigration. *See* Dispersal.

Endangered Species Act: conservation strategy, 147-151, 154, 158, 160, 189-192; delisting/removal, 22, 27, 147, 191-193; distinct population segment, 191, 192; listing, 5, 42, 92, 186, 192; litigation, xi, 22, 192; reasons for listing grizzly bears, 19, 147, 150; recovery plan, 24, 42, 187, 191; recovery zone, 37, 41, 42, 44, 125, 141, 146, 148,154.

Energy/Energetics: definition, 201; digestible energy intake, 47-49, 58, 84; effects of gestation and lactation, 36, 60; hibernation, 26, 36, 48, 53, 56, 58, 60, 61, 65, 104, 105, 174, 203; hyperphagia, 36, 56, 65, 78, 204; metabolic rates, 53, 60, 174, 198, 203, 205.

Estimate (abundance/numbers/population size). *See* Counts.

Estrus: 30, 34, 201.

Euro-Americans: colonization and settlement, xv, 13, 142; definition, 201; extirpation of grizzly bears, xv, 24, 91, 178; interactions with bears, 24, 91, 104; native peoples, 24.

Europe: 1, 53, 94, 99, 178, 201.

Evolution. *See* Adaptive capabilities; Gene/Genetics.

Executive Order: 180.

Extirpation: 167, 178.

Eyesight. *See* Vision.

Fat. *See* Nutrition; Nutritional condition.

Fecundity. *See* Birth; Demography.

Feeding economies/strategies, of bears: 49-55, 77. *See also* Garbage.

Fights: 3, 79.

Fire: x, 56, 137, 161.

Fish. *See* Trout.

Fishing Bridge: 183.

Fitness: 92, 201, 204.

Food: army cutworm moths, 4, 5, 52, 57, 58, 82, 84, 85; autumn/fall, 5, 8, 53, 54, 56; elk, 5, 7, 49, 51, 53, 56, 64, 76-78, 80, 81, 84, 87-89; grasses, 5, 51, 77, 140, 141; human, xv, 9, 12, 15, 54, 104, 155; meat, 4, 8, 47, 49, 50, 53-57, 76, 81, 84, 85, 198, 208; nutritional quality of, 47-49, 51, 53-55, 58; quantity consumed, 49, 58, 80, 84; spring, 49, 51, 56; summer, 49, 51, 53, 56; trout, 4, 5, 7, 26-27, 47, 51, 52, 55, 76, 78, 82, 87-89, 161, 162, 175; whitebark pine nuts/seeds, xii, 4, 5, 8, 23, 35, 50, 52, 53, 56, 59, 61, 85, 122; ungulates, 4-8, 32, 49-51, 53-55, 64, 76-83, 85. *See also*

Food habits; Garbage; Nutrition; Nutritional condition.

Food-conditioning: begging, xv, 14, 119; definition, 201; factors contributing to, 14-17, 104, 105, 115, 126; garbage, 14-18, 104, 151, 155; human injuries from, 10, 18, 106-108, 110, 111, 138, 155; managing people, 18, 20, 106, 115, 120, 126, 129, 132-134, 155, 163; prevention of, 15, 18, 25, 26, 106, 115, 119, 129, 132-143, 144, 145, 151, 155, 160, 163; property damage from, 10, 18, 105, 121; removals of bears, 15, 18, 134, 163; slogans, 155, 163, 164; trends in, 10, 18, 104-106, 119, 159. *See also* Human-bear conflicts; Garbage.

Food habits: by forage classes, 4, 5, 8, 50; composition, 4, 5, 8, 50, 53, 54, 77, 78; flexibility/switching, 18, 51, 53, 54, 87-89; historical, 7, 14, 15, 18, 54, 55, 77; human influences, 14, 15, 18, 20; location in ecosystem, 51, 52, 57, 58, 78; proportion of meat to plant matter, 4, 54, 55, 86; selection, 47, 49, 51, 54, 77; shifts in, 18, 20, 51, 53, 54, 87-89; strategy, 54, 77, 78.

Food storage: boxes/containers, 18, 105, 106, 134, 136, 138, 145, 149, 150, 155, 163, 185, 188; campsites, 18, 134, 135, 138, 185; hanging devices/poles, 18, 134, 135, 150, 155, 163, 185, 188; patrols, 123, 134; regulations/enforcement, 10, 18, 20, 37, 44, 115, 118, 119, 134, 135, 138, 155, 163, 188-193.

Food web: 85-89, 201, 209. *See also* Omnivory.

Forage. *See* Food; Food habits.

Forbs. *See* Food; Food habits; Grassland ecosystems; Habitat; Vegetation.

Forest Reserve Act: 179.

Forests. *See* Habitat.

Frontcountry: attacks/injuries, 107, 110-112; bear encounters, 110, 111, 119; bear safety guidelines, 113, 132, 133, 157, 163, 164; bear spray use, 106, 110, 113, 114, 115, 135, 138, 139, 144, 163-164; campsites, 18, 107, 108, 110-112; definition, 201; food storage, 138, 148, 150, 155, 163, 185; Grand Teton National Park, 122, 123, 133; hiking, 106, 108, 109, 112, 113; overnight stays, 111; trails, 107-113; Yellowstone National Park, 18, 110, 111, 133.

Fur: 1, 36, 55, 84, 170, 208.

Gait: xiii, 2, 10, 21, 48, 172.

Garbage: acquisition, xv, 9, 12, 15, 54, 104, 155; bear-resistant cans, 15, 18, 105, 106, 134, 145, 150, 155, 163, 184, 185, 188; dumps, xv, 6, 9, 12, 15, 16, 35, 54, 92, 93, 119, 178-180, 182-187; dumpsters, 15, 18, 105, 106, 134, 155, 163, 184, 185, 190; effects on reproduction and survival, ix, x, 16, 18, 19, 35, 92, 115, 119, 183, 184, 186; management/regulations, 18, 20, 92, 115, 134, 145, 150, 151, 155, 163, 184, 185, 188.

Gardiner, Montana: 142, 186.

Gene/Genetics: alleles/chromosomes, 93, 172, 197; bottleneck, 9, 93, 198; clade, 99, 199; definitions, 201, 202; depression, 92-94, 204; distance, 94-97, 202;

diversity, 9, 92-95, 162, 202; drift, 99, 101, 202; effective population size: 92, 99-101, 200; effects of management, 9, 148, 162; effects of population reductions, 9, 91-94; founder effect, 9, 198; flow, xvi, 9, 94-96, 162, 202; heredity, 201-203; heterozygosity, 93-95, 203; human influence on, 91-93; inbreeding, 9, 69, 91-97, 162, 175, 204; integrity, 162, 202; isolation, 9, 91, 94-97, 162; kinship, 82; microsatellites, 93, 205,; mitochondrial DNA, 96, 99, 205; viable population size, 9, 92-94, 99-101, 162; worldwide, 96, 99. *See also* Adaptive capabilities; Movements.

Generation time: 31, 93, 202.

Geographic isolation/separation: 9, 91, 92, 162. *See also* Gene/Genetics.

Geothermal: x, 2, 111, 202.

Gestation. *See* Pregnancy.

Glacier National Park: 54, 55, 127, 184.

Grand Teton National Park: 2, 81, 103, 107, 110, 117, 118, 121-125, 127-129, 132-135, 202.

Grasses. *See* Food; Food habits; Grassland ecosystems; Habitat; Vegetation.

Gray wolves. *See* Wolves.

Greater Yellowstone Ecosystem: bears in, xvi, 2, 5, 6, 14, 16, 19, 22, 40, 71, 154, 159; distribution of forages in, 52; geography of, Table of Contents, xvi, 2, 96, 97, 153; people in, 11, 24, 25, 61, 131-151, 154, 157-160, 163.

Green-up, of vegetation: 64, 203.

Growth, of bears: 30, 36, 37, 54, 56, 57. *See also* Weight.

Habitat: degradation/encroachment, xvi, 11, 13, 14, 26, 140-143; displacement from, 4, 84, 123, 127, 141-143; influence of climate warming, 161, 162; influence of hunting, 143, 160, 161; influence on home range and movements, 44, 63, 64, 68, 69; influence on reproduction, 31, 32, 35, 44, 84, 154; influence on survival, 14, 38, 44, 84, 125, 154; loss of, 13, 19, 147; protection, 5, 15, 19, 27, 106, 126, 128, 136, 138, 144, 145, 147, 148, 151, 153-155, 158, 159, 167, 187; recolonization of, 6, 22, 63, 69, 105, 132, 141, 145, 159, 160; roadsides, 118, 123, 125, 129, 133, 164; secure, 20, 44, 136, 137, 148, 154, 155, 159, 163; types of, 50-52, 63, 203; whitebark pine, 52, 53, 85.

Habituation, of bears: bear viewing opportunities, 10, 26, 118, 122, 127-129, 155, 164; benefits of, 118, 119, 122, 126-129, 164; challenges from, 10, 26, 118, 120-126, 128, 129, 155, 160, 164, 166; definition, 10, 118, 203; factors contributing to, 20, 21, 118-125, 155; Grand Teton National Park, 122-125; management of, 10, 21, 119-125, 127, 136, 163, 164, 198; roadsides, 20, 21, 26, 119-125, 133, 155, 163, 164, 166; susceptibility to human-caused mortality, 124, 125, 155; trends in, 20, 21, 119-125, 155, 166; Yellowstone National Park, 20, 21,

119-122. *See also* Bear jams; Roadside bears; Viewing.
Hair. *See* Fur.
Harrison, Benjamin: 179.
Harvests. *See* Hunting/Harvests.
Hayden Valley: 53, 112.
Hazing: 21, 119, 120, 142, 157, 203.
Hearing: 2, 171.
Herbivore: 203, 209.
Heredity. *See* Gene/Genetics.
Hibernation: birth, 32, 36, 48, 60, 203; body condition, 36, 48, 56; body temperature, 60, 172, 174; emergence, 3, 32; heart rate, 60, 172, 174; length, 3, 32, 36, 59, 60, 61; metabolism, 60, 174; nitrogen recycling, 60; nutrition during, 36, 48, 53, 58-61, 174; respiration, 60, 172; timing, 32; waste products, 60, 174; weight loss, 36, 56, 174.
Home ranges: annual, 66, 67, 69, 72, 170; crossing roads within, 96; cubs, 64, 66, 67, 170; definition, 66, 67, 203; factors influencing, 63, 64, 67-69; females, 44, 64, 66-69, 72, 170, 175; lifetime, 66-68, 170; males, 30, 64-69, 72, 170, 175; overlap in, 30, 175; seasonal, 64; sizes of, 66-69, 72; subadults, 66, 67, 69, 170, 175; trout, 51, 88; whitebark pine, 35, 44, 53; yearlings, 64, 66, 67, 170.
Human activities: agriculture, 13, 19, 145; development, 7, 13, 14, 16, 18, 19, 26, 37, 95, 104, 107, 108, 110, 118, 126, 127, 129, 132, 133, 142, 148, 154,157, 159; hunting, 7, 14, 24, 26, 27, 39, 41, 53, 73, 78, 80, 106, 110, 124, 132, 143, 144, 160, 161, 178, 182-184, 186, 188; livestock grazing, 13, 20, 37, 38, 41, 106, 138, 140-142, 148, 151, 154, 159; mining, 19, 25, 138, 142-144; recreation, 11, 25, 105, 110, 111, 113, 117, 118, 127, 131-137, 157, 181, 187; timber harvests: 19, 140, 179, 180; tourism, x, 11, 14, 15, 20, 25, 26, 118, 119, 126. *See also* Climate change; Culling; Human land use practices; Hunting.
Human-bear conflicts: apiaries, 145; beehives, 104-106; conditioning to human foods, xv, 10, 14-18, 104-108, 110, 111, 115, 119, 126, 129, 132-134, 151, 155, 159, 163; factors influencing, 7, 9, 10, 11, 72, 73, 104, 105, 110, 115, 121, 126, 140, 143, 164; fruit trees, 104, 105, 145; gardens, 104-106, 145; hunters (ungulates), 7, 39, 41, 53, 73, 78, 80, 106, 110, 124, 143, 144; influence of natural foods, x, 10, 18, 21, 54, 104, 105, 119, 122, 123, 137; influence on public support for bears, xi, 5, 7, 16, 20, 25, 45, 61, 105, 106, 111, 123, 126, 127, 145, 147, 150, 155, 157-160, 166; livestock, 7, 104, 105, 118, 119, 145, 160; number of, 10, 104-108, 110, 111, 125; on private lands, 72, 73, 105, 106, 111, 127, 145, 147, 154, 167; orchards, 105, 106; prevention of, 11, 15, 18, 25, 26, 104, 106, 107, 113, 115, 119, 127, 129, 132-145, 150, 151, 153, 155, 157, 160, 163, 167; property damage, 10, 18, 105, 121; range expansion and, 13, 14, 72, 73, 106, 141-143, 154; removals of bears, 15, 18, 134, 163; wilderness, 21, 22, 41, 132, 133, 144, 145, 153, 157.

Human-bear encounters/interactions: attacks, xvi, 20, 42, 106-108, 110-112, 138, 177, 182; backcountry, ix, 10, 26, 107, 110-113, 119, 135, 138; Bear Management Areas, 136-137, 158; bear reactions to, 106-111; bear spray, 106, 110, 113-115, 135, 138, 139, 144, 163-164; campsites, 18, 21, 22, 26, 107, 108, 110-112, 133-137, 157, 188; factors influencing, 7, 72, 73, 104-111, 137, 140, 143, 159, 160, 164, 184, 185, 188, 189; frontcountry, 107, 110-112, 119; historical, 9, 10, 13-24, 184, 185, 188, 189; human deaths and injuries, 107-111; influence of hunting (elk, black bears), 7, 18, 39, 41, 53, 78, 80, 106, 110, 124, 143, 144, 180; influence of human group size, 113; numbers of, 104-107, 112, 121; off-trail, 107, 108, 110; risk of, 107-111; roadways, 108, 110, 111, 121, 125, 133, 140, 143; trails, 107, 108, 110, 111, 113; visitation, 10, 103, 110.

Human foods. *See* Foods.

Human land use practices: agriculture, 13, 19, 145, development, 7, 13, 14, 16, 18, 19, 26, 37, 95, 104, 107, 108, 110, 118, 126, 127, 129, 132, 133, 142, 148, 154,157, 159; livestock grazing, 13, 20, 37, 38, 41, 106, 138, 140-142, 148, 151, 154, 159; mining, 19, 25, 138, 142-144; recreation, 11, 25, 105, 110, 111, 113, 117, 118, 127, 131-137, 157, 181, 187; timber harvests: 19, 140, 179, 180; tourism, x, 11, 14, 15, 20, 25, 26, 118, 119, 126. *See also* Roads.

Human safety: 5, 21, 22, 25, 26, 45, 104, 106107, 111, 113, 115, 117, 128, 129, 135-138, 150, 155, 159, 160, 163, 166, 198.

Hunting/Harvests: concerns about, 24, 26, 27, 132, 160, 161; historical, 14, 178, 182-184, 186, 188; sport hunts of bears (post-delisting), 160, 161; ungulate hunter-bear conflicts, 7, 39, 41, 53, 73, 78, 80, 106, 110, 124, 143, 144.

Hyperphagia: foods, 78; length, 36; purpose, 36, 65, 204; timing, 36, 65; weight gain, 56.

Idaho: xvi, 2, 19, 96, 127, 128, 131, 145, 148, 160, 183, 186-190, 202, 209.

Inbreeding. *See* Genetics.

Independent-age bears: 37-39, 44, 45, 73, 204. *See also* Age distribution.

Indians. *See* Native Americans.

Infanticide. *See* Cubs.

Information and Education Working Group: 150. *See also* Education.

Injuries. *See* Human safety and Mortality.

Interagency Grizzly Bear Committee: 20, 37, 134, 135, 154, 166, 187-190.

Interagency Grizzly Bear Study Team: xi, 6, 19, 22, 27, 38, 39, 158, 161, 186, 192, 193, 205.

Inter-birth interval. *See* Birth; Pregnancy.

Invertebrates: 4, 66, 204.

Isolation. *See* Gene/Genetics.

Jackson, Wyoming: 110, 123.

Kinship recognition: 33, 82.

Known-fate monitoring. *See* Surveillance.

Lacey Act (National Park Protective Act of 1894): 14. *See also* Hunting.

Lactation: costs of, 60; effects on subsequent pregnancy, 36; intake by cubs, 36, 174; milk content and production, 48, 174; timing of, 32, weaning, 175. *See also* Nutrition; Nutritional condition.

Lamar Valley: 49.

Landowners. *See* Private landowners.

Landscape-scale processes. *See* Grassland ecosystems; Dispersal; Vegetation.

Land use. *See* Human land use practices.

Learning: about bears, 16, 20, 164, 197; by bears: 18, 21, 48, 104, 118, 183.

Leopold, Aldo: 15, 20.

Leopold Report: 184, 185.

Lewis and Clark expedition: 177.

Life span. *See* Demography.

Litigation: xi, 22, 192.

Litters: adoption, 31, 33; density and, 35; effect of age of mother, 33, 175; factors influencing, 18, 33; lifetime, 31; loss of, 34, 204; mass, 30, 36, 37; mixed age, 31; sires, 3, 30, 173; size, 30, 33, 34, 174; size influence on cub growth, 36, 37; weaning, 31, 34; whitebark pine and, 35.

Livestock and cattle: conflicts with bears, 7, 104, 105, 118, 119, 145, 160; depredation, 7, 41, 77, 105, 106, 124, 141, 142, 178; effects on bears and habitat, 13, 37, 91, 138, 140, 141; grazing allotments, 20, 41, 44, 105, 141; mitigation, 37, 41, 44, 106, 141, 142, 148, 151, 154, 159; removals (of bears), 7, 39, 77, 106, 124, 141, 142, 160, 178.

Maintenance. *See* Nutrition; Nutritional condition.

Management: adaptive management, 161, 197; backcountry/wilderness, 21, 22, 132, 133, 136, 137, 144, 145, 157; campgrounds/campsites, 18, 133-138; current, 26, 131-151, 153-167; developed areas, 132, 133; food storage, xvi, 18, 20, 44, 104, 119, 129, 134, 145, 151, 155; garbage, xvi, 16, 18, 20, 119, 129, 151; hunting, 27, 143, 144, 160, 161; issues regarding, 159-166; jurisdiction, 2, 20, 52, 105, 119-125, 131, 138-151, 153; multiple use, 138-151; of people, 10, 120, 122, 129, 132, 133, 144, 150, 157, 158; paradigm/strategies, xi, 15, 16, 19, 21, 25, 119-121, 129, 133, 134, 136-151, 157-167; population guidelines and objectives, 147-151, ; road corridors, xi, 21, 119, 120, 132, 133; successes, xi, 18, 19, 123, 128, 129, 136, 137, 153-158; zones, 21, 22, 44, 45, 132, 133, 136, 137.

Mass. *See* Weight.

Maternal care: 31, 36, 37, 174.

Mating. *See* Breeding.

McKinley, William: 180.

Meadows: 2, 10, 20, 21, 26, 77, 119, 122, 140, 164.

Meat: 4, 8, 47, 49, 50, 53-57, 76, 81, 84, 85, 198, 208. *See also* Carcasses/Carrion; Foods; Food habits; Ungulates.

Memory: 2.

Metabolism/Metabolizable energy: 53, 60, 174, 198, 203, 205. *See also* Nutrition.

Microsatellites. *See* Gene/Genetics.

Migration: 64-66.

Milk. *See* Lactation.

Mining (mineral extraction): 19, 25, 138, 142-144.

Mitochondrial DNA. *See* Gene/Genetics.

Monitoring/Research: aerial flights, 39; Bear Management Areas, 136, 137; bear numbers, 22, 158, 188; bear spray compliance, 113; body condition/mass, 36, 55, 56; carcasses, 38, 82; climate warming, 161; Conservation Strategy, 147, 148, 158; Craighead (Frank, John), 16, 18, 184; Demographic Monitoring Area, 7; distribution, 22; food resources/webs, 16, 19, 77, 86, 87, 89; genetics, 82, 92, 95, 99; ground monitoring, 39; habitat, 19, 140, 147, 158; habituation, 164; human-bear conflicts, 19; hunting, 27, 160, 161; Interagency Grizzly Bear Study Team, 19, 22, 27, 38, 158, 186; known-fate, 38, 204; mortality, 39, 147; movements/home ranges, 68-71, 82, 95, 96, 136, 137; nutrition, 58; population dynamics, 19; remote cameras, 82; reproduction, 31, 33, 36; safety messaging, 113; social interactions, 82; survival, 38, 39; telemetry/radio collars, 31, 38, 39, 68-70, 82, 128, 140, 207; visitors, 113; Washington State University Bear Research Center, 36; whitebark pine, 33; Yellowstone Ecosystem Subcommittee (Interagency Grizzly Bear Committee), 20. *See also* Management.

Montana: xvi, 2, 14, 16, 19, 22, 55, 67, 72, 95, 127, 128, 131, 142, 145, 148, 160, 177, 178, 180, 182, 184-190, 192, 202, 209.

Moose: 76, 209, 211.

Mortality: causes of death, 7, 39, 41-44, 105, 106, 119-121, 126, 151, 157, 158, 164, 174; closing dumps and, ix, x, 16, 93, 119; effects of range expansion on, 41, 72, 73, 106, 159, 160; human related, 7, 19, 39, 41, 42, 91, 105, 106, 125, 143, 151, 157-160, 174, 180; hunting related, 41, 106, 143, 144, 160, 161; livestock related, 41, 106, 141; poaching, 39, 106; prevention of, 5, 11, 19, 20, 25, 26, 37, 115, 118, 119, 147, 148, 151, 154, 158-160, 166; spatial patterns in, 40, 41, 72, 73; trends in, 19, 39-42, 45, 73, 91, 105, 106, 120, 121, 141, 154, 159, 160. *See also* Survival.

Moths. *See* Army cutworm moths.

Mountain lions: 8, 75, 80, 81, 89, 212.

Movements: annual, 66, 67; daily, 64, 65; factors influencing, 63-67, 69, 96; females, 66-69; historical, 71-73; hyperphagia, 36, 56, 65, 78, 204; males, 66-69; patterns and routes, 69, 70, 72; rates of, 65; seasonal, 64. *See also* Distribution; Dispersal; Home Range; Range expansion.

Multiple use management: 131, 132, 139-145, 157.

Murie, Olaus: 183.

National Forests: 2, 20, 37, 42, 54, 105, 111, 138-145, 153, 154, 179, 181-183, 188-190, 192, 193.

National Park Protective Act of 1894. *See* Lacey Act.

National Park Service: bear management, x, 16, 18, 19, 105, 163, 182-186; mandate/mission, 14, 131; protection of wildlife, 14, 148, 182.

Native Americans/peoples: 19, 20, 24, 54, 147, 160, 166, 190, 192, 206.

Native Fish Conservation Plan: 162.

Natural selection: 101.

Niche: 75-89, 206.

North Continental Divide Ecosystem: 162.

Northern Pacific Railroad: 179.

Nursing. *See* Lactation.

Nutrition: annual variations in, 49-57; autumn, 5, 51, 53-57; dietary energy and protein, 53, 54, 57, 58, 60, 198; digestion and digestive capacity/efficiency, 4, 47, 48; energy content of forage, 52, 54, 57, 58; hibernation and, 48, 56, 59, 60; hyperphagia and, 56; importance of meat, 4, 49, 50, 54, 55; influence of plant maturity (senescence), 4, 51; seasonal changes in, 4, 5, 49-55, 57; spring and summer, 5, 49, 51, 53, 56, 57.

Nutritional (body) condition: body fat content, 4, 48, 55-57, 161, 198; body mass and dominance rank, 48, 56, 84, 85; effects of garbage, 54, 56, 61; effects on growth and survival, 56, 61; effects on pregnancy and lactation, 48; factors influencing, 48, 56, 57, 84, 161; fat deposition and metabolism, 56-58, 60, 84, 85, 198; habitat productivity and, 44, 55, 57, 58, 161; hibernation, 26, 48, 56, 59, 60; muscle anabolism and catabolism, 60, 84, 198; protein metabolism, 60; seasonal strategies, 49-56. *See also* Pregnancy; Survival.

Offspring. *See* Cubs.

Omnivore/Omnivory: 47, 49, 85-89, 175, 206. *See also* Food web.

Organic Administration Act: 179, 180.

Parturition. *See* Birth.

Pelican Creek, Yellowstone National Park: xiii.

Phenology. *See* Vegetation.

Photography: 21, 26, 112, 118, 120, 122, 126, 164-166. *See also* Bear jams; Habituation; Viewing.

Physiology: 47, 169.

Pinchot, Gifford: 181.

Plant communities. *See* Vegetation.

Plant phenology. *See* Vegetation.

Poaching: 14, 20, 39, 106, 178.

Pocket gophers: 77, 212.

Politics: xvi, 205.

Population: carrying capacity, 6, 43, 44, 189, 199; dynamics, ix-xi, 5, 6, 9, 19, 20, 29, 37, 44, 45, 92, 99-101, 148, 162; effects of culling and harvest, 10, 13, 14, 19, 106; historical estimates, 5, 6, 13, 14, 22, 42, 91, 92; rates of increase (or decrease), 6, 9, 22, 42; regulation (density dependent), 6, 22, 42-45, 64, 67; size, xi, 5-7, 13, 14, 19, 20, 92, 99-101, 162, 186, 187, 206; viability, 9, 92-94, 99-101, 162.

Precipitation. *See* Snow and snowpack.

Predation/Predatory: bear cubs, 42, 64; bison, 49, 52, 76, 77, 80; black bears, 77, 81; elk, 7, 49, 50, 51, 76-78, 87, 89; meat consumption, 76, 84; moose, 76; pocket gophers, 76, 77; rates (elk calves), 49, 51, 77, 78; smaller mammals, 76, 77; trout, 51, 76, 87-89; ungulates, 8,50, 76-78; voles, 76, 77; wolves, 5, 49, 80. *See also* Competition; Ecological role; Livestock and cattle; Population dynamics; Ungulates.

Pregnancy: age of first, 32, 33; blastocyst, 30, 198, 199; body condition, 36, 48; delayed implantation, 30, 173, 199; effects of lactation, 31, 36, 48, 60; estrus, 30, 34, 201; factors influencing, 34, 35, 48; gestation length, 30, 173; inter-birth interval, 33, 34, 174, 204; offspring to mother body mass, 30; parturition, 30, 32; rates of, 35; sexual maturity, 34, 35; sex ratios, 42, 173. *See also* Demography; Nutrition; Nutritional condition.

Primary Conservation Area: bear distribution/management units, 71, 97, 146, 148; connectivity (of habitat), 148; development, 148, 154, 159; habitat standards, 148; hunting, 160, 161; implementation/evaluation, 150; information/education, 150; Interagency Grizzly Bear Study Team, xi, 6, 19, 22, 27, 38, 39, 158, 161, 186, 192, 193, 205; jurisdiction, 148; livestock grazing allotments, 148, 154, 159; management actions within, 148,, 150; National Park Service, 148; population standards, 148; roads, 148, 154, 159; secure habitat, 148, 154, 159; size, Table of Contents, 146, 148, 154; U.S. Forest Service, 148.

Private landowners: 2, 18, 72, 73, 105, 106, 111, 127, 145, 147, 153, 154, 167.

Productivity. *See* Demography; Vegetation.

Property damage and public safety. *See* Humans; Human safety.

Protein. *See* Nutrition; Nutritional condition.

Public engagement: xi, 7, 16, 20, 45, 106, 123, 126, 128, 138, 144, 145, 150, 155, 157, 158, 166, 167, 189-191.

Radio collar. *See* Telemetry.

Radio telemetry. *See* Telemetry.

Range expansion: challenges from, 45,72, 73, 106, 141-143, 145, 154, 155; effects of culling and harvest on, 40, 41, 106, 160, 161; effects of density/population growth, 22, 96; effects of learning, 20; factors influencing, 3, 22, 58, 68-72, 96, 106; human-bear conflicts, 13, 14, 72, 73, 106, 141-143, 154; influence of roads, 22, 96, 143; livestock conflicts, 41, 142; mortalities, 40, 41, 45; private lands, 72, 73, 145; subadults, 67-69, 73; trends in, x, xi, 22, 40, 41, 69, 71, 72, 97. *See also* Dispersal; Movements.

Recovery. *See* Restoration; Endangered Species Act.

Recreation: 11, 25, 105, 110, 111, 113, 117, 118, 127, 131-137, 157, 181, 187.

Recruitment. *See* Demography.

Red squirrels: xiv, 5, 59, 77, 85, 212.

Regulations: approaching wildlife, 113, 129, 157, 163; Bear Management Areas, 136-137, 158; Endangered Species Act, 186, 191-193; feeding wildlife, 10, 18, 180, 184; food storage, 10, 16, 18, 115, 118, 119, 134, 135, 138, 150, 155, 163, 185; hunting, 14, 144; protecting predators, 25.

Relocation, of bears: 9, 15, 21, 77, 94, 96, 119, 134, 142, 162, 207.

Removals, of bears: conflicts in developed areas, 15, 18, 39, 41, 106; food conditioned, 15, 18, 134, 163; from protection under the Endangered Species Act, 24, 27, 147, 191-193; livestock depredation, 7, 39, 41, 77, 106, 141, 142; property/human injuries, 15, 120, 121; recommendations regarding, 5, 19, 163.

Reproduction. *See* Pregnancy.

Reproductive cycle/transition: factors influencing, 30-37; influence of density, 22, 32, 35, 42, 43, 45; influence of habitat (such as whitebark pine), 31, 32, 35, 43, 44, 154; inter-birth interval, 33, 34, 174, 204; length, 34, 35, 174, 175; longevity, 21, 30, 38. *See also* Weaning.

Reproductive rates. *See* Demography.

Research. *See* Management; Surveillance.

Resource extraction: 11, 13, 19, 25, 132, 138-143.

Resources. *See* Foods; Habitat.

Restoration: x, xvi, 6, 7, 10, 11, 13-27, 37, 41, 42, 44, 45, 55, 63, 125, 136, 141, 143,
146-148, 151, 153, 154, 157, 159, 160, 187, 189, 191, 208.

Roads: bears feeding along, xv, 14, 15, 118, 119, 122, 123, 126, 155; bear viewing, ix, x, xvi, 9, 10, 20, 21, 118, 119, 122, 126; crossing of, 96; disturbances to bears, 108, 110, 129, 132, 138, 140, 142, 143, 148, 154, 159, 166; influence on survival, 22, 37, 118, 119, 122, 126, 129, 132, 143, 154, 159, 164; signs, 107. *See also* Bear jams.

Roadside bears: factors contributing to, x, 20, 21, 118, 119, 122, 126, 164; food conditioned, xv, xvi, 14, 15, 119, 126, 164; habituated, 20, 21, 26, 108, 110, 118-124, 127, 128, 132, 133, 155, 164, 166; management of, x, xi, xv, xvi, 9, 10, 21, 26, 119, 120-122, 127, 128, 132, 133, 143, 157, 163, 164, 166; park entrance fees and, 128; photography of, 164. *See also* Bear jams.

Roosevelt, Theodore: 180, 181.

Russell, Osborne: 177.

Scandinavia: 31, 33, 43, 99.

Scavenging. *See* Carcasses/Carrion.

Seed dispersal: 86.

Selkirk Mountains: 94.

Senescence: in reproduction, 32, 34, 35, 175; in survival, 208; in plants/vegetation, 51. *See also* Demography; Vegetation.

Sex and age composition. *See* Age distribution.

Sexual maturity: 32-35, 197, 208.

Sheep: allotments, 141, 191; grazing, 20, 105, 178; predation on, 105, 178.

Sheridan, Philip: 179.

Smell: 2, 8, 54, 78, 171.

Snow and snowpack: carrion and, 80; denning and, 3, 64, 173; melt, 49, 56, 77, 202; trends in, 161.

Social interactions (bears): 4, 76, 80-85, 87-89, 96, 175, 200.

Social organization. *See* Behavior.

Social tolerance: 106, 126, 157-160, 167, 208.

Species: xi, xii, 1, 4, 8, 14, 29, 30, 39, 61, 66, 73, 75-77, 80, 81, 85, 87, 89, 92, 99, 112, 120, 123, 128, 140, 141, 147, 150, 151, 158, 161, 167, 169, 175, 183, 184, 192, 199, 202, 206, 208, 209.

Stable isotope analyses: 55, 84, 86, 208.

Stakeholders: xii, 154, 159, 160, 208.

Starvation: 5, 8, 39, 42, 80.

Subadult. *See* Age distribution, of grizzly bears.

Summer ranges. *See* Distribution.

Surveillance. *See* Management; Monitoring.

Survival: adults, 6, 18, 22, 35, 37, 38, 43, 44, 174; cubs, 18, 30, 32, 39, 42, 43, 45, 174; effects of density on, 32; effects of development on, 22, 37, 132; effects of garbage on, 18, 35; effects of hunting on, 132; effects of public lands on, 22, 38, 132; effects of roads on, 22, 37, 132; effects of whitebark pine on, 43, 44, 122; influence on population dynamics, 5, 6, 22, 29, 37, 42-45; subadults, 37, 38, 174; trends in, 22, 38, 39, 44, 45; yearlings, 39, 42, 45, 174. *See also* Demography; Mortality.

Sweden: 33.

Teeth: 1, 107, 172.

Telemetry: 16, 31, 33, 34, 38, 39, 68-70, 76-78, 82, 83, 95, 96, 128, 136, 137, 140, 204, 207.

Temperature, air. *See* Climate; Weather.

Teton Forest Reserve: 180.

Thermal. *See* Geothermal.

Threats, to bears: 4, 5, 19, 26, 27, 63, 82, 91, 92, 115, 159-167.

Timber harvests: 19, 140, 179, 180.

Tolerance: beliefs and values, 19, 24-25, 157-160; effects on dispersal, 72, 73, 106, 162; issues regarding, 11, 27, 72, 73, 126, 157-160, 167.

Tourism: x, 11, 14, 15, 20, 25, 26, 118, 119, 126. *See also* Visitation.

Trails: bear encounters along, 10, 26, 108, 110, 111, 112, 138, 155; closure of, 22; front/backcountry, 18, 26, 108, 110, 111, 113, 134, 135, 155; hiking off/on, 107, 108, 112, 113, 136, 163; signs, 107.

Translocation. *See* Relocation.

Travel corridors: bears, 2, 76, 108, 137; roads, 108, 110, 123, 132, 133, 157. *See also* Recreation; Roads.

Tribes. *See* Native American tribes.

Trophic cascades/levels: 85-89, 208, 209.

Trout: cutthroat, 4, 5, 7, 26-27, 47, 51, 52, 55, 76, 78, 82, 87-89, 161, 162, 175, 211; lake, 51, 76, 87, 211.

Trout Creek dump: 15, 185.

Truffles: black, 53, 212; false, 50, 53, 54, 56, 212.

Uncertainty: xi, 27, 161.

INDEX 271

Undernutrition. *See* Energetics; Nutrition.

Ungulates: bear predation on, 53, 76,77, 81; competition with bears, 80,81; consumption of, 4, 8, 32, 49, 50, 51, 53, 64, 78, 80, 81, 83, 85, 175; hunters of, 7, 39, 41, 53, 73, 78, 106, 141; nutrition from, 4, 54, 55; species, 209, 211, 212.

U.S. Department of the Interior: 181, 186, 187. *See also* National Park Service; U.S. Fish and Wildlife Service; Yellowstone National Park.

U.S. Fish and Wildlife Service: xi, 19, 22, 37, 131, 147, 186, 187, 189, 191-193.

U.S. Forest Service: attractant storage devices, 144-145, 188; grazing allotments, 41; Interagency Grizzly Bear Study Team, 19, 186; mandate/mission, 131-132, 141; mining, 143; Organic Administration Act, 179, 180; Primary Conservation Area for bears, 148; wilderness, 144; wildlife management, 144-145.

U.S. Geological Survey: 19, 180, 182, 192.

Ursidae: 30, 169.

Vegetation: berries, 8, 48, 50, 53, 54, 56, 57, 81, 141, 161; climate warming and, 161; forbs, 5, 47, 50, 51, 53, 140, 141; grasses/graminoids, 3, 5, 50, 51, 77, 140, 141; leaves, 48; management of, 140-145; phenology, 56, 64, 203; roots (and bulbs, corms, tubers), 1, 8, 48, 50, 51, 53, 81, 86, 87, 175; seeds, 4, 35, 51, 53, 57, 77, 85-87, 89, 122, 161, 175; types of, 4, 50-54. *See also* Whitebark pine.

Vehicles: accidents, 122; damage by bears, 104, 145; strikes of bears, 39, 106, 120, 121, 124, 127. *See also* Bear jams.

Vertebrates: 38, 43, 209.

Viewing, of bears: appropriate distance, 113, 129, 157; benefits of, x, xvi, 24, 25, 122, 125, 126-128, 157, 164, 166; Grand Teton National Park, 122-125; management of, x, xi, 21, 120-125, 127-129, 133, 157, 164, 166; visitor experience, xv, xvi, 10, 20, 54, 117-129; Yellowstone National Park, xv, xvi, 10, 20, 25, 54, 119-122. *See also* Bear jams; Photography.

Vision: 2, 170, 171, 175.

Visitation: activities, 14, 15, 20, 21, 26, 117-129, 164; effects of, 15, 20, 21, 26, 104-112, 117-129, 132-151, 155, 157, 164; Grand Teton National Park, 103, 118, 122-125; influence on human-bear interactions, 9, 10, 15, 20, 21, 104-112, 132-151, 155, 157, 164; levels of, xvi, 10, 103, 110, 111, 118, 127; timing of 26, 103; trends in, 7, 10, 14, 15, 103, 107, 110, 111, 118; Yellowstone National Park, 10, 26, 103, 107, 110, 111, 118-122, 127.

Visitors and interactions with wildlife: economic benefits, 126-128; effects of management on, 20, 21, 104-112, 132-151; expectations of, 14, 15, 21, 26, 127, 128; experience of, ix, x, xv, 10, 15, 21, 24, 25, 117-129; numbers to Yellowstone, 10, 26, 103, 107, 110, 111, 118-122, 127; origins of, 103, 104, 166; reasons for visiting, 24, 25, 127, 128. *See also* Bear jams.

Vital rates. *See* Demography.
Voles: 77, 212.

Watching, of bears. *See* Viewing.
Water: xiii, 5, 7, 15, 18, 49, 50, 51, 53, 76, 78, 79, 82, 87-89, 91, 98, 112, 123, 135, 156, 161, 162, 174, 177, 180, 182, 183, 185, 189, 194, 199, 203.
Weaning: age, 4, 31, 33, 34, 37, 124; from human foods, 20; from mother, 3, 4, 31, 175, 209.
Weather: climate, xvi, 26, 61, 80, 106, 161, 162, 167; drought, 76, 161; snow, 3, 49, 56, 64, 77, 80, 161, 173, 202; temperature, 3, 80, 161, 162. *See also* Climate warming; Yellowstone National Park.
Weight (mass): adults, 55-56, 171; army cutworm moths and, 57-58; birth, 30; carcasses and, 84; climate warming and, 161; cubs, 36-37, 48; dominance and, 30; hibernation, 36, 56, 60, 174; human-provided foods and, 56, 105; importance of, 48; seasonal, 55-57; subadults, 37; whitebark pine and, 44; yearlings, 2, 37.
West Yellowstone, Montana: 15, 185, 187, 188.
Whirling disease: 51, 76, 212.
Whitebark pine: annual use, 5, 8, 23, 50, 53, 56; bear jams/viewing and, 122; bear population demographics/dynamics and, xi, 35, 44, 56-57, 61, 161; climate warming and, 26, 61, 161; cone production, 35; cone caches (middens), xiv, 59, 85; distribution, 52; fire, 56, 161; home ranges of bears and, 53; importance of, xi, 4, 35, 140; litigation and, xi, 22, 192; mortality, xi; nutritional value, 4, 35, 53, 85; other foods and, 53-54, 56-57, 77-80, 85-87, 122; pathogens, 56; red squirrels and, xiv, 85-86; seeds (nuts), 35, 53, 59, 85; trends in, xi, 8, 53, 54, 56-57, 85. *See also* Climate; Foods.
Wild/Wildlife/Wildness: bears as a symbol of, ix, xii, xv, xvi, 9, 14, 15, 19, 72, 127; definitions, 205, 209; ecological role, 7, 8, 75-89; genetic recommendations of, 9, 91-101; public support (or lack of) for, 11, 15, 16, 19, 25, 26, 73, 127, 128, 150, 151, 157-159, 166, 167; restoration of bears as, xv, xvi, 9, 13-26, 107, 127, 132, 133, 144, 150, 151, 153-155, 157, 163, 166, 167. *See also* Adaptive capabilities.
Wildlife Brigade, Grand Teton National Park: 123, 125.
Wind River: Range, 69, 72, 181; Reservation, 19.
Winter-kill. *See* Starvation.
Wolves: x, 5, 8, 39, 49, 53, 55, 60, 75, 78, 80, 81, 87, 89, 212. *See also* Predation.
Wyoming: xv, xvi, 2, 19, 123, 127,128, 131, 145, 148, 160, 180, 181, 183, 186-190, 202, 209.

Yaak Mountains: 95, 96.
Yearlings: age, 30, 173, 199, 209; body weight (mass), 2, 37; climbing trees, 175; home range, 66, 67; maternal care, 30, 31, 39, 82; roadside habitat use, 123, 124; survival, 39, 42, 45, 174; weaning, 4.

Yellowstone ecosystem. *See* Greater Yellowstone Ecosystem.

Yellowstone Ecosystem Subcommittee: 20, 154, 166, 187, 189, 190.

Yellowstone Forest Reserve: 180, 181.

Yellowstone Grizzly Coordinating Committee: 147.

Yellowstone Lake: 5, 7, 49, 50, 51, 53, 76, 78, 87-89, 156, 162, 177.

Yellowstone National Park: establishment of, 14, 178, 209; historical narratives of, 14-22, 104, 178-189; map of, Table of Contents; number of grizzly bears, 2, 16, 189; bear attacks/conflicts/encounters, xvi, 20, 42, 106-108, 110-112, 138, 177, 182; bear management approach, 16, 17, 21, 127, 136-138, 178-189; bear viewing, xvi, 20, 119-122, 127-128; bear management areas, 136-137, 158; camping, 134-135; safety messaging, 137-138, 163-164; visitation, 10, 20, 26, 127-128, 163.

Yellowstone Park Timber Land Reserve: 179-181.

Yogi Bear: xvi, 25.

# AUTHOR AFFILIATIONS

**Daniel D. Bjornlie**
Wyoming Game & Fish Department, Lander, Wyoming

**Amanda M. Bramblett**
National Park Service, Yellowstone National Park, Mammoth, Wyoming

**Steven L. Cain**
National Park Service, Grand Teton National Park, Moose, Wyoming
(retired)

**Tyler H. Coleman**
National Park Service, Organ Pipe National Monument, Ajo, Arizona

**Jennifer K. Fortin-Noreus**
Grizzly Bear Recovery Program, U.S Fish and Wildlife Service, Missoula, Montana

**Kevin L. Frey**
Montana Fish, Wildlife & Parks, Bozeman, Montana

**Kerry A. Gunther**
National Park Service, Yellowstone National Park, Mammoth, Wyoming

**Mark A. Haroldson**
U.S. Geological Survey, Northern Rocky Mountain Science Center, Interagency Grizzly Bear Study Team, Bozeman, Montana

**Pauline L. Kamath**
School of Food & Agriculture, University of Maine, Orono, Maine

**Eric G. Reinertson**
National Park Service, Yellowstone National Park, Mammoth, Wyoming

**Charles T. Robbins**

School of the Environment and School of Biological Sciences, Washington State University, Pullman, Washington

**Daniel J. Thompson**

Wyoming Game & Fish Department, Lander, Wyoming

**Daniel B. Tyers**

U.S. Forest Service, Custer Gallatin National Forest, Bozeman, Montana

**Frank T. van Manen**

U.S. Geological Survey, Northern Rocky Mountain Science Center, Interagency Grizzly Bear Study Team, Bozeman, Montana

**P. J. White**

National Park Service, Yellowstone National Park, Mammoth, Wyoming

**Katharine R. Wilmot**

National Park Service, Grand Teton National Park, Moose, Wyoming

**Travis C. Wyman**

National Park Service, Yellowstone National Park, Mammoth, Wyoming

NPS Photo/Jim Peaco

*Grand Prismatic Spring with its distinctive bands of color—the result of brightly-pigmented microbes living in the superheated waters.*

# YELLOWSTONE
# FOREVER

The official nonprofit partner of Yellowstone National Park

WE PARTNER WITH Yellowstone National Park to create opportunities for all people to experience, enhance, and preserve Yellowstone forever.

Our combined operations include 11 educational Park Stores with gross sales of over $4.9 million; the Yellowstone Forever Institute, which offers more than 600 in-depth programs each year; a supporter program of over 50,000 Yellowstone enthusiasts raising funds to support critical park priority projects; and an online community of over 300,000 worldwide.

Yellowstone Forever's mission of engagement and support through education and fundraising for the park will ensure Yellowstone remains for generations to come.

Please visit Yellowstone.org or call 406.848.2400 to learn more.

CPSIA information can be obtained at www.ICGtesting.com
Printed in the USA
LVIW01n0508220617
538624LV00001B/1